Revolutions of the Heart

Art by Agostino Arrivabene (with permission of the artist)

Revolutions of the Heart

Literary, Cultural, & Spiritual

YAHIA LABABIDI
foreword by David Lazar
preface by Sven Birkerts

RESOURCE *Publications* · Eugene, Oregon

REVOLUTIONS OF THE HEART
Literary, Cultural, & Spiritual

Resource Publications
An Imprint of Wipf and Stock Publishers
199 W. 8th Ave., Suite 3
Eugene, OR 97401

www.wipfandstock.com

PAPERBACK ISBN: 978-1-7252-6494-6
HARDCOVER ISBN: 978-1-7252-6495-3
EBOOK ISBN: 978-1-7252-6496-0

Manufactured in the U.S.A.   03/27/20

This book is dedicated to all who long for transformation.

Activism is the rent I pay for living on this planet.

—ALICE WALKER

Find a subject you care about and which you in your heart feel others should care about. It is this genuine caring, not your games with language, which will be the most compelling and seductive element in your style.

—KURT VONNEGUT

Make yourself a "capacity" and I will make myself a "torrent."

—ST. CATHERINE OF SIENA

Contents

CONVERSATIONS & FICTIONS

Foreword

On Lababidi's *Revolutions*

YAHIA LABABIDI HAS A generous sense of the spiritual and a generous sense of the essay. He combines these two generosities in the reviews, essays, and meditations in *Revolutions*, a title that captures the multiple sides of his interests, politics and aesthetics. Lababidi is interested in change—new movements, new thought, new ideas, whether they're from symbolist poets or Christian mystics, the Koran or contemporary essayists. The "new" is what changes things, is revolutionary in some form, and its force can last for centuries.

Revolution also means to turn, and Lababidi turns repeatedly from the literary to the spiritual, from the intimacy of personal thought and experience ("I did not think that I, a recovering existentialist, would find myself one day slipping through the back door of Islam") to the general notions of philosophy. The first person plural imprecations and questions of aphorism are sprinkled throughout his work ("What if we were to view our wounds as peepholes, through which to view the world and open us up to the wounds of others, and our planet, as an extension of our larger body?") and which he also speaks to and about, eloquently.

Rilke, Heraclitus, Leonard Cohen, Rumi, Alaa Al Aswany . . . Lababidi is an internationalist in his literary tastes, but he returns again and again to the turmoil in Egypt, the promise and failures of the Arab Spring, and the poignancy which colors the work, his work as an expatriate viewing the literature and politics of homeland from a great distance. This hardly mutes his passion, engagement and self-aware positionality in considering the Middle East. As he writes, "Broadly speaking, I do this by best trying to represent my region through my person, offering an alternative to the simplistic and often negative portrayals of Arabs/Muslims in the US media. In that way, I believe Art is the best form of cultural exchange and diplomacy."

To this we might add that Lababidi's art is the best form of cultural exchange and diplomacy.

This is a rich, complex, multifaceted volume of prose. Give yourself over to this supple and extraordinary writer.

DAVID LAZAR

Preface

MY FIRST CONTACT WITH Yahia Lababidi was some years ago—an over the transom meeting that happened when he submitted work to AGNI, the literary magazine I edit. Reading submissions, I look for work that freezes my reading attention and says "Here!" Which is exactly what happened with the generous sheaf of aphorisms that Lababidi had sent. Aphorisms—we never get aphorisms. But these were, further, aphorisms of a compelling spiritual sensibility, which we likewise never see. I made my way down the page with a feeling of imminent revelation. The little awakenings came, one after the other, and I had the reader's hope that I might at any moment arrive at some unanticipated larger wakefulness.

That did not happen, quite. A series of aphorisms, however pointed or wise, can't carry a reader the full distance. That is the work of devotion and discipline. What they did accomplish, however, was important. They reminded me—and these days we all need reminding—that it is not only possible, but necessary to find ways to speak freely of the mysteries and intimations that reveal our deep human need, a need that in our time has been sidelined by the cynical ethos of the media and our vast collective distractedness, and which draws attention, when any attention is drawn, mainly in its wispier spiritual find-your-inner self public offerings. The aspirations of the mystical, the applications of inwardness—these have little place in our culture nowadays, and finding a way to talk openly about the soul or the revelations of beauty is very difficult. We live in the age of the eye-roll.

Which is why it was so bracing to come upon Lababidi's spiritual probes. They were not apologetic, or defensive, or shy. They addressed openly the search for meaning and a connection to forces or entities larger than the self, even as they promoted no particular faiths or sects. Keeping faith with the themes found in spiritual writings throughout history, they

xiii

not only legitimized the search for deeper integration, they modeled it in a literarily compelling way. Lababidi is at once an honest and graceful writer.

I stress these things because this is the spirit that moves and fluctuates throughout Lababidi's *sui generis* gathering of meditation, memoir, social commentary, poetry, and, of course, aphorism.

I have talked so much about this form, one of Lababidi's's first chosen modes of expression, so let me cite a few aphorisms from the submission that so caught my attention, for these set a tone for all the work brought together here.

Where there are demons there is something precious worth fighting for.

The grades of love we are ashamed to confess: from the playground crush to Divine madness.

A poem arrives like a hand in the dark.

The lines, clean and unornamented, resonate in the mind and inevitably enlarge our apprehension of things.

I used the word "attention" above, and I note it again here because it is a central tenet of Lababidi's thinking. He himself cites Simone Weil's well-known assertion: "Absolute unmixed attention is prayer," and follows its implications throughout his writing. For attention, open and directed focus, is the endangered art of giving things their due, be they objects in the outer world, or the inward stirrings we feel when we consider larger frames of reference—when we ask about meaning and purpose, and when we confront the extraordinary unlikeliness of our being here at all. Lababidi transmits on this frequency. The work is full of inklings of what might lie just beyond.

Revolutions of the Heart offers a broad portfolio of Lababidi's exploration of this state of awareness. He brings together his ruminations on mysticism with compelling accounts of his own progress through stages of awareness; he searches the work of favorite writers in order to set out the connection between the literary and the transcendental; he pays heed to the aspiration and strife of contemporary Egypt, his culture of origin. He also assesses strains of popular culture and matters of the moment, looking at the singer Morrissey, and the paradoxes of Marianne Williamson's presidential candidacy.

In an essay called "Spiritual Tourism," Lababidi confronts what he considers his own spiritual fickleness, the fact that he can't confine himself to any one religion, but must instead keep on testing, sampling, taking from this and from that as he keeps looking for what he needs. I think he is being unnecessarily self-deprecating. I see him not as tourist, but pilgrim, and these diverse reflections show us the path of his progress.

SVEN BIRKERTS

Essays, Appreciations, Reflections

The Books We Were

Certain cherished books are like old loves. We didn't part on bad terms; but it's complicated, and would require too much effort to resume relations.

IF ONE'S FIRST LOVE is for Letters, people tend to come second (or possibly third). Yes, books are ink-and-paper relationships that can supplement and, at times, displace flesh-and-blood relations.

Such was my breathlessly intense, and evidently unhealthy, understanding of literature as an impressionable, voracious teenager. I read to get drunk and, to paraphrase Baudelaire, hoped to stay that way. A clutch of slim volumes altered my intellectual landscape and, at the risk of melodrama, saved my life. Past the intoxicating, escapist, aesthetic experience (style always mattered for me), these early loves knew me before I knew myself and confessed my secrets—speaking the yearnings of my still-inchoate soul far more eloquently than I could ever dream at that tender age. Sensing my desperation and need, I believed these books opened themselves up to me so that they were a more real and alive world than any other I inhabited.

The first, which made me suspect I might (want to) be a writer was Wilde's Picture of Dorian Gray. Its relentless cleverness made for a heady ride, and I might have underlined every other line while highlighting the rest. By donning a mask of brilliant wit, Wilde seemed to have split himself in two and outdistanced his pain. This was a trick worth learning, my sixteen-year-old self intuited wordlessly, as was his apparently effortless knack for pithy summary. "I summed up all things in a phrase, all existence in an epigram: whatever I touched I made beautiful," Wilde would go on to say in *De Profundis* (which I devoured shortly afterward, along with all his immodest utterances, in various genres). Yet, fond as I am of this early crush, I cannot bear to return to Wilde's Gray. Past his glittering style, I find the cynicism suffocating. As Franz Kafka is supposed to have said to Gustav Janouch of Wilde's work: "It sparkles and seduces, as only a poison can. . . . It is dangerous, because it plays with truth. A game with truth is always a game with life." Then, there was Kafka, and his sublime self-loathing and life-recoil. He also came to me in my teens, when I was particularly susceptible to that volatile cocktail. Those hallucinatory short stories, especially his "A Hunger Artist," hit me like a dark epiphany: "I have to fast, I can't help it. It is just that I couldn't find the food I liked. If I had found it, I would have stuffed myself like you or anyone else." Afterwards, came the exquisite masochism of his diaries, which I inhaled like a guilty pleasure, and concluded with his choice aphorisms. Of all his work, actually, it is the aphorisms that I can return to, which are, somehow, greater than the sum of the man and his torment.

Before I turned twenty, I was to encounter the love of my life—the one that would set my world spinning and take me nearly two decades to recover from: Nietzsche. His Zarathustra combined everything I needed to hear at the time: rebellious philosophy, stylish nihilism, vicious humor, and something akin to prophecy. He spoke the soul-splitting contradictions I hardly had words for—"*Body and soul*, I am more of a *battlefield* than a human being"—and, in my intemperate enthusiasm, I can say that, for the next decade or so, he was nearer and dearer to me than any living soul. Incredible, now, to think it!

Nietzsche handed me over to that other hysterical prophet: Dostoevsky. And, if memory swerves correctly, I was so caught up in his *Notes from Underground* that I hardly noticed that the train I was riding had derailed. When I did (because everyone else was panicking and scrambling to get off the tram), I proceeded to disembark, in measured pace, without tearing my eyes off his delirious pages. And so it was: one Existentialist horror writer after another kicked me around for a bit then passed me, the besotted lover, off to their buddies to have some violent fun with.

Which is why when, belatedly, I recovered my senses and bearing, I had to set these seductive invalids aside for some time. For, just as they'd oxygenated my days, they'd also left me in a moral, spiritual daze. I felt I'd just barely managed to escape their clutches and could not afford to flirt with their frailties any longer—from fear I might be dragged to that treacherous space where they initially found me. They began to all seem like otherworldly, gilled creatures thrown upon the earth, gasping for a breath from their home atmosphere. I just couldn't bear to pity any more suffering—each one, forever, on the verge of nervous collapse. I'd combed their letters, I'd inhabited their journals, I'd read between their lines. Quite simply, I had to keep these once too-dear books at a distance, as I was afraid of what echoing responses they might draw from me.

I was able to formally say good-bye to these formative influences in a book of conversations: The Artist as Mystic. In this love letter to my early masters (including Kierkegaard, Rimbaud, Baudelaire, and the usual suspects), I was finally able to see, with the 20/20 vision of hindsight, that what I was attracted to in these dark thinkers was an anguished yearning, a longing to utter what's ineffable: in short, the Light. It's just that with my night vision, at the time, I could only take so much glare, and could not find my sustenance in sunlit spaces . . . yet.

"At the end of my suffering / there was a door," writes Louise Glück in The Wild Iris. That door would lead me to poetry that was at the threshold of revelation. The sort of poetry that had set me alight in Eliot's Four Quartets and Rilke's Duino Elegies (two loves from my past that I can and do return to). And, past poetry, further along on the other side of that door, I made a somewhat destabilizing, liberating discovery: I found that not only did I care far less for the tyranny of the mind and its chew toys, which I previously cherished, but "literature" also seemed to matter much less. To quote Rumi, who spoke of the limitations of poetry when he had become a celebrated poet: "What, after all, is my concern with Poetry? In comparison with the true reality, I have no time for poetry. It is the only nutrition that my visitors can accept, so like a good host I provide it."

And, just like that, my early love for Western philosophical literature slowly came to be replaced by Eastern mysticism. First, through that little inexhaustible marvel of a book, the Tao te Ching, bursting with fruitful paradoxes and then, in quick succession, mystics of all stripes: Buddhist, Christian, Sufi. Maybe this sounds odd, but through the eyes of love (quietly gazing past the loud surface differences) I find that I can see the luminous spirit of Rumi in Nietzsche, only stunted. I recognize that I am drawn to the captivating contradictions in both, the serious play and their radical ecstasy. But I see the example of scholar-become-poet, who then goes on to make of his entire life a work of art, more beautifully and spiritually realized in the Persian master.

"What you are seeking is also seeking you," Rumi says. Certain cherished books, like old loves, find and transform us at decisive stages of our lives. Thus, they remain emblazoned on our minds and hearts, whether we like it or not. And when we must address these emissaries of the past (as I find that I am doing, now) we should try to speak of them with the respect and tenderness befitting a ghostly self. If I might be permitted one parting quote from another Sufi mystic, Al-Ghazali, "Only that which cannot be lost in a shipwreck is yours." The rest is flotsam.

Every Subject Chooses Its Author

How strange that someone can be an authority on a life, other than their own. How odd, that in setting themselves aside—to better imagine another, *objectively*—a biographer often ends up producing a sort of veiled autobiography. Yet, perhaps, self is not meant to be sacrificed entirely, in the art of biography, but only long enough to return as another.

In many ways, biography comes down to a question of temperament, a borderless affinity stretched across time and space. Something of a spiritual kinship must exist in order to be able to channel another's spirit. This is the mysticism of the biographer: one who knows without knowing, whose "facts" unearthed during the hard work of research only go on to confirm initial intimations. (And the work itself is a labor of love, or perhaps an exploration of unlived possibilities.)

"Every writer is a man given over to an obsession" writes Graham Greene. The biographer is no exception. The act of biography is a kind of possession and exorcism. The biographer who dedicates years of their life, sometimes decades, to explore another's must also experience all sorts of intensities, initiation rites, and illuminations. Somewhere along the way, a life is transformed into a work of art.

How much can actually be known for certain of another person cannot be said. Yet, in the hands of an inspired biographer, a figure may emerge from the mist, summoned from the dead, and made to walk and talk among the living. In this sense, a biographer must be seen as a creative artist in their own right. Whereas 'nothing alive can be calculated' as Kafka tells us, it can be approximated.

In The Artist as Mystic, a collection of ecstatic conversations I had with author and editor, Alex Stein, we attempted something of this literary séance, daring to summon the spirits of Nietzsche, Rilke, Kafka, Kierkegaard,

Baudelaire and others. In Stein, I'd found a serious playmate who had read, and (imaginatively) lived with, many of the same poets and thinkers that had shaped my intellectual landscape. Decades later, we were both ready to unburden ourselves of their influence, while acknowledging our debt. We did not have a name for this odd genre-bending form that we embarked on, I think we settled on lyrical interviews, but we did have a theme.

Broadly-speaking, we were sifting through the (sometimes dark) inheritance of these writers for the Light: the prophet in Nietzsche, the God-seeker in Kafka, the secret ascetic in Baudelaire. Always, we groped for the gold thread of the artist as mystic—high above their small, tortured self—as makers of beautiful things, seeking to harness that beauty to their great longing, in their life-long pursuit of transformation.

In the process, the lines often blurred between Stein's utterances and mine, or even the specificity of the artists under consideration. What remained was an inhabited intensity that each of our illustrious subjects vibrated with when we attempted to speak them from the inside out. In this joint attempt at creative biography writing, we found we were also sounding our own truths, more freely, by donning masks of our great dead friends.

Sometimes in writing poetry, for example, it is necessary to become the poem—one agonizing line, or liberating verse, at a time. Something of this living-through was also required of us in attempting to translate the inner lives of our literary masters. Modern American poet, Gregory Pardlo, in an extraordinary essay *Choosing a Twin* echoes this truth while discussing a different discipline: "Translation is a practice of empathy," he writes, "like choosing a twin, where affinity and kinship is a declarative act and not a passive discovery."

Rimbaud's Spiritual Battle

WHAT BECOMES A LEGEND most? Great talent, suffering, and mystery . . . three ingredients that French poet Arthur Rimbaud possessed in spades. General readers will be familiar with the broad lines of the Rimbaud legend: child prodigy and *enfant terrible* who, between the ages of fifteen and twenty, revolutionized modern poetry, only to abruptly stop writing at twenty-one, disappear in Africa, and die at thirty-seven. In Arthur Rimbaud (2018), part of Reaktion Books' Critical Lives series presenting the work of leading cultural figures, Seth Whidden seeks to fill in the blanks of this enigmatic life. Whidden, professor of French at the University of Oxford and co-editor of a scholarly journal of Rimbaud studies for a decade, loves his subject and knows well the milieu that produced him, demonstrating how the life and poetry of our precocious protagonist inform one another.

At the outset, Whidden emphasizes the importance of flight for Rimbaud's life and art: away from the provincial mind-set of his hometown, Charleville (which he fled and returned to frequently throughout his short, peripatetic life), as well as running away from what he viewed as the stifling restrictions of the pretty, stuffy poetry of his time: the Parnassians' "art for art's sake." Often quoting from Rimbaud's original French poetry (and translating it himself), Whidden sketches the development of the young poet's art from the pastoral, to the political (beginning with the Franco-Prussian War), onto the erotic and mystic. As a voracious reader and prodigious linguist (he would go on to learn/teach English, German, Spanish, Italian, Russian, Arabic, and Greek), Rimbaud was always familiar with the rules of language that he would gleefully break throughout his brief literary career.

Reading Whidden's study feels like sitting in on a poetry class, featuring close (at times, technical) readings and perceptive analysis, which deepen our appreciation of Rimbaud's art. The reader experiences the thrill

of being granted a front-row seat to the precocious becoming and prema-
ture undoing of our young hero. In addition, we are treated to facsimiles
of Rimbaud's original manuscripts featuring his beautiful penmanship and
the cast of characters whose influence he often quickly outgrew: family,
teachers, artists, and friends. As a gifted teenager, Rimbaud does what many
young poets do: writing to the poets he admires, introducing his work, and
announcing himself with supreme confidence.

In one of his two letters referred to as the Lettres du voyant (letters of
the seer), Rimbaud famously declares, at the tender age of sixteen:.

> . . . I am working to make myself a *Seer* . . . It's a question of
> reaching the unknown by the derangement of *all the senses.* The
> sufferings are enormous, but one has to be strong, one has to be
> born a poet, and I know that I am a poet. This is not all my fault.
> It is wrong to say: I think. One ought to say: I am thought . . . I is
> another. Too bad for the wood that finds itself a violin.

Precisely this reckless daring, of one embarking on a tremendous ad-
venture of the Spirit with sublime indifference to its personal cost, is the
larger-than-life heroism of Rimbaud that continues to capture our imagina-
tion today.

It does not take long for the young visionary with his promise of a
"new literature" to secure the attentions of Paris's literary elite, but, as the
saying goes, familiarity breeds contempt. Just as Rimbaud's radical art
gains the respect of literary giants of his time, his gross misbehavior (which
Whidden carefully catalogs) proves our boy hero can be quite ugly up close,
using and abusing those he encounters like a spoiled brat. Nowhere is this
more apparent than in Rimbaud's disastrous relationship with poet Paul
Verlaine, over a decade his senior. "Come, great dear soul, we call you, we
are waiting for you" is Verlaine's fateful invitation to Rimbaud to visit him
in Paris, at the start of a violent romantic relationship that would last for
two years—leaving the older poet's marriage in shambles, culminating with
Verlaine shooting Rimbaud and receiving a two-year prison sentence for it.

At this point in the horror story, we encounter a more sober, chastened
Rimbaud taking stock in the only book he published himself, the influential
A Season in Hell (1873). Tellingly, this "notebook of the damned," as he calls
it, is addressed to the devil and makes this mystic pronouncement:

> We are moving toward the *Spirit.* I tell you it is very certain, it
> is prophecy. I understand it, and not knowing how to explain it
> without using pagan words, I prefer to be silent.

After the torturous, unconscious living we have been privy to in his life so far, with its litany of monstrosities, one can't help but wonder: *Who speaks here?* It is the Other that Rimbaud alluded to earlier, the Wood-That-Finds-Itself-a-Violin, striking a much-needed note of self-knowledge and, beyond that, recognizing the necessity for transcendence

The mysterious poet continues his confession from the depths, in "Hell," addressing the incorruptibility of the soul and his spiritual longing, in this way:

> Yes, my eyes are closed to your light. I am a beast, a savage. But I can be saved . . . Do I know nature yet? Do I know myself?—*No more words* . . . My innocence would make me weep. Life is the farce we all play . . . So trust in me, faith relieves, guides, and cures.

A Season in Hell is a hallucinatory, remarkable repudiation of his past life and, with its new clarity, carries a suggestion of transformation and redemption:

> . . . the gnashing of teeth, the hissing of fire, the reeking sighs abate. All filthy memories fade out. My last regrets scamper off . . . A spiritual battle is as brutal as a battle of men.

As Whidden sums it up in his reading of this fascinating text, Rimbaud "arrives at an optimism: 'Adieu' is an offering to God ('à Dieu'), leaving behind Satan and hell, and with them there is at least a suggestion of leaving the West."

By twenty-one, the "man with soles of wind" had stopped writing poetry and would apply his restless, desperate energy elsewhere, traveling outside Europe and taking odd jobs—including manual labor at docks and quarries, selling everything from coffee to guns and just stopping short of trading in slaves. Asked by a friend around this time if he still thought of literature, an amused Rimbaud replies that he no longer bothers with such things, regarding it as "dregs" from a past life of general drunkenness. Whidden is keen to emphasize, however, that Rimbaud still wrote but that it was far from literary, more of an explorer's means to describe other worlds. For the same reason, the ex-poet takes up photography in Africa a decade later; a few evocative pictures from this inscrutable period of Rimbaud's life are reproduced in Whidden's stylish, slim volume.

Ironically, just as he has definitively turned his back on literature (after desperately yearning to make a name for himself as a feverish youth), Rimbaud's work was beginning to appear in print and his name circulating with mounting appreciation. In an anthology entitled The Damned Poets,

Verlaine generously introduces his long-lost friend (declared dead several times) to a new and sympathetic audience, including in the book a number of poems by the child-genius, which would prove influential—even inspiring the symbolist movement.

Although Rimbaud was outliving himself in a sense, he was also dying in another and wracked with regrets. In a letter from Africa sent to his mother (a relationship that grew less embattled as he matured), he makes this plaintive confession:

> I regret having never gotten married or had a family . . . I'm condemned to wander . . . What's the point of all these comings and goings, this exhaustion, these adventures with people of strange races, these languages that fill up my memory, and these nameless difficulties?

To add insult to injury, the mute poet now learns he is to become an amputated wanderer. Here he is again, wailing:

> . . . how tiring and how sad when I think of my old travels . . .
> And, now, I'm a one-legged cripple . . . I who had just decided
> to return to France this summer to get married! Goodbye marriage, goodbye family, goodbye future!

And before he can fully process this major life change, his cancer spreads and he rapidly deteriorates. Rimbaud's final weeks before his death, at thirty-seven, are heart-rending: he weeps, is in a daze, and still dreams of future plans.

The last chapter of Whidden's gripping study is entitled "Afterlives" and considers the many posthumous lives of an unfathomable character who died and was reborn while still alive. We learn of forgeries, influences, and his undying connection to artists and readers alike (apparently, he continues to receive enough mail for authorities to place a mailbox in his cemetery at Charleville-Mézières).

Despite his uncommon achievements, it is difficult not to regard the life of Rimbaud as a kind of cautionary tale or moral fable. Claimed by the surrealists, he was pronounced by their leader, *André Breton*, as "a god of puberty." Perhaps this blasphemous epitaph gets at the pitiable heart of it all: that such an immense gift should have been entrusted to rebellious, destructive adolescence and emotional immaturity—in short, one inadequately suited to it. As we see in his abbreviated life example, debauchery, eventually, ushers in virtue; but there are less vicious paths, such as patience. Also, might it be that the difference between diabolical and divine inspiration is the duration of pleasure afforded?

Contemplating this almost mythological life leaves us meditating on larger questions, spiritual and existential. *Who was Rimbaud? What is the nature of inspiration? Were the sacrifices his vocation entailed worth it?* (By this I mean the protracted torment inflicted upon Rimbaud and those in his inner circle). Could it be that, from the start, the thing he sought, this demon-angel, was always just *outside* the page? That, after swimming the length of the alphabet, with fine gills and deranging senses, he created an opening for others but a trap for himself? If so, then slipping through those watery bars was imperative, a chastened mysticism—and freedom to write in the air, to be . . . human.

To his credit, Whidden offers no easy answers, honoring the fundamental mystery at the core of Rimbaud's fate and suggesting that the answer to these riddles, and others raised by his extraordinary life, are to be found in his art.

That Particular Intense Gaze

An Appreciation of John Banville

THE IRISH WRITER JOHN Banville is a novelist of ideas whose prose aspires to
the condition of poetry. Whether meditating on the truths of art or science,
investigating the nature of reality or mortality, or forever trying to pinpoint
the elusive self, this modern master demands to be read slowly and thought-
fully. Of course, Banville is hardly unknown, but until he won the UK's Man
Booker Prize in 2005, for The Sea, Banville labored in relative obscurity for
around three decades, his finely-wrought thirteen previous novels selling
fewer than 5,000 copies in hardback. To be sure, this has something to do
with his uncommercial concerns and purportedly "difficult" style.

Like his professed mentor, Samuel Beckett, whom he has written about
perceptibly and whose shadow is never far, Banville, too, for all his arsenal of
jeweled words, seems always to be straining at the limits of the sayable. ("So
much is unsayable: all the important things," he writes in The Newton Let-
ter.) Also, as with Beckett, it is not an ethical truth (moral, value judgment)
that can be trusted, but an aesthetic one (form, language) that we return to
time and again. *Only describe* might be the mantra here, as faithfully and
truly as you possibly can. This is, at most, what the artist is capable of. "You
cannot even speak about truth. That's what's so distressful. Paradoxically, it
is through form that the artist may find some kind of a way out. By giving
form to formlessness. It is only in that way, perhaps, that some underlying
affirmation may be found." This is Beckett in conversation, but it might as
well be Banville.

Besides describing, there's imagination: perhaps, the artist's version of
compassion. In Banville's morally ambivalent universe, it is failure of imagi-
nation that permits one of his sympathetic monsters, Freddie Montgomery,
to take a life in The Book of Evidence. Passionate as Banville is about the
life of the mind, the drama to be found in his work is, generally speaking,

internal, as his articulate characters strive to eavesdrop on their soul's dialogue with itself. In Eclipse, for example, one of his typically introspective male narrators, actor Alexander Cleave, retires from life and the stage to his childhood home to do just that: better overhear himself. When he turns outward, his ambitions are at once modest and profound; he is after the essence of things.

As Cleave sets about to study commonplace things—an open window, a chair, flowers—he finds "the actual has taken on a tense, trembling quality. Everything is poised for dissolution. Yet never in my life, so it seems, have I been so close up to the very stuff of the world . . ." This tremulous awe in the face of the ordinary is reminiscent of Rilke, who in the ninth *Duino Elegy*, asks: "Are we, perhaps, here just for saying: House, Bridge, Fountain, Gate, Jug, Fruit tree, Window—possibly: Pillar, Tower?" In so doing, Rilke does not believe he's merely mouthing names, but almost mystically endowing things with a special life force ("such saying as never the things themselves / hoped so intensely to be").

Banville, also, shares in this concept of the artist as a sort of mystic. In an interview at Powells.com (April 5, 2010), he illustrates his "method" in these memorable words: "You know, the artist concentrates on the detail of the object until it blushes in the way the love object blushes when a lover gazes at it with that particular intense gaze. That is what art should do. It should make the world blush and give up its secrets."

Style is not merely a superficial concern in Banville, it is how he conjures the secrets he is after. He approvingly quotes Henry James: "In literature, we move through a blessed world, in which we know nothing except through style, and in which everything is redeemed by style." As a novelist slightly irritated with the form and limitations of the novel, Banville has defiantly expressed disregard for most aspects associated with it, professing "little or no interest in characters, plot, motivation, manners, politics, morality or social issue . . . " In their stead, it seems that his abiding interest is nicely suggested in the opening lines of Czeslaw Milosz's magisterial "Ars Poetica": "I have always aspired to a more spacious form / that would be free from the claims of poetry or prose." This "spacious form" is one that Banville inhabits quite well in his oeuvre, which is rich, allusive, playful, and existential at the same time.

As a barely closeted aesthete, and also in his capacity as a long-time book reviewer (for the *New York Review of Books*, etc.), it is evident Banville believes in the civilizing influence of beauty and literature. It was his stated duty, for example, as editor for the *Irish Times*, "to get people to read good books." In fact, more than once, Banville has confessed: "The world is not real for me until it has been pushed through the mesh of language."

However, such an aesthetic sensibility is not antithetical to reality, but complimentary, in the sense Joseph Brodsky meant when he wrote: "Art is not an attempt to escape reality but the opposite, an attempt to animate it. It is a spirit seeking flesh but finding words."

Which is why finding the right words is paramount for Banville. In further defense of the importance of style, here is Nietzsche—whom Banville quotes, often and admiringly, referring to him a "superb literary stylist." Far from being a trivial concern, the philosopher writes: "Improving our style means improving our ideas. Nothing less." And elsewhere, Nietzsche effuses, lyrically:

> Oh, those Greeks! They knew how to live. What is required for
> that is to stop courageously, at the surface, the fold, the skin,
> to adore appearances, to believe in forms, tones, words and the
> whole Olympus of appearance. Those Greeks were superficial
> out of profundity.

Something of this paradox is at the heart of Banville, who claims only to concern himself with the world of appearances yet is clearly enmeshed in the mysteries of consciousness. This aesthete's philosophy, being "superficial out of profundity" seems at the root of his thought-tormented, solitary heroes. Mostly outsiders, these scientists, artists, murderers, spies, and actors are taunted by intimations of transcendence or transformation. In their desperate pursuit of clarity and understanding, they seek far and wide for, as he puts it in Kepler, "world-forming relationships, in the rules of architecture and painting, in poetic meter, in the complexities of rhythm, even in colors, in smells and tastes, in the proportions of the human figure." But first they must wrestle with themselves, these unreliable filters of reality, and here is where the emphasis on style comes into play:

> When we were children, we used to say of show-offs in the
> school playground they were only shaping; it is indeed some-
> thing I never got out of the habit of; I made a living from shap-
> ing; indeed I made a life. It is not reality, I know, but for me it
> was the next best thing—at times, the only thing, more real than
> the real.

This is Cleave from Eclipse again, musing on his professional, and personal, tendency to fashion masks ("a making-over of all [he] was into a miraculous, bright new being"). The same desire for self-fashioning, or re-creation, could apply to Cleave's fictional predecessors, such as Freddie Montgomery in The Book of Evidence or Victor Maskell in The Untouchable.

In an aphorism titled, "One Thing Is Needful," Nietzsche summarizes this art of living thus:

> To give style to one's character. A great and rare art. He exercises
> it who surveys all that his nature presents in strength and weak-
> ness and then molds it into an artistic plan, until everything
> appears as art and reason and even weakness delights the eye.

Of course, this aesthetic project extends past simply giving style to one's character (or characters) and ultimately to life itself—which appears in need of order and harmony, amidst so much absurdity or chaos.

Throughout it all, there is no escaping the sheer pleasure of Banville's singing prose—his wondrous-strange manner, which boasts a profusion of gifts and an uncommon sensitivity to the ineffable. We're confronted with the work of a muralist and also a miniaturist, someone equally at ease tackling the large themes—time, memory ("The past beats inside me like a second heart," he writes in The Sea), authenticity, alternative existences—as he is capable of devoting loving attention to the details that make up our world. We emerge from his novels, senses tingling brightly, somehow more aware of our possibilities. And Banville honors "the ordinary, that strangest and most elusive of enigmas" through his allegiance to indeterminacy, often content to leave mysteries unresolved, thrumming.

In justifying the existence of the controversial Western Canon, critic Harold Bloom states that a key facet to great writers "is strangeness, a mode of originality that either cannot be assimilated or that so assimilates us that we cease to see it as strange." Banville, whom Bloom admires, is eligible by these standards as a distinguished heir to a tradition of great European prose stylists. As a novelist, he seems to write with his entire nervous system (rendering country light, for example, as "the hue of headaches" in The Infinities) and as readers we are deeply rewarded by paying close attention to his considered and concentrated art.

Poetry and Journalism of the Spirit

It is difficult to get the news from poems, yet men die miserably every day for lack of what is found there.

—William Carlos Williams

PHYSICAL DISTANCE IS DIFFICULT because of the helplessness it engenders. To see one's world unraveling continents and oceans away and to feel that you can't do anything can be terribly frustrating. But with distance, one also sees more clearly. Art, as I understand it, and this includes philosophy, is about cultivating a certain distance so that we might, in turn, lend our vision to those in the thick of historic events. Which is to say, one cannot evaluate the play while sharing the stage with the actors. At least this is how I justified my decision, as an Egyptian, to remain in the United States, my adopted home, during the Arab Spring Revolution.

Since the Egyptian Revolution began, discerning the meaning of poetry in trying times has been a quandary very much weighing on my heart and mind. Until then, I pretty much viewed art and politics as separate spheres. Journalism, I thought, was better suited to tackle the here and now, like Kierkegaard's parable of the "matchstick" men: upon their head is deposited something phosphorescent, the hint of an idea; one takes them up by the leg, strikes them against a newspaper, and out comes three or four columns. Artists were creatures of another order, I suspected; they were closer to Nietzsche's lovers of truth (in *Zarathustra*): "Slow is the experience of all deep wells: long must they wait before they know what fell into their depth."

Of course, Kierkegaard is not being entirely fair to journalists, and there is a place and a need in this world for both: speed of coverage and

17

slowness in reflection. For a journalist to achieve his highest function, which is to serve as a kind of moral watchdog, it might be necessary to rush—to the battlefield and to print—to keep their eye on the moment and to tell the story as it unfolds. Such near-sightedness is a virtue. For their part, artists and thinkers excel in a form of far-sightedness, somehow seeing just past the moment, over its head, to tomorrow. That is how they are able to lend us their vision.

And so it is that I have come to realize the role of poetry in times of crisis: Vision. By "vision" I mean that unblinking witness is only half of the equation. This is what I mean by seeing over the head of the times. It is not enough to bear witness to *now*; journalists, to an extent, do that. Poetry lends us a third (metaphysical) eye, one that collapses distances, at once reminding us of our essential selves and who we can become. This vision provides more *insight* than mere sight.

Back to the *here and now*. There is a very touching story (one of many that do not receive media attention) that came out of the Egyptian revolution that I'd like to share. A middle-aged man learns of a young activist having been (deliberately) blinded in scuffles with the Supreme Council of the Armed Forces, and calls in to a television show offering to donate one of his eyes to the unfortunate young activist:

> "I've heard the dead can donate their eyes for transplants," he reasons, "and so this should work since I'm alive."
> "And, you'd do this? Donate one of your eyes for a complete stranger?" the TV broadcaster, asks incredulously.
> "Yes," the caller confirms, with feeling. "That young man lost his eyes fighting for freedom, for all of us. So, while I can't offer him both my eyes, I'd like to offer him one, *to split the cost of freedom*."[1]

Poetry, at its finest, can restore our sight. The pen is the seismograph of the heart, Kafka is supposed to have said in conversation with Gustav Janouch. If writers are equipped with sensitive instruments to register inner quakes, then how can they fail to note when the entire world itself is in a state of convulsions? Yet, in order for the art not to be poorly digested, it might take artists time to process what has fallen into their depths.

An excellent instance of such witness-art, a form of spiritual journalism, really, is Libyan-American poet Khaled Mattawa's poem on the aftermath of Muammar Gaddafi's death, "After 42 Years." More drawn out than the uprisings in Tunisia or Egypt, the human cost in Libya's revolution was (and remains) sickening—not unlike the current carnage in Syria. Enough was too much, and there seemed no end in sight. Then, out of the blue, we learned of Gaddafi's capture. How to make sense of all the suffering, the waste of human lives, and to restore to the living their dignity, lost years and possibilities? This is the catharsis Mattawa's masterful poem offers.

I wept, as I imagine countless others must have, as the poet traced the outline of Libya's pitiable history, beginning with the bloodless coup: "The country like a helpless teenage girl / forced into marriage hoping her groom will be kind." Sparing us no detail of the vicious atrocities, humiliations, and daily deprivations endured by his people over decades, as well as the psychological toll:

> What and who taught you, O' sons of my country, to be so fearless, cruel?
> "Him," they say. 42 years, 42 years of him.
> Who taught you to be heroic in this way?
> The no-life we had to live, under him . . .
> There were holes in the air that was full of death.
> We managed to hold our breath and live our lives.

And, then, after suffering of such magnitude the poet (with his pen-cum-seismograph-of-the-heart) knows that closure will not be easy or quickly forthcoming:

> How can you say "over" when it took 42 years . . .
> history like a rat, hiding in a sewer drain . . .
> the astonishment unbearable that would kill you if it lasted too long . . .
> O' Lord how little our lives must be when so much can be buried lost . . .
> There is no "after" until we pray for all the dead.

This is what poetry can do in difficult times, to speak our silences and make sense of our pain, harnessing the anguish of so many souls—what Kafka, in a letter (to Oskar Pollak) says about books being "an axe for the frozen sea within us." Someone once said: if you want to know what the moon is *truly* like, send a poet. Mattawa's report from planet Libya on the moral aftermath of Gadaffi's rule is heart-rending and more meaningful in a way than any of the coverage in print or on television. Why? Because it is journalism of both the outer *and* inner lives of a people; his poetry dares to carry upon its back the otherwise unimaginable agony of countless souls.

State of Siege by the late, great Mahmoud Darwish is another magisterial instance of witness-art: a smashed vase of a poem, not unlike Eliot's *Wasteland* ("these are the fragments I have shored against my ruin") only in this case it is the very real wasteland of Palestine that Darwish surveys. It makes sense, in a time of war or siege, to speak in shards; in such times of duress, the world appears shattered, and fragments are what the artist is left with when they can muster the concentration, the energy, and the faith to put pen to paper and write something down.

Like Eliot's *Wasteland*, the void is never far in Darwish's *State of Siege*. Unlike the parched faith of *Wasteland*, however, *State of Siege* is seared by a near mystical love; amid the rubble, an affirmation of earth and angels in the same breath. Faced with the abyss, hope obstinately arises. Hate is transmuted, and enslavement has the poet dreaming freedom: "A little, absolute blue / Is enough / To ease the burden of this time / And clean the mud of this place." But first pain must be set aside, as an unsteady burden preventing one from traveling light, "like those who ascend to God do." Interestingly enough, trafficking as Darwish does here with eternity as the nearest hope, the poet refuses to relegate poetry to a secondary concern, lamenting the cost of violence on art:

> . . . the work that remains to be done in language.
> In addition to the structural fault that
> Damage poem, play and incomplete painting . . .
> words that besiege me in my sleep
> words of mine that have not been said
> that write me then leave me, looking for the remainder of my sleep.

Out of the other side of his mouth, though, Palestine's national treasure expresses an ambivalence, warning us against loving (his) words overmuch, during hard times: "We do not care much for the charm of adjectives . . . Do not trust the poem . . . Writing is a small puppy biting nothingness . . ." Instead, the poem expresses a deeper allegiance to the tribe of humanity, to beauty, to Home as a state-of-being. Things that people everywhere can appreciate, or should.

In this manner, the poet reconciles the false distinction between the active life and the contemplative life, since his words are also actions. Specifically, in those first heady days of the Egyptian revolution, a great deal of pent-up creative energy was unleashed in the streets, and much of it took the form of poetry. Before and after things got ugly—courtesy of the previous regime's rent-a-mob—Al Jazeera reported spirited poetry readings at Tahrir Square.

Protestors heartily sang the punchy poems of legendary Egyptian poet Ahmed Fouad Negm who, in his bold verse, has been using puns and colloquial speech to critique the state and mock its corrupt leaders for a few decades. A much younger poet, Tamim al-Barghouti, also came to be regarded as one of Egypt's revolutionary voices. Though he couldn't be in Egypt during the demonstrations that ousted Mubarak, al-Barghouti faxed a new poem back home after the government-imposed Internet blackout. His poetry was photocopied and distributed throughout the square and, when people erected two massive, makeshift screens in Tahrir, al-Barghouti was able to virtually participate in the revolution, after all, by reading his words to the gathered crowds.

Despite these instances of political poetry, I believe that, at its heart, poetry is apolitical—even if it is sometimes employed in the service of politics—since it cannot take sides. In addition to serving as a witness in times of crises, poetry can act as a sort of (inner) alarm system, activated when we've strayed, trespassed or tripped into unholy territory. Reminding us, like American soldier-poet Brian Turner does in his exemplary *Here, Bullet* that: "it should break your heart to kill . . . nightmare you." This is what I mean by poetry as spirit journalism, a report on the life of our collective spirit, a reminder of our higher estate, and allegiances to one another and life.

On that note, I will end with a cherished work emblematic of what poetry can offer in bleak days. Here is an excerpt from W.H. Auden's *September 1, 1939*, a poem that many reached for after 9/11 and will continue to turn to, so long as we need reminding by the better angels of our nature:

> All I have is a voice
> To undo the folded lie,
> The romantic lie in the brain
> Of the sensual man-in-the-street
> And the lie of Authority
> Whose buildings grope the sky:
> There is no such thing as the State
> And no one exists alone;
> Hunger allows no choice
> To the citizen or the police;
> We must love one another or die.
> Defenseless under the night
>
> Our world in stupor lies;
> Yet, dotted everywhere,
> Ironic points of light
> Flash out wherever the Just
> Exchange their messages:
> May I, composed like them
> Of Eros and of dust,
> Beleaguered by the same
> Negation and despair,
> Show an affirming flame.

1. The program, "Akhbar Baladna" (News of Our Country), is hosted by Reem Maged on ONtv. As an aside, I'd like to add that the caller was Coptic, while the activist was a Muslim, showing another face to the sectarian violence covered by the media.
2. Gustav Janouch. Conversations with Kafka: Second Edition. (New Directions, 1971): 47

Seeking the Light Through Literature

THE HUMAN HEART ABHORS a vacuum. With organized religion losing ground, all sorts of substitutes rush in to fill the god-shaped hole. One particularly effective and time-honored balm for the aching human heart is literature. For some, poetry is how we pray, now. In these skeptical times, there still exists an Absolute Literature, in the coinage of Italian writer Roberto Calasso, where we might discern the divine voice. Such pre and post-religious literature shares aims and concerns similar to belief systems: sharpening our attention, cultivating a sense of awe, offering us examples of how to better live and die—even granting us a chance at transcendence.

Mysteriously, certain strains of literary art are capable of using words to lose words, ushering us to the threshold of that quiet capital of riches: Silence. It is, after all, in silent contemplation that difficulties patiently unfurl and entrust us with their secrets. By deepening our silences, such literature allows us to overhear ourselves and can lend us a third (metaphysical) eye. We are able not only to bear witness to the here and now but, past that, calmly gaze at eternal things, over the head of our troubled times, in order to try and understand our spiritual condition (where we've come from and where we're heading).

Currently, in our fractured world, beset by so much physical suffering and political turmoil, as a kind of (unconscious?) corrective, more people are reading and writing literature that addresses the life of the spirit, overtly or otherwise. One manifestation of this renewed spiritual hunger that is being met by literature is the publication of a giant anthology, The Poet's Quest for God: 21st Century Poems of Faith, Doubt and Wonder (Eyewear, 2016), featuring over three hundred contemporary poets from around the world and of great value (as the jacket blurb indicates) "to those for whom poetry has become a resource or replacement for faith-bound spirituality."

Likewise, more literary-spiritual oases are appearing in the desert of popular culture to slake the great thirst of seekers. Among the ones I'm aware of, and turn to for sustenance and inspiration, are edifying podcasts such as Krista Tippett's *On Being* and Godspeed Institute, or interfaith literary journals such as *The Sun, Parabola, Tikkun, Tiferet, Sufi,* and many others.

But, since we cannot step into the same river twice, what *does* a return to religion look like? There are poets, writers, and artists who pursue direct paths to God through their art. And there are readers, myself included, who study the lives and utterances of saints and mystics for moral guidance and uplift. For example, in Brad Gooch's valuable new biography, *Rumi's Secret,* where the celebrated mystical poet and the world he lived in (around eight hundred years ago) come to life, we develop a deeper appreciation of why this Muslim saint matters to us so much at this historical moment.

Gooch, in conversation with ambitious Rumi translator Jawid Mojaddedi, quotes Mojaddedi as saying to him: "Rumi resonates today because people are thinking post-religion. He came to see mysticism as the divine origin of every religion." This is a subject that Mojaddedi further unpacks in his illuminating piece, "Following the Scent of Rumi's Sufism in a Postreligious Age."

Coleman Barks, regarded as one of the great popularizers of Rumi in English, concurs: "I do believe that Rumi found himself going beyond traditional religion. He has no use for dividing up into the different names of Christian and Jew and Muslim. It was a wild thing to say in the thirteenth century, but he said it, and he was not killed."

Nowadays, there is also a more ambiguous literature (as well as audience) that finds it needless to name their nameless yearning and sees no contradiction in drawing on different traditions to make a patchwork quilt of their inchoate longing. This peculiarly modern pilgrim, unencumbered by dogma, is unembarrassed to treat organized religions as an archaeological site to be excavated for durable ruins—unearthing fragments of Beauty, Grace, Wisdom wherever they might find them and leaving behind what does not resonate, spiritually.

In such literature that is not directly religious, all sorts of spirits are invited, random relics thrown into the spiritual pot to prepare a nourishing bone broth. Amid culture wars dominating the headlines and airwaves, prayerful prose or poetry and mystic art grant us the opportunity to share Good News, or to *make a joyful noise.* One way of doing so is by giving thanks, even in the midst of suffering, or "try[ing] to praise the mutilated world" (Adam Zagajewski). In a hymn of a poem, "Brief for the Defense," Jack Gilbert urges:

We must have
the stubbornness to accept our gladness in the ruthless
furnace of this world. To make injustice the only
measure of our attention is to praise the Devil.

Belief, in the midst of chaos, remembers the indestructible world. And
we are fearless once we recall that we are also deathless. Belief also teaches
us to deeply trust, in spite of appearances, in the innate and inexhaustible
goodness of life, and how we might contribute to it by caring for our souls.
Instinctively, out of self-preservation in the encroaching darkness, we seek
out the light with greater urgency—recognizing the necessity for transfor-
mation, reevaluation of values, evolution . . . We are called to sanctify our
days, in the phrasing of Kahlil Gibran:

Your daily life is your temple and your religion
Whenever you enter into it take with you your all.

Thus, literature in the service of belief, though mindful of other disci-
plines, is also shrewdly aware of their inadequacies—how the consolations
of psychology, philosophy, science, even language, cannot quite address the
mysteries of the human heart. Mystical art addresses a mute center in us,
initiating us into hardly communicable secrets, numinous states of being
and a knowing (gnosis) at the very limits of our self or ego.

In these skeptical times, poems are hymns. For me, too, as a poet,
poetry is how I pray. Past the personal, poets sing for those who cannot:
registering our awe, making sense of our anguish, and harnessing the long-
ing of countless souls. Unlike prose, poetry can keep its secrets—deepening
our silences, so that we might overhear ourselves.

Lately, I'm consumed with the idea of the artist as a kind of mystic,
and abiding by the laws of beauty as a form of prayer. How, in Persian poet,
Omar Khayyam's deceptively simple utterance, I pray by admiring a rose,
one finds the connection among the visible, invisible, and indivisible laid
bare. Theologian and Sufi mystic, Al Ghazali, puts it thus: "This visible
world is a trace of that invisible one and the former follows the latter like a
shadow."

One year before his death, Rilke is meditating upon the inseparability
of the material and spiritual worlds, in these memorable words:

It was within the power of the creative artist to build a bridge be-
tween two worlds, even though the task was almost too great for
a man . . . Everywhere transience is plunging into the depths of
Being. It is our task to imprint this temporary, perishable earth
into ourselves, so deeply, so painfully and passionately, that its

essence can rise again, invisible, inside of us. We are the bees of
the invisible. We wildly collect the honey of the visible, to store
it in the great golden hive of the invisible.

Reverence for the visible world is not in opposition to the invisible
one; in the same way that it is through the body we access the life of the
spirit. Remembering we are "bees of the invisible," sweetens the suffering
and even cheats death of its ultimate sting. We are saved by the very idea of
a back and forth, between a Here and There. Bodies are like poems that way,
only a fraction of their power resides in the skin of things. The remainder
belongs to the spirit that swims through them.

Beauty, far from being a superficial concern is essential, and can be
a turnstile that leads us from the visible to the invisible world. To return
to Khayyam, yet again, by admiring the rose—its inscrutable architecture
and scented essence—we are made finer morally, spiritually even. This is
how aesthetics can serve as an ethical code, and prayer is "the soliloquy of a
beholding and jubilant soul" (Emerson's definition).

Poets, philosophers and mystics, by their nature, seem especially
well-suited to exposing the false divisions between the visible and invisible
worlds. While a calling in the life of an artist might be divorced from the
strictly religious sense of the word, it still requires similar renunciations,
obedience and sacrifice. I can't say I've studied the lives of mystics as closely
as I have those of artists, yet the profound similarities seem difficult to
dismiss.

The artistic-philosophic landscape is teeming with seers of this type.
The power and aura of these fiery spirits derives as much from the truths or
realities they have revealed as what they've had to sacrifice along the way; it
is an authority born of the tension between what is accomplished and what
is suffered.

What such poets or thinkers have in common is a life-long struggle
to build a bridge between the two worlds—an uncommon commitment to
bear better witness and Be, more fully. To travel to and fro, between the
visible and the invisible, required a kind of vanishing act of the traveler,
what Foucault called "a voluntary obliteration that does not have to be rep-
resented in books because it takes place in the very existence of the writer."

Marianne Williamson & the New Spirituality

I ADMIT, INITIALLY, I was excited to learn of US presidential candidate Marianne Williamson. I found Williamson's emphasis on ethics and our inner lives as well as her call for a moral and spiritual awakening refreshing. This was a far cry from the language of the current occupant of the White House and not quite the sort of thing one, typically, hears from presidential hopefuls.

In her cultural diagnostics and aspirational language, addressed to the *better angels of our nature*, I heard echoes of spiritual teachers I admired, such as Muslim mystic, Rumi:

> "Perhaps, you are searching among the branches, for what only appears in the roots."

Also, by placing the condition of our hearts at the center of our calamity and reason for why we allowed ourselves to stray so far off course, I was reminded of these soulful words by Trappist monk and activist, Thomas Merton:

> It is true, political problems are not solved by love and mercy. But the world of politics is not the only world, and unless political decisions rest on a foundation of something better and higher than politics, they can never do any real good . . .

Then, I learned that Williamson was one of the original popularizers of something called *A Course in Miracles*, a self-help book with a cult-like following that I'd vaguely heard of. Following that, I heard Oprah (an early champion of Williamson) introduce her as "my spiritual counselor." Hmm, I thought. From what I'd seen, so far, it seemed like Williamson's heart was in the right place, only now I was concerned that she might turn voters off by pretending to know more than she truly did or playing (up) the role of guru. Friends suggested that her presidential bid was some sort of publicity stunt and that she had framed it in her mind as part of a 'love ministry.'

But, this was not my feeling. My concern was that in the land of the blind, the one-eyed woman is queen. To get a taste for the blind ambition and utter absence of modesty symptomatic of our confused times, head over to Instagram, for example, to read some of the outlandish titles that the spiritually immature assign themselves: *prophet, sage, visionary, authenticity expert, freedom coach, transformation facilitator, inspirationalist, lightworker, alchemist . . .* The list is as long as it is tragicomic.

Which is not to suggest that Williamson is a complete con. But, in a cynical age, ignorant or suspicious of organized faith, I was afraid that this vacuum was increasingly being occupied by far too many students-posing-as-teachers, or other opportunists who styled themselves as 'life coaches' and 'metaphysicians' (a term Williamson used to describe herself during her presidential announcement). I worried that this patina of spirituality, actuality, might be a disservice to genuine seekers by seducing them to stop short of pursing the real deal, while surrendering their longing to another spiritual 'entrepreneur', bandying about seductive buzz words.

With organized religion on the wane and spiritual-but-not-religious seekers on the rise, self-help books and self-made gurus appear to be omnipresent and omnipotent. That such books have mushroomed into a lucrative industry at a time of collective lostness and laziness is no real surprise. Yet, that Williamson, self-help guru to the stars (before Oprah and the Kardashians, she was friends with Barbara Streisand, Elizabeth Taylor and countless glittering others) was running for the highest office in the land seemed like a further form of compromise.

I know I'm not alone in feeling disillusioned by corrupt politics and immoral politicians. But I'm also dismayed by these so-called spiritual leaders who presume to speak for The Universe. The background, learning and practice of these 'teachers' matters a great deal. Williamson claims to be uncomfortable with the term New Age, as she feels it invites mockery and disqualifies her from being regarded as a serious thinker.

Yet, her inspiration and how she made her name, A Course in Miracles (ACIM), is a 'channeled' self-help book that was allegedly dictated by Jesus Christ, no less—over a period of seven years, claims its helpless scribe. In 1965, Helen Schucman claimed Christ, suddenly, began to speak to her, saying "This is a course in miracles. Please take notes."

Which is to say, Williamson is hardly a scholar in the traditional sense, say, of the Tao te Ching, for example, or any of the time-honored books of respected spiritual or philosophic traditions. In fact, it is precisely this sort of spiritual pastiche that makes reasonable people wary of New Age philosophy, with its tendency to cherry pick terms or ideologies out of context to create its cozy patchwork quilt.

Uprooted from tradition, or the direct source of light, New Age ideas are like a shadow of a shadow. In my modest experience and readings, truly holy persons—mystics, saints, masters—are humble and tend to shun attention or power. As ancient Chinese philosopher, Lao Tzu, memorably put it: "He who knows, does not speak. He who speaks, does not know."

I suspect that to a traditional Christian, ACIM's view of itself as the words of Jesus and "Third Book" of the Bible (after the Hebrew Bible and Christian New Testament) would be viewed as downright blasphemous. Despite its Christian-sounding language, ACIM is heretical in its treatment of the doctrine of salvation (referring to such teachings as "attack" philosophies) and claiming there is no sin, suffering or need to perfect oneself, since we are all perfect/divine. Students and teachers of the ACIM made further outrageous claims, such as self-proclaimed "modern-day mystic" David Hoffmeister, who not only regularly heard from Jesus, too, but suggested he could raise the dead!

I suspect such false revelation and distorted theology, with its profusion of miracles, raised the blood pressure of Franciscan Catholic priest, Benedict Groeschel. Groeschel was a former student of the author of ACIM, Schucman at Columbia, and went on to become a psychologist like Schucman and a close friend in the last dozen years of her life. More than once, Schucman told Groeschel, "I hate that damn book" (referring to ACIM), just as she repeatedly disavowed its teachings and the cult it created.

Ultimately, Groeschel believed that ACIM might have been based on a diabolical entity, and wrote "This woman who had written so eloquently [in ACIM] that suffering really did not exist spent the last two decades of her life in the blackest psychotic depression I have ever witnessed." ("A Still, Small Voice, A Practical Guide On Reported Revelations," by Fr. Benedict J. Groeschel, C.F.R., Ignatius Press 1993). Groeschel summed it up this way, to journalist Randall Sullivan (in his book, The Miracle Detective, Grove/Atlantic): "I decided that ACIM was a fascinating blend of poorly understood Christianity . . . and poorly understood Christian Science . . . all of it filtered through some profound psychological problems."

However, for the uninformed who seek the comfort of faith, without the inconvenience of a commitment, ACIM offers easy solace. This curious project undertaken by two co-heads of the psychology department at Columbia College (as their answer to "there must be another way") continues

to enjoy a disturbingly broad appeal with its moral relativism and panthe-
ism, and is even referenced in church settings.

Now, here is unconventional presidential candidate, Marianne Wil-
liamson, demanding that America dig deeper and examine its soul while
voting for her as our moral leader. Williamson's credentials are inseparable
from her self-help career (in addition to calling herself an activist, she iden-
tifies as an entrepreneur).

Only in an age of shameless advertising, is it desirable for a human
being to become a 'brand'. Considering the seriousness of the position Wil-
liamson is campaigning for, it's difficult not to be put off by the superfi-
ciality of her belief system. To present ACIM as poetry or a collection of
meditations is one thing, but to champion it as scripture is blasphemous
and dangerous.

Given the current mess we're in, I maintain it's refreshing and neces-
sary to hear Williamson introduce morality, spirituality, love and mercy into
the national discourse as an antidote to the rampant fear and loathing we
live with. Yet, questions around her qualifications remain. For example:

> Does Williamson pose a risk as a false prophet or a sign of the
> times: the spiritual equivalent of fast food for the starved and
> undiscerning? How discerning and intelligent is she; how morally
> rigorous to be duped by a hoax like ACIM and make it her life's
> work? Is she naive or a shrewd celebrity guru preying on the hun-
> ger and ignorance of the powerful, in order to further her ambi-
> tions? In voting Williamson, do we usher in a potential cult leader
> as president, or an intellectual and spiritual lightweight posing as
> deep thinker and profound spiritual teacher?

This is not Williamson's first foray into politics; in 2014, she ran for
Congress in California, unsuccessfully (finishing in fourth place). And, of
course, the issues Williamson is promoting are not all New Agey, but also
non partisan and touch on how we all live. Notably, she addresses festering
race relations in America, for example, and proposes a $100 billion in slav-
ery reparations. Perhaps, the charitable thing in considering Williamson as
a candidate is to try to look past the facile self-help talk, and see her broad
message of love and healing as a necessary corrective to our unconscious
living.

C.S. Lewis & the Spiritual Tipping Point

WHEN I WENT TO see the play, *The Most Reluctant Convert*, I knew next to nothing about its subject. Other than that C.S. Lewis was the author of one of my favorite books when I was a child, his spiritual life was a mystery to me. As a sensitive and imaginative pre-teen, I was set alight by The Lion, The Witch and the Wardrobe, the first volume in Lewis's "Chronicles of Narnia." I was utterly aware at the time of Narnia's sacramental undercurrents, that Aslan (a major character in the Chronicles and also known as The Great Lion) represented a sacrificial Christ figure or that Lewis was a 'Christian apologist' (as he has been dubbed). None of that holy apparatus mattered to me then. Yet, it is intimately relevant to me, now, as is the subject of this new play: religious conversion.

How *does* a diehard atheist become, in effect, one of the most successful evangelists of the twentieth century? Remarkably, Lewis's inner life and spiritual pilgrimage serve as the plot, action and characters of this extended monologue, executed with wit and great feeling, by award-winning actor Max McLean. There is no set change in this one man play, we mostly see McLean—who is also the playwright and director of this ambitious work—standing, center stage, and reminiscing. Nor does he ever leave throughout the performance the book-lined room meant to represent Lewis' study at Oxford, in 1950, an academic position he assumed at the age of twenty-six. Only rarely will McLean-as-Lewis stroll across this stage—on one end to light a pipe, on another to fix a drink.

Notably, there was also no intermission during the eighty minute, sold-out performance I attended in Fort Lauderdale's Parker PlayHouse theater (the play is, also, touring the country). Yet, despite its demanding subject matter and simple stage set, there was never a dull moment. In fact, it's been years since I've attended a play where the audience (in this case, some 1,200 souls) seemed to be active participants in the play, punctuating the text with hearty laughter and, occasionally, sighing meaningfully. It's a testament to McLean's charismatic stage presence, intimate knowledge of the material and droll delivery that he manages to hold our attention, and capture our imaginations for as long as he did with as little distractions as he had.

McLean as Lewis cuts a commanding figure and seems to embody the brilliant Oxford Don through his journey from staunch materialist to one of the most beloved Christian authors. The Lewis we first encounter, speaking in his own words (mostly taken from his autobiography, Surprised by Joy and augmented by his letters) is an arrogant, young intellectual. A scientifically-minded, voracious reader he contemptuously rejects the Christian tradition of his father, and presents himself as mocking of faith, lusty, and beyond guilt. In one of the many memorable pronouncements throughout this play, he declares: 'Cowardice drove me to hypocrisy, and hypocrisy to blasphemy.'

As an ex-agnostic, myself, a student of Existentialist philosophy maddened by my own music and mistaking the totality of my mysterious being for the limitations of my mind, I recognized my college self in this early portrait of the author. Thus, I joined the audience in the laughter of recognition, as Lewis lambasted the vanity of his former self. I knew all too well from my own recent history the futility of persuading such a short-sighted, argumentative creature that they could be wrong, or that there might be more to the story than their 'logical' and spiritually-immature self can comprehend.

To assist in this story of a man telling himself his life, the back of the stage is composed of a series of projected photographs depicting key characters in the development of the author, which become larger and seem to come alive as Lewis recollects their significance. After our young atheist has spent a good half hour ranting about the horror of the Christian Universe, with its lack of an Exit Door or treaty with reality, the passionate bibliophile encounters Yeats. The Irish poet—not a Christian, but one who rejects materialist philosophy—offered Lewis a *Perhaps*, a world beyond that of his senses. With it, Lewis confesses to experiencing a desire for the occult, the supernatural, a spiritual lust that takes him "from eccentricity to perversity." The fact that the occult was scorned by atheists and rationalist, alike, appeals to the rebel in Lewis, and leads him astray, to flirt with diabolical fantasies.

As it turns out, this dabbling in the occult does not last long and soon comes to seem sordid to this unconscious seeker, who confesses shortly after that his "imagination was baptized" . But, after a taste of this numinous new desire he experiences, it also proves short-lived, the 'world turned common, again' and he is frightened by his greed to have it, once more.

I admit, I was more than a little surprised to learn of the name Lewis assigns to this elusive desire: Joy. As a questing young man, in my late teens / early twenties, I had come up with a similar formula, which I thought original and included it in my first book of aphorisms, Signposts to Elsewhere: "Pleasure may be snatched from life's fists, but joy is granted."

It was humbling to hear that, once again, truth agrees with itself, and Lewis had used more or less the same wording to describe his yearnings, recognizing that while pleasure is in our power, *Joy* never is (and must be Divinely granted).

Arriving at Oxford University, at eighteen, the once-atheist finds the remnants of his old word view assaulted from all sides. The first chink in his armor takes the form of reading Christian writer, Chesterton, which was followed by the conversion of his intellectual sparring partner, Owen Barfield, from materialist to theist. This leads Lewis to question the reliability/supremacy of his mind, and to come at the realization that 'rock bottom reality had to be intelligent'. As he encounters more Christian writers, the young reader admits to a wider disturbance and Lewis declares, mock-dramatically, 'all my books were turning against me!'

A central figure in the conversion of this book-based seeker to Christianity is George McDonald, Scottish poet, fantasy writer and minister. At this point, Lewis amusingly confides to the audience that 'Christianity was beginning to sound more sensible, apart from its Christianity' and, in contrast, Voltaire and company to seem more thin. Yet, he still cannot utter the word God ('I called Him Spirit').

All this dramatization of Lewis' spiritual biography occurs before the theologian-to-be and literary scholar turns twenty-six years of age. In spiritual time, in the words of Lewis, it is before 'God closed in on him'. At this decisive moment, our protagonist feels he was offered a moment of free choice. He thought he wore a suit of armor and he could, now, unbuckle it. The Spirit had become personal for him.

The audience might have collectively gasped at this change of heart and I found myself in tears, recalling my own embattled relationship with organized religion, growing up as a cultural Muslim, and a skeptic for far too long. In turn, I remembered, how deeply I'd been moved, just a few years ago, by a poem that my wife's high school religion teacher shared with me, Francis Thompson's *Hound of Heaven*. Permit me to quote the opening of his prayer-like verse for those unfamiliar with it:

I fled Him, down the nights and down the days;
I fled Him, down the arches of the years;
I fled Him, down the labyrinthine ways

Of my own mind; and in the mist of tears
I hid from Him, and under running laughter.
Up vistaed hopes I sped;
And shot, precipitated,
Adown Titanic glooms of chasmèd fears,
From those strong Feet that followed, followed after.
But with unhurrying chase,
And unperturbèd pace,
Deliberate speed, majestic instancy,
They beat—and a Voice beat
More instant than the Feet—
'All things betray thee, who betrayest Me.

After such a transformation, Lewis confesses (in words that contin-ued to resonate deeply with the arc of my own spiritual awakening) that he could play at philosophy no longer, the Absolute had arrived. Having been broken open this way and humbled, we find him undergoing profound soul-searching: "What I found appalled me—depth after depth of pride and self-admiration—a zoo of lusts, a bedlam of ambitions, a nursery of fears, a harem of hatreds. My name is legion."

Even though Lewis had given in and prayed, recognizing that the 'hardness of God is kinder than the softness of man,' his journey Home is not yet complete—for he has only converted to theism, he tells us, and not fully to Christianity. Yet, he was curious and longing to learn more about the Lord from any source, he says. Likening paganism to the childhood of religion, he was keen to learn where it had achieved maturity.

It's at this stage, that another important figure in Lewis' conversion story enters the picture, English writer and fellow Oxford teacher, J.R.R. Tolkien. In a heady conversation with Tolkien, on the truth of myths and the prison of rational materialism, his slightly older friend finally convinces Lewis of Christianity with the following words: 'Christ is a myth working on us in the same way as the others, but with this tremendous difference that it *really happened*.'

Before Lewis' ultimate surrender to Christianity, we are confronted with (for me) the one unsavory moment in McLean's play[1], or the return of the unbecoming contempt of earlier-Lewis. In embracing Christianity as the-myth-that-really-happened, he recognizes that the Incarnation of Jesus is the main point separating Christianity from other religions. In contrasting its claim that God became a man, we hear Lewis' rightly says this would be considered as blasphemous to other faiths, such as: Judaism, Islam, Buddhism.

Yet, he is not content to leave it at that, and uncharitably ridicules Prophet Mohammed, for cheap laughs from the audience. Given the current state of Islamophobia, I winced at McLean's inclusion of this low blow directed at the messenger of Islam and his clumsy characterization of the faith. My hope is that the more mature Lewis, as a practicing Christian, did not permit himself such rigidity and intolerance.

Aside from this unnecessary and distasteful moment, we see Lewis back on track, recognizing he has taken the last and necessary step, comparing his conversion to awakening and a search for Joy. In the ecstatic closing scene, Lewis declares a series of epiphanies:

> I was made for another world . . . We are to drink Joy at the fountain of Joy . . . We are at present at the wrong side of the door . . . There are no ordinary people, all are immortals . . . only humility . . . I, now, Believed.

With that, the lights dim and only the face of Mclean's Lewis is illumined, before a background of the vast universe.

I thought it a fine decision to end with the birth of Lewis, so to speak, as a Christian and author who would go on to make his mark on the world. When I gathered my wits, wiping more tears from my face, I joined in the enthusiastic standing ovation and applause. In focusing on the reluctant religious passage of one famous atheist, the play had succeeded in delivering a communal spiritual experience, in its own right, giving shape and language to the ineffable power of revelation and submission. C.S. Lewis On Stage is a powerful work of (he)art with something to say to all of us today, whether we belong to the doubting, cynical camp or, at the other end, the spiritual-but-not-religious group.

Because I thought Islamophobia unworthy of the integrity of this play, I sent the following letter its playwright:

> Dear Max McLean,
>
> I thoroughly enjoyed C.S. Lewis On Stage: The Most Reluctant Convert and, in turn, I hope you will appreciate my review.
>
> Yet, I'm also deeply disturbed by your reluctance to remove the ignorant and hateful line re: Prophet Mohammed "cutting off the head" of someone who asked him if he was Allah (Despite the emails you admit to receiving, which encourage you to take the offensive line out, I don't understand why you've defiantly decided to keep it in).
>
> Buddha and Socrates when asked the same hypothetical question, regarding Brahma or Zeus politely laugh it off, finding it ludicrous. Yet, it is Mohammed who has the hysterical and

murderous response—tearing his clothes, first—thereby reinforcing discriminatory views of Islam as savage and bloody.

Your justification, Sir, for keeping the unfortunate line in are equally inadequate and revealing.

You tell us Lewis said it.

So what? Lewis said a lot of other things, too; but creating thoughtful art is about selection and omission.

Theater is provocative.

Meaning what? Does he not realize it is irresponsible and dangerous to enforce such fear and loathing, at a time when Islamophobia and attendant hate crimes are on the rise?

The historical record supports it.

False. Mohammed got along and even protected those of different faiths, such as Jews and Christians. Also, he was known to be kind and forgiving to those who insulted him.

A rare instance of prosecution for blasphemy in the Muslim historical record was of a Christian accused of insulting the Prophet Muhammad.

It ended in an acquittal in 1293.

That said, ultimately, do you find it fitting in a play of such a spiritual nature to make this type of low blow, for cheap laughs, at another (much beleaguered) faith?

Is it really necessary to pit the world's second largest religion, nearly 2 billion souls, against Christianity—in order to present the latter as the One True Way?

As the founder and artistic director of the Fellowship for the Performing Arts (FPA), surely, this does not fall under your noble mission to produce 'compelling theatre from a Christian worldview that engages a diverse audience'?

This is beyond 'political correctness' as you brush it off in your written defense; this is more about moral integrity and respecting people of all faiths.

It is my hope, dear Sir, whose one-man-show this is, that you will reconsider removing this problematic line, which only sullies an otherwise inspiring, sophisticated work of art and faith.

Thank you,
Yahia Lababidi

Spiritual Tourism

A Confession

The life of sensation is the life of greed; it requires more and more. The life of the spirit requires less and less . . .

— ANNIE DILLARD

DESPITE BEING RAISED A cultural Muslim and only recently, in the last five years or so, finding myself deeply drawn to its mystical branch, Sufism, I also frequent churches with my dear wife, a practicing Catholic, from time to time. In fact, I frequently refer to a line from a sermon I heard while visiting a church in Buenos Aires, and seek to apply it whenever I am stuck (in either life or literature): *El misterio necesita silencio y contemplación* (the Mystery requires silence and contemplation).

Yet, on account of a quirk in my temperament, that I only partially understand, I am not a practicing *anything* (other than artist). I realize that Paths are also relationships and, to be meaningful, they require fidelity. I also know that it's all very well being a spiritual tourist, keeping in mind that one cannot truly *know* a place until you live there. To put it slightly differently, the Sufis say that a person who tries to find water by digging a little here and there will die of thirst. Whereas, the one who digs deeply in one spot, will find water to drink and share with others.

Thus, I've come to regard unfortunate spiritual tourists or erratic diggers, such as myself, as being the playboys of religion, perpetually thirsty— with a glut of choices, overfed, yet undernourished. What I'm describing, of course, is not unique; it's almost a modern predicament. So, despite finding great beauty, meaning and solace in different religious expression and traditions, to my regret, I find that I'm unable to fully commit to any one (and, in turn, reap the benefits of a sustaining discipline). Instead, I continue to pore over the lives of saints and mystics for guidance—Daoist, Buddhist, Jewish, Christian, Muslim—longing for transformation as I continue to fashion my queer artist's metaphysics.

Is there "resolution" in matters of the Spirit? All we can do is to share what we have. What I have, at this stage, is a profound and abiding appreciation of mystical literature as soul-transforming, and a calling. In turn, I attempt through my writing (poetry, aphorisms, even meditative prose pieces) to take readers *There*. Despite the personal impasse I find myself at, I've come to an understanding of my vocation. With humility and wonder, I view the artist as a kind of mystic, and art a form of prayer.

There is a quotation by Frederick Buechner that I find myself returning to, regularly, to better explain my literary-spiritual predicament: "The place God calls you to is the place where your deep gladness and the world's deep hunger meet."

Which is to say, not only are callings mysteries to the bewildered persons being summoned, but it's also marvelous how our inner longings correspond with outer needs.

I would never have imagined, for example, as a reactionary Existentialist (in my teens and twenties) who turned my back on my culture's oppressive religiosity—by throwing the luminous baby out with the sordid bath water—that I would one day find myself drawn to mysticism, specifically Sufism, or called to serve as a type of apologist for the vilified faith of my Home: Islam.

Yet, such is where my deep gladness and the world's deep hunger met. Strange to say but, recently, I've come to think of myself as something of an ex-writer, no longer enamored by art for art's sake, or purely literary concerns. Instead, what I try to do, lately, as an immigrant and poet living in the divided states of America and our wounded world, is to share the beauty I find in Sufism in hopes this might bring about some peace and healing—encouraging readers to question received wisdom, move past the false idols of popular culture and begin the difficult work of heart purification.

Much of my book of 800 original aphorisms, Where Epics Fail, is composed under the influence of Sufi literature, which I increasingly turn to for sustenance and inspiration. Aphorisms, are connected to a Sufi-informed world view in the sense that Rumi meant when he stated in his discourses, *Fihi Ma Fihi* (It Is What It Is) that: 'The best words are those that are few and to the point.' So, aphorisms are connected to wisdom literature, in general and, Sufism in particular. Ibn Ata Illah, for examples, is an important Sufi saint and sage of 13th century Egypt, who bequeathed us his treasured Kitab al Hikam (Book of Wisdom) composed of aphoristic writing.

I define aphorisms as 'what is worth quoting from the soul's dialogue with itself'. Which is to say that, out of the ongoing conversation I have with myself, occasionally, I'll overhear a line that I think is good enough to stand alone and represent the subject I've been musing on. My hope is that my spiritual aphorisms, found in my latest work, might serve as a form of peace offering and balm in these troubled times. Below, is a mixed bouquet from Where Epics Fail: Meditations to Live By:

> The contemplative life is not a passive one.

> Our most profound prayers hardly reach our lips—they are made with our entire being.

> The divided self is spiritually immature. Divine union begins with self unity.

> Wings are, always, on loan.

> Think of existence as a great love story: every shy creature or timid truth wants to be courted; every secret wants to be told—cultivate the art of listening.

Radical Love
Mysticism in Islam

Theologians may quarrel, but the mystics of the world speak the same language.

—Meister Eckhart

We live in unexemplary times, maddened by fear, murderous ignorance, and mistrust of one another. Even though Muslims make up around a fourth of the global population, or around two billion souls, for many, the faith has become besmirched with backwardness and violence. Islamophobia is a widespread, too painful reality, and hate speech is not without its cost. It is a proven fact that hate crimes against Muslims are on the rise, from bullying in the classroom to racial slurs, as well as more grave offenses, such as mosque burnings, even murders. Which is to say, hate and violence (on either side) begin in minds and hearts before finding their way to our lips and, soon enough, translating into heinous actions against (oftentimes, dehumanized) Others.

As an immigrant, Muslim, and writer living in Trump's alarming America, as well as a citizen of our increasingly polarized world, I will not deny that speaking out on behalf of Islam has become something of a burden and sweet responsibility. I find that I must begin most conversations on this subject, including this one, by stating the obvious: "Terrorism has no religion and most victims of terrorism are moderate Muslims."

It's tiresome to be continually on the defensive, which does not always bring out the best in us or the most charitable, gentle responses. A German Muslim scholar, when asked about the connection between terrorism and Islam, went on this rant:

> Who started the first world war? Not Muslims. Who killed 6
> million Jews in the Holocaust? Not Muslims. Who killed about
> 20 million Aborigines in Australia? Not Muslims. Who sent the
> nuclear bombs of Hiroshima and Nagasaki? Not Muslims. Who
> killed more than 100 million Indians in North America? Not
> Muslims. Who killed more than 50 million Indians in South
> America? Not Muslims. Who took about 180 million African
> Muslims as slaves obliged them to leave Islam, 88% of whom
> died and were thrown overboard into the Atlantic Ocean? Not
> Muslims . . .

Which is not to say that I believe, as a Muslim community, we are
entirely off the hook either. I agree with many theologians and scholars of
Islam who call for profound self-examination and a better understanding
of the faith, such as Hamza Yusuf's formula for "a renovation of the abode
of Islam . . . to make new again, repair, reinvigorate, refresh, revive our per-
sonal faith." It seems self-defeating and willful to deny that something is rot-
ten within the Muslim community, and that we need serious housekeeping.

As I said, we must begin, of course, by declaring to ourselves and the
world in no uncertain terms: *we condemn all violence, especially, in the name
of faith.* There is a damning quote, by Canadian author Robertson Davies,
that sums up how I feel about so-called "religious" fanatics in a handful of
words: "Fanaticism is overcompensation for doubt." To distance ourselves
from the blasphemous-murders-who-would-sabotage-faith, we need to
embody the peace, love, forgiveness, and sacrifice we find in the spirituality
that sustains us, and extend it to those who do not know any better.

For those who wish to throw out the luminous baby, Faith, with the
sordid water of current events, it is wise to recall the timeless words of a
religiously inspired proponent of nonviolence, the great Martin Luther King
Jr.: "Darkness cannot drive out darkness; only light can do that. Hate cannot
drive out hate; only love can do that."

Meantime, for those who wish to deepen their understanding of the
Muslim faith and its ecstatic dimension, I recommend Omid Safi's Radical
Love: Teachings from the Islamic Mystic Tradition (Yale University Press,
2018) as a fine point of entry. A leading scholar of Islam, Safi's Radical Love
arrives on the troubled scene with a peace offering, to clear the good name
of a much-maligned, widely misunderstood religion. Showing Love to be at
the very essence of Islam, the Divine, and, by extension, everything in exis-
tence, Safi's stirring collection of excerpts then goes on to expertly illustrate
how grossly terrorists (in the news and political office) have misperceived
the faith.

Which is to say, in the scorching heat of public debate on whether all Muslims are dangerous and should be banned from the civilized world, this book serves as an oasis. Safi presents us with a cool spot to sit and reflect on a religiously inspired state of bliss that, of necessity, precludes violence. After all, in honoring Beauty—as the Quran does, unmistakably, by declaring that God is beautiful and loves beauty—we learn to better appreciate the sanctity of life, all life, and recognize violence, any violence, as the cowardice, failure of imagination, and heresy that it truly is (irrespective of who tries to manipulate which holy text to suit their devious ends).

It is remarkable, for example, during this historical moment of Islamophobic panic, that a thirteenth-century Sufi mystic, Mawlana Jalāl ad-Dīn Muhammad Balkhi (known as Rumi in the West), is not only a best-selling poet but the most popular poet in the US! This is doubly interesting, since Rumi was also a refugee who lived in a turbulent time of religious persecution, not entirely dissimilar from our own. For the millions who appreciate Rumi's poetry, Safi's anthology offers an opportunity to better understand the Arabic/Persian traditions that produced him as well as the Muslim holy book, the Quran, that is fertile soil for Rumi's soul and art.

After all, isn't it another form of (insidious?) Islamophobia, given Rumi's current stature in popular culture, that the appreciation of his art should come at the expense of erasure of Islam from his work—as though this beloved, mystical poet is only palatable to the masses if entirely dissociated from the seeming stain of Islam?

Safi's own translations, here, seek to rectify this subtle violence, by making clear the ongoing conversation with Islam, or love letter addressed to the Divine, that inspires Rumi's poetry:

> The mystics of Islam see themselves as being rooted unambiguously in the word of God . . . their poems and stories are "Qur'an-ful," filled with both direct and indirect references to scripture.

Selections from the holy Quran are featured in Safi's Radical Love alongside sacred sayings of the Prophet Muhammad (Hadith Qudsi), emphasizing self-knowledge and mercy as a counterbalance, one hopes, to the ugliness and ignorance that blaspheme in the name of Faith:

> The remembrance of God
> brings serenity
> to hearts.—Qur'an 13:28

> To know God
> intimately

> intimately know yourself
> "He who knows his own soul
> knows his Lord"—Hadith Qudsi

Also featured in this fine spiritual compendium are mystical utterances and teachings of Divine love by celebrated Sufi poets, such as Attar, Hafez, and other key Muslim mystics, carefully selected and translated by Safi.

Page after page, we encounter these "intimates of God" (awliya', in Arabic) all love-drunk, engaged in the alchemy of transformation and advocating the hard work of overcoming ego and seeking Divine intimacy:

> Love of a human being
> is an ascension
> toward love of God. —Ruzbehan Baqli
> My heart takes on every form
> a pasture for gazelles,
> a cloister for monks,
> the idol's temple . . .
> I follow the religion of Love:
> Whichever way this caravan turns,
> I turn. —Ibn 'Arabi

Before reviewing this book, I had just completed another rather intriguing book on Islamic mysticism, entitled Ahmad Al Ghazali, Remembrance, and the Metaphysics of Love (2016), by Joseph E. B. Lumbard. The titular mystic, Ahmad, whose life and work are under study in this radical book, was the younger brother of Abu Hamid Muhammad Ghazali, regarded by many as the most important Muslim theologian.

Yet, according to both Lumbard and Safi, the path of radical love in Islamic mysticism found its most articulate spokesman in the lesser-known Ghazali, whose "Sawanih" (a short meditative prose text) Safi refers to as "the love child of Platonic dialogues and Shakespearean sonnets in a Persian Garden."

All this beginningless and endless love, naturally, circles back to the Divine, who is quoted in Safi's book as saying:

> I was a Hidden treasure
> and I loved to be intimately known
> So I created the heaven and the earth
> that you may know Me
> Intimately. —Hadith Qudsi

Safi separates his book of teachings into four parts: "God of Love" ("not just in God, but as God"); "Path of Radical Love" ("meditations on this overflowing"); "Lover and Beloved" ("the dance of love, being and becoming"); and "Beloved Community" ("how to achieve this in the here and now").

"Here and now" are words that Safi repeats quite often throughout his short, passionate introduction, in case readers mistakenly assume that mystics are only concerned with the next world:

> To be a mystic on the path of radical love necessitates tenderness in our intimate dealings, and a fierce commitment to social justice in the community we live in, both local and global.
> Again, Safi underscores this important point by circling back to the source, the Quran: "This is God's command: love and justice."

Think of this book as an extended hand, holding an olive branch. Or, in Safi's words,

I invite you to join us on this journey of love. May you find in these poems, in these luminous and fierce teachings of radical love from the heart of the Islamic tradition a mirror—one to reflect to you the beauty of your own soul.

We live in confusing times, where Islam and its practitioners need their friends. Sufism, generally speaking, remains relatively untarnished in the public imagination. But "What is Sufism to Islam?" a friend once asked me. The short answer is that it is its mystical branch. Books, of course, can be composed on this subject—and they have, including the valuable one currently under review. But, I think it's safe to say that Sufism is the heart of Islam. It is both the husk and flower of the faith.

Yes, mysticism is not for everyone. One must crawl, first, before one can fly—hence the suspicion ecstatics provoke, in those who do not soar (even within the faith itself). Sufism, in turn, is the (open) secret of Islam, the poetry and beauty, when you've boiled everything else away (dogma, etc.). I did not think that I, a recovering existentialist, would find myself one day slipping through the back door of Islam. Yet, led by an abiding longing, I crawled like a refugee to Sufism, for succor and inspiration. To paraphrase Rumi, I let myself be silently drawn by the strange pull of what I love, and it did not lead me astray.

As Safi reminds us in his helpful anthology: "Radical love is channeled through humanity. It has to be lived and embodied, shared and refined not in the heavens but right here and now, in the messiness of earthly life."

It is difficult, I think, in times like ours, not to become radicalized . . . by Pity. May this book help heal and illuminate broken hearts and open hardened ones. I leave you with one parting quotation, which features at the opening of this love manual, by a pioneering teacher of love in the Islamic tradition, the aforementioned Sufi mystic, Ahmad Al Ghazali:

> I will write you a book on Radical Love
> provided you do not bifurcate it
> into Divine Love
> and Human Love

Ballad of the Global Patriot

Script for a short film, by Academy Award®-nominated director Jehane Noujaim, for Sundance Now

"DAMAGED PEOPLE ARE DANGEROUS, they know they can survive." That line affected me, deeply, the first time I heard it as a young man, in the movie adaptation of Damage, by Josephine Hart.

In context, it was delivered as a perverse badge of courage and also a cautionary tale, or warning. As an embattled teenager, growing up in an unconventional household, I suppose I related . . . I suppose, on some level and in some way, we all do.

When our hearts break, do they break open, or do they harden? I suspect both, at some point, at different stages of life, we experiment with various ways of pain management, which can be another term for continuing to live. We can live like a hardened scab, impervious to mighty winds of the mutilated world around us, or like an open wound, sensitive to the slightest breeze of suffering or injustice we encounter.

I believe most of us try both ways and oscillate between one and the other. "The opposite of love is not hate, but indifference." This quote was coined by Holocaust survivor, Elie Wiesel. A global patriot is someone who recognized this, profoundly, our wound and the world wound is one.

Our larger allegiances are to one another, past the narrow-heartedness of mere nation-state and what that big-thinking and vast spirit, Einstein, referred to as: "an infantile disease . . . the measles of mankind: Nationalism."

There is no exchange rate for human suffering. Daring to care about the pain of others is not an option, but a shrewd form of self-preservation.

45

As world conscience, Martin Luther King Jr. reminds us: "Injustice any-
where is a threat to justice everywhere."

How it is, then, that we are told never to forget 9/11 and the nearly
3,000 innocent lives taken, and yet in the same breath we never remember
the unjust 'war' exacted in retribution and the hundreds of thousands Iraqi
civilian lives, for example.

All human life is sacred and all murder unholy. Like American soldier-
poet Brian Turner tells us in his devastating report from Iraq, Here, Bullet:
"it should break your heart to kill . . . nightmare you."

If we do choose to turn our back to the wailing of our mutilated world,
and carry on amusing ourselves to death, violence, like a karmic serpent will
wind its way to our doorstep.

Maybe we ask *What is Aleppo* and why should we care, and find our-
selves confronted with gun violence in our schools, or police brutality in
the streets, or the unhealing horrors of race relations in America, or the
unstoppable plaintive cry, as old as the creation of a nation, of American
Indians in Standing Rock, or physically and psychologically damaged war
vets, homelessness, uprootedness, refugees, Isis—all terrorists in the shape
of our shadows, all side-effects of the our pandemic of indifference.

If all this does not wake the sleepwalker, they are confronted with an-
other type of violence: the eruption of hateful reactionary politics at the
voting booths in the US and throughout Europe, leaders with vision or in-
tegrity, that don't reflect our longings or the better angels of our nature. If
we don't speak in unison, and declare: Not in our Name, we find ourselves
cutting off our nose to spite our face. And, waiting on the world to change.

But, you can't bury pain and not expect it to grow roots. What we can
do is try to tend, tenderly, to its bitter-sweet fruits.

I learned this lesson, in becoming an artist, just as I was becoming
an adult. 'The creative adult is the child who has survived' says Ursula K.
Le Guin. This encouraged me to try and see my personal pain as a gift. I've
come to see myself as having been lavishly gifted a pain, as thick and rich
as oil paint. By pushing that pain round the page, I've learned to make Art.

In time, I've come to be fascinated by wounds (a student of my own
condition?) and how to best put them to use. What if we were to view our
wounds as peepholes, through which to view the world and open us up to
the wounds of others, and our planet, as an extension of our larger body?

These words by Leonard Cohen's became my anthem,

> The birds they sang
> At the break of day
> Start again

I heard them say
Don't dwell on what
Has passed away
Or what is yet to be

Yeah the wars they will
Be fought again
The holy dove
She will be caught again
Bought and sold
And bought again
The dove is never free

Ring the bells (ring the bells) that still can ring
Forget your perfect offering
There is a crack in everything (there is a crack in everything)
That's how the light gets in.

Long before Cohen, another virtuoso of suffering, another Global Citizen, Rumi, voiced this timeless insight: "The wound is the place where the Light enters you." If the wound is where the Light enters us, then how can we keep our wound clean?

One way is to recognize that we are all wounded and wounding, exceptionalism is dangerous nonsense, we inflict pain knowingly and unknowingly. And, if this is so, we may try to forgive damaged people (including ourselves) since they can hardly imagine the pain they inflict on others.

Here's another perverse human truth that we as Global Patriots must be mindful of if we are to break this vicious cycle, this time from Auden:

I and the public know
What all schoolchildren learn,
Those to whom evil is done
Do evil in return.

Another human perversion comes to mind, how bullies seek to the play the role of victims. And I look at the dangerous folly of the Middle East, and I look at the self-defeating arrogance of the US, and I see the same gaping world wound, seeping, because it is not being compassionately tended to . . .

Another quote, from another Global Patriot with a prescription how we might begin to connect, and heal: (American psychiatrist) Morgan Scott Peck:

How strange that we should ordinarily feel compelled to hide
our wounds when we are all wounded! Community requires the
ability to expose our wounds and weaknesses to our fellow crea-
tures. It also requires the ability to be affected by the wounds of
others . . . But even more important is the love that arises among
us when we share, both ways, our woundedness.

We forgive to live. Because, as an Arab-American bridge-of-a-man, by
the name of Gibran, reminds us: 'Hate is a dead thing. Who of you would be
a tomb?" How is it that we readily accept that we are governed by physical
laws, like gravity, yet believe that we cannot afford to turn our backs on
age-old spiritual laws (Love, Compassion, Forgiveness, Mercy, Trust, Hope)
without paying too high a price.

What if we were to consider that every time we betray our conscience,
we strangle an angel? And, yet, it's not certain that we are allotted an infinite
supply of winged pardons.

Open Letter to Israel

*He who fights monsters should see to it that, in the process, he does not
become a monster.*
—Nietzsche

Tell me, what steel entered your heart,
what fear made you rabid,
what hate drove out pity?

How could you forget
that how we fight a battle
determines who we become,
when did you grow reckless
with the state of your soul?

We are responsible for our enemy,
compassion is to consider the role
that we play in their creation.

If you prick us, do we not bleed?
. . . If you poison us, do we not die?
and if you wrong us, shall we not revenge?

Strange, how one hate enables another;
how they are like unconscious allies,
darkly united in blocking out the Light.

Yes, we can lend ideas our breath, but ideals —
Peace, Justice, Freedom—require our entire lives

and, all who are tormented by such ideals
must learn to make an ally of humility.

Truth, and conscience, can be like large, bothersome flies
—brush them away and they return, buzzing louder
nearly 2,000 dead, in Gaza, 500 children
no, these are unbearable casualties to ignore
To speak nothing of the intangible casualties:
damage done to our collective psyche, trust, and sleep
no more nightmares, please, give us back our dreams
we can still begin, again, and must
wisdom is a return to innocence.

What Makes for Good Conversation?

IN OUR INCREASINGLY POLARIZED world, I've begun to ask myself what makes for a good conversation, what is the essential criteria for an engaging exchange. Is it being heard, learning something new, human connection, or something else, altogether?

With most of us living behind screens, I'm afraid that we might be getting rusty at the vital art (and sport) of face-to face, civilized exchange. As someone who lives for and through good conversations, here are some reflections from my personal experience of what I think contributes to valuable human interaction.

'Attention is the rarest and purest form of generosity' said Simone Weil, French philosopher, mystic and political activist. This is doubly so, in our hurried and distracted times. To truly listen—with our eyes, ears, mind and heart—is the first step. Conversation is not a series of interrupted monologues, where we are impatiently waiting for the other person to stop talking so that we can sound off. Interested people are more interesting to know and good listeners make for better talkers.

Hear and try to take in the other person with genuine interest. Try to consider how they might have arrived at the positions they hold, for better or worse. Even if their views might seem odious to you, try and see yourself in the other person, and the other person in you. Now, go further; flex your spiritual muscle, and seek the Divine in them. If we are able to see others in this light, then there is no one that we cannot speak with, and we are able learn from everyone.

Conversation, at its finest, is no small matter. It is a chance to touch the soul of another and expand our own. Put differently, we can forge a profound human connection with a perfect stranger because, ultimately, there are no strangers. We might think of others as the missing pieces of our puzzle—the more we know them, the more we know ourselves (and vice versa). Approaching another with openness, detachment, empathy and humility, we stand to discover something new about the world or ourselves. If we maintain curiosity and reverence for our conversational partner, while remaining willing to be surprised, we might emerge from our talk with them improved, perhaps, transformed.

A hearty talk is also an opportunity to practice radical honesty. If we are not willing to lay our heart bare, and give of ourselves meaningfully, why should they? It's the first person on the dance floor, willing to make a fool of themselves, that gets the party started. To be that person requires taking a risk and courage, as all important human interaction does. Pre-Socratic Greek philosopher, Heraclitus, puts it this way: "Man is most nearly himself when he achieves the seriousness of a child at play." That's what conversation is: serious play.

In a sense, all of life is conversation, really—with ourselves, others, this world and the Next. In conversation, as in real life, violence is a failure of imagination and an admission of defeat. Polite provocation can spark a healthy debate, where we are challenged and challenging. But, if a passionate, spirited, enthusiastic discussion devolves into one that is angry, vicious, or condescending, all the latent good of the exchange is lost. Good talk is an art, like dance, where we take turns leading and come back together. It is also a sport, but not a competitive one with winners and losers, rather one where the shared goal is to keep the ball up in the air.

Paradoxically, good conversation must also respect silence. The same way having something to say comes from quiet contemplation, and writing is born of reading, so non-verbal exchange in a conversation is as significant, if not more, than what is actually being said. Try not to rush the silences, yours or another's, out of nervousness, fear or awkwardness. Give time for what is said to sink in and be processed. It's a rare privilege to be allowed to think, wordlessly, in the presence of another and an act of trust.

Ultimately, conversation is a living thing, and nothing alive can be calculated or anticipated. There are no hard and fast rules for social intercourse that cannot be broken or rewritten. But, if we keep these basic guidelines, loosely, in mind next time we interact with a fellow human being in real time, we might be rewarded with a conversation that is revelatory, entertaining, civilizing.

Short Meditations on Inspiration and Hope

A poem arrives like a hand in the dark.

WHO KNOWS WHERE INSPIRATION comes from, and where it goes. I submit that even artists don't, at least, not yours truly. After something of a dry patch, where I began to refer to myself as an "ex-writer," I find that I'm writing poetry, again. In late 2019, I produced three new pieces I'm pleased with, actually, within three days: a feat that I've not achieved in years, possibly decades.

Blogging—something that I swore up and down I'd never do—has, certainly, helped to kickstart my creativity. For one, it forced this old dog to learn new tricks, since I began posting on a social blockchain by the name of Steem, where I was paid for my efforts in cryptocurrency. Also, one of the boons of joining a new community that thinks differently has been collaborating with other creative souls: visual artists who illustrated my writing as well as accomplished musicians who put my words to song, or transformed them into new art.

Inspired by this dynamic online platform and challenged by this new network of creative thinkers that I've become a part of, I find that I'm writing more and differently—so much so that I've begun to polish prose and poetry pieces I've posted on Steemit in order to include them as part of a new book.

Ultimately, I think the mysterious creative process has something to do with humility, desperation even, and the intensity of the conversation we are having with ourselves. Then, there is the spiritual dimension to consider. As

SHORT MEDITATIONS ON INSPIRATION AND HOPE   53

with life, perhaps, the fewer expectations we have of our art, the more fully we are able to surrender. Admitting to ourselves that creativity is, ultimately, beyond our control, we are more likely to be visited and helped by our muse.

Art, after all, is a product of authenticity. However artists might lie to themselves or others in their personal lives, art-making is involuntarily truth-telling. When we truly dare to lay our soul bare, we find that we are able to reach strangers; only what springs from the heart reaches the heart. Increasingly, I am concerned with how to ease souls in these troubled times we live in. Mostly, poetry is the best answer that I have. Below, is one of my new poems, reminding us to keep hope alive.

The Light-keepers

Hope is a lighthouse
(or, at least, a lamppost)
someone must keep vigil
to illumine this possibility

In the dark, a poet will climb
narrow, unsteady stairs
to gaze past crashing waves
and sing us new horizons

Others, less far-sighted, might
be deceived by the encroaching night
mistake the black for lasting, but
not those entrusted with trimming wicks

Their tasks are more pressing —
winding clockworks, replenishing oil-
there is no time for despair
when tending to the Light.

Does a Sex Beast Lurk in the Breast of Men?

In After Zen, Jan Willem van de Wetering's humorous, thoughtful account of his time at a Zen monastery, we meet monks behaving like adolescents in an all-boys boarding school. We learn, for example, from the gently-disillusioned author that 'Pam-pam was what the monks called the Western-type sandwiches I sometimes prepared in my room. The way sliced bread got cut, buttered and smacked together reminded them of [sexual encounters] they went after when they climbed the temple walls at night . . . '

Willem van de Wetering concluded 'the sex drive does not get sublimated spiritually . . . sexual longing is programmed into human genes; frustrate it and it becomes demonic.'

If this is the case with Zen monks, then what can be expected of Hollywood directors, executives, actors and comedians, where the "casting couch" seems to be a shabby, yet cherished, piece of furniture since the entertainment industry began. But, even then, who would have anticipated that the ninety-three year-old former president, George H.W. Bush, was getting handsy, from his wheelchair! Or that Garrison Keillor, a national treasure, and admired TV journalist, Matt Lauer, would lose their jobs the same day, before we knew why?

The list is long and it goes on. Lately, every week an icon is toppled and their feet of clay exposed. The serious Charlie Rose a serial flasher? The gentle, spiritual Russell Simmons, now, stepping down from his Def Jam empire after another damning sexual assault allegation. All contrite (to be caught?) offering partial apologies, professing bad memories and faulty understanding of mutual consent. Most promise to soul search, get help and step out of the public limelight (though others don't, like Al Franken, Roy Moore, President Donald Trump).

As Simmons acutely noted, following his second accusation:

> This is a time of great transition. The voices of the voiceless, those who have been hurt or shamed, deserve and need to be heard. As the corridors of power inevitably make way for a new generation.

Yes, women are finally fed up and disinclined to keep silent any more, emboldened by the increasingly large numbers of sexual victims coming out of the woodwork—witness the overwhelming reach of the #metoo campaign, began by activist Tarana Burke, over a decade ago. The old excuses are wearing thin ('boys will be boys') and abuse of power is being called out, with more woman occupying positions of power and less afraid of the consequences of speaking out. Also, thanks, to social media 'the voice of the voiceless' is getting amplified and heard.

Times are changing, indeed, and along with them so are sexual mores and gender roles. What once passed for 'innocent' is being called to task. "I really loved the '60s and '70s when life was so simple and you could slap a woman on the butt and it was taken as a compliment, not as sexual harassment." This (tone-deaf) remark made by former INXS guitarist, Kirk Pengilly, brought on a Twitter storm.

To step outside the US, for a moment, to my other home, Egypt, I must ask myself: How did we (as Egyptians) go from allowing men in ancient times to take time off of work to care for menstruating daughters and wives, to modern Cairo being named the most dangerous megacity for women? Admittedly, this devolution took place in the space of a several millennia, and an unholy mix of insecurity, patriarchy, failed politics and volatile religiosity are to blame for our current predicament. Yet, corruption aside, Egypt is quite different from, say, India where modern-day matriarchies do exist alongside an alarming rape crisis.

So, where did it all go wrong? Have men always been latent monsters at heart? An ancient Greek tragedist, Sophocles seems to think so, likening the male sex drive to being 'chained to a lunatic'. One way of taming this beast, we're learning, is to say enough is enough, which seems to be, finally, happening at this cultural moment, an overdue time of reckoning. The rules of the jungle are changing, and the line between aggressive, unwanted flirtation and sexual harassment obliterated.

Yes, history is littered with instances of powerful male figures acting badly, political actors and artists, alike. The difference, today, is that there seems to be public consequences, and for the slightest infraction. Women, and men of conscience, are standing up and denouncing such misbehavior. Decades-long careers can, now, be destroyed overnight through public shaming.

No longer is the private life of a public figure viewed as separate from their work or art. It is difficult, for example, to laugh light-heartedly at the jokes of Bill Cosby or Louis C.K., without acknowledging how their sexual misconduct infects their art and smears their legacies. Furthermore, we are beginning to recognize that the depravity of our cultural heroes affects our core values, too; which is to say, what we're willing to overlook or pardon says a lot about our own priorities, who we are and who we wish to become.

> When scandal breaks, and we get to see the humanity of the great and the powerful revealed, naked and dumb in front of us, there's always a cry for new rules or at least some new awareness that will prevent this from ever happening again.
> —Garrison Keillor, 1994

The Opposite of Virtue

Despite my better judgment, I allowed myself to get into a "debate" about whether pornography is bad for you, forgetting Wilde's wise counsel that: 'it is only the intellectually lost who ever argue.' In view of the sexual harassment scandals that seem to be unfolding daily, and the moment of cultural reckoning we are having, regarding what constitutes permissible behavior, I marvel at how little the connection seems to be made among pornography, misogyny, addiction and violence.

The person who took exception with what I had to say works in the sex industry and tried, as best as she could (English is not her first language) to convince me that I took too narrow a view of pornography. Men are natural predators, she argued (in more graphic terms) and women are quite alright being sex objects. It would be worrying, she added, if she were *not* seen as one.

In response, I was forced to assume the deeply unfashionable position that, despite 'liberal' protestations, pornography actually does us/our relationships harm. In turn, it is responsible for its share of societal ills, by normalizing extreme and depraved behavior. I cited a Buddhist principle I thought apt, namely, that sex divorced from love or spiritual connection, was like licking honey from a very sharp blade. Further, I proposed that, viewed regularly, porn erodes our moral compass until we are lost at sea, without bearings. In the dramatic formulation of I.B. Singer, "a morally neutral human being is a monster."

'Well, then, half of Western culture is bleeding' retorted the porn advocate, informing me she was a Buddhist herself, and that I was being naive.

Maybe so, but I do maintain that we are more than sensual apes, rubbing our private parts for pleasure. Nothing is without its price. Short-term gratifications *do* have long-term consequences and one need not be a porn addict to realize how it can be ruinous to mind, body and spirit. Yet, we live in contrarian times, where self-evident virtues—such as: restraint, ethics, integrity—are contemptuously overlooked, in favor of self-defeating, self-indulgence.

Sex sells, we are told (and shown) everywhere we turn. If it feels good, go for it; you first, you deserve it; and so on and so forth . . . Here's a poem of mine that explores these timeless spiritual truths:

The Opposite of Virtue

One might say, a vice is a vise
never mind if metal or moral,
it's basically the same device

With cunning moveable jaws
designed to fix us in place
and cheat us of a chance at grace

Impervious to all advice, habit
hotly whispers false reassurance
while tightening its iron grip

It takes no effort to slip into vice,
but virtue is trickier to stick to
like the back of a bucking bronco.

Holy Mess

AMID THE COUNTLESS BLESSINGS, something dark happened in the Spring of 2019. Something so dark that I cannot speak of it, directly—perhaps, my closest encounter with Evil. Let's just say I spent time that summer, in New York, professionally covering the high profile trial of an infamous cult leader and, to my shock, found uncanny echoes in my personal life. To deal with an odious hate crime directed at me, orchestrated by an unstable individual in my inner circle, I was required to hire two criminal lawyers and found myself entangled in court hearings, for the better part of that year.

What saw me through this soul-trying crisis was the fierce support of family, friends, prayer, work and the stubborn conviction, even in the bleakest of times, that, ultimately, Justice & Truth *will* prevail. Whether or not I liked it, I came to realize this could be a growing experience, and was told as much by elders in my life that I respect. My fear, however, was that the growth might be malignant and, if I was not careful, I might emerge from this ugly ordeal hard of heart and embittered.

Gradually, I began to undergo a strange acceptance that this hurt and betrayal were necessary, somehow, for my spiritual development. If I paid attention and did not fight it, I might extract something good, healing and possibly even transformative from this poison. As I understand it, poetry is an expression of the intolerable. Through it, one can confess in code and attempt to articulate what is unutterable. Enduring this harrowing period, I did what I had done, previously, in dealing with life's difficulties: I turned to poetry for solace and to overhear my higher self.

But, in this trying instance, I found that my voice and vision were not enough. I needed another poetic soul to unburden myself to, who could talk back to the veiled intimacies that I shared and walk me through them. So, I submitted the partial poem I had composed to a poet and friend I admire,

Laura Kaminski, and the result is this fuller work of (he)art—a steadying
call and response as well as a kind of breathing meditation.

Holy Mess

Overnight, your once blessed existence
might reverse course
become an alien thing
and you stand accused
of unspeakable crimes

Never mind, you are innocent
of these base horrors—
as Kafka says, in his Trial,
'Guilt is never to be doubted'

Walk softly then, in sock-feet
across the floor that's in your mind
until you reach the alcove
between the two open windows
that serve as sockets for your eyes

inhale through the nose
exhale through the nose

Be grateful, then
there are still dreadful sins
in our fallen world
of which you are blameless

Then move to the left window
lift the pitcher full of water
just beneath it to the sill
and pour it out

inhale through the nose
exhale through the mouth

Cross over to the other window
and look out, cross your arms over
your chest and clasp your shoulders

Now, tell me, how will this crucible
change you? Then show how this
unasked-for crisis is
blessing, allow it to assist
the birth of your longed-for self

inhale through the mouth
exhale through the nose

Slowly, return to descend
the spiral staircase of your spine
until you reach the landing
level with the Heart —

Thank God, for this Holy Mess —
Open the window, air it out

inhale through the mouth
exhale through the mouth.

Poem by Yahia Lababidi & Laura Kaminski

My Close Encounter with a Dangerous Cult

In the summer of 2016, an announcement in a reputable site for journalists (JournalismNext.com) caught my attention. It stated that an Ethical Media Scholarship and three prizes ($10,000, $3,000 and $1,000) would be granted by a 'media watch dog' proposing to 'revolutionize the way we read news'. The monetary awards included a full expense paid scholarship to take a training program (worth $7,000) which would assist applicants towards becoming writers and analysts with the company, covering world news or opening local bureaus. To be eligible for this prize and scholarship, applicants must submit their resume, along with an essay (in English or Spanish) on the importance of ethical standards in media for our modern society.

Furthermore, The Knife of Aristotle (as they were called) were looking to 'inspire a culture of questioning, critical thought and ethical communication'. I was delighted to read all this since, as I writer, I believe I shared those noble values in my seven published books of prose and poetry, as well as in the way I perceived our world. Rushing home from the beach, I locked myself in my room and laid my heart bare in the form of an essay. A few hours later, I was ready to submit it. The difficult news cycle that followed the next week or so, covering gun violence and angry politics, reminded me anew of the necessity of ethical journalism: the subject of the essay submission. I was positively delighted when I shortly heard back from The Knife that they wished to set up a Skype interview, in the upcoming days.

The interviewer, a journalist younger than myself told me he previously worked for Bloomberg and Time magazine and was easy to talk to. I reiterated what I had written in my submission, that since people cannot be everywhere, at the same time, we must trust the media to be our eyes and by, extension, our conscience. Quite simply when we know better, we do better. Which is why, I thought, applying ethical standards in the media stands to saves lives, and this seemed especially important in our divisive time.

My interlocutor ambiguously, but amiably, explained to me that they had devised a unique methodology (which is why I needed to sign a confidentiality agreement) that was able to extract spin and slant from news, in order to offer readers raw data. 'We want the news to read more like science, less like fiction,' he stated as their mission, and so 'we train prospective analysts in logic as well as critical thinking'. All very well, I thought, and told him it sounded almost too good to be true—Utopian, even. If you guys weren't real, I offered, if would make good material for a movie. 'But, the good thing is,' he replied with a smile, 'is that we *are* real.'

When it was time for me to ask questions, I wondered why there wasn't more information on their website. They were working on that, he assured me, solemnly adding that their system/tools cost a great deal to develop. They do not rely on advertising, he elaborated, which could pose a conflict of interests, and subscribers would be able to see the full site, soon. Fair enough, I thought. As a parting comment, the editor-in-chief checked my availability for the thirty day intensive training (to be held in Albany, NY the following month) and I confirmed it.

Less than a week later, I received a form letter stating that The Knife of Aristotle sees in me 'a rare commitment to ethics and integrity and building a better world'. For this reason, and the skill I'd demonstrated in my essay, I'd won the 2nd place prize ($3,000) which would entitle me to a full scholarship and require a work commitment, of at least, 18 hours a week for a minimum of a one year period. All I needed to do was, again, confirm my interest and availability and a check for the prize money would be mailed to me with further details.

This was great news! Squeamish about talking money, I'd not asked how much *exactly* the compensation for my work would be, once I was verified, but I figured that would come later. My other, more practical half did not think so. Instead, my wife recommended that, before committing to anything, I reply with a few hard-nosed questions, regarding salary, and if they covered room and board, for training, etc . . . Meanwhile, she and my mother-in-law also suggested I do some further research, trying to learn more about my possible employers.

Unable to fall asleep that night, and searching the internet, I learned that I'd had a close encounter with a dangerous cult. What I read, through the night and early morning, filled me with disbelief, dread and morbid fascination. The cult I was about to join, was an offshoot of the infamous NXIVM—a 'life improvement' coaching company founded by Keith

Raniere, a depraved, megalomaniacal individual who kept a rotating harem of nearly twenty woman (underage, too) and had driven previous students to madness, bankruptcy, even death.

Worse, he continued to do so, through a vicious mix of mind control, perverse sex and years of harassment. Those who try to defect or speak out (former followers, loves, journalists, a cult expert, etc . . .) are intimidated in a variety of ways, aided by the unstinting financial support of the Bronfman sisters, heiresses of the Seagram fortune. Besides, The Knife, there were other Raniere-influenced groups I discovered online, which try to down-play their connection to NXIVM: acting classes, yoga-themed, and more self-help nonsense.

Although some of Raniere's thousands of followers have uprooted their lives from other countries to be near him in New York, the cult leader fled the US to Mexico (seeking to avoid arrest). Why Mexico? Perhaps, because Carlos Salinas, the former president, and Alejandro Junco, the country's largest newspaper publisher, both have children in Raniere's cult. Which reminded me that, during my Skype interview I was told that, if I did well, maybe I could set up a branch of The Knife of Aristotle in my home coun-try? Because, that's just what Egypt needs, more Fake News, overseen by another power-hungry psychopath!

As the sun was rising it dawned on me, in the words of someone less fortunate than myself, who had barely escaped Raniere's clutches: "I thought what I was supporting was humanity. I recently realized it was just the per-version of a sick man." I still had to draft a reply to politely decline their training and award, and all day long debated the wisdom of writing this piece you're reading.

But, further considering the damage this cult leader had inflicted upon innocent others —financial, psychological, sexual, at times, and fatal—I re-alized I had no choice. The same impulse that had driven me to submit to their essay competition, now, compelled me to expose this wicked scam and the self-proclaimed 'smartest man in the world' and 'spiritually-evolved guru' behind it.

In closing, here's the opening paragraph from my "award-winning" essay on the need to reclaim our conscience through a more moral media:

> We are, by nature, ethical creatures. Instinctively, we seek truth
> and meaning and beauty. We wish to live virtuously. But, it is
> also human nature to be lazy, and forgetful. It takes time and
> continuous effort to meet the rigorous standards of these ideals.
> In the bold words of Malcom X: "If you're not careful, the news-
> papers will have you hating the people who are being oppressed,

and loving the people who are doing the oppressing." Which is why, when it comes to staying abreast of world affairs and making informed decisions as concerned citizens, we need a media that we can trust and look up to.

UPDATE

In early 2018, Raniere was arrested following accusations that NXIVM was involved in a master-slave sex-cult, where women were starved, branded with Raniere's initials and bullied into having sex with him. Seagrams heiress, billionaire Clare Bronfman footed the bill for lawyers in federal court. During the summer of 2019, I attended Raniere's court trial, while working on an HBO docu-series, "The Vow," covering the NXIVM cult (released in Spring, 2020).

Reverence for the Visible and Invisible Worlds

This visible world is a trace of that invisible one and the former follows the latter like a shadow.

—AL GHAZALI

LATELY, I'M CONSUMED WITH idea of the artist as mystic, and the appreciation of beauty as a form of prayer. Following a dream contributing to his conviction of having been "called" philosopher Ludwig Wittgenstein wrote in a letter at the age of 31, "I had a task . . . to become a star in the sky." In his conception of philosophy—as a means of authentic existence equally concerned with logic as ethics—the spiritual, artistic, and metaphysical aspects of a calling are nearly fused.

At a feverish pitch, we see this ascetic philosopher flirting with poverty, giving away an immense family fortune to pursue his ideal of living and working with the rural poor; with solitude, spending years alone in Norway and Ireland, to meditate and write; and with death, in the trenches of World War I, in the belief that he did not deserve to live unless he created great work.

The artistic-philosophic landscape is teeming with seers of this type. The power and aura of these fiery spirits derives as much from the truths or realities they have revealed as what they've had to sacrifice along the way; it is an authority born of the tension between what is accomplished and what is suffered.

On a personal note, I observe that something is taking place within me, a shift as decisive and imperceptible as a continental drift. I, who once identified with my mind, have come to feel I am standing at the very edge of it, and that it's thin and flat. The time came to leap. My way into the life of the spirit began, unwittingly, when I first began experimenting with silence in university. I would attempt to go on silent fasts for days, rationing words, and speaking only when I must—perhaps a mouthful in class, or even less if someone absolutely needed to hear from me. Otherwise, friends understood that I'd "gone under" and only the very committed continued leaving me voice messages or, braver still, tagging along, noiselessly.

The idea at the time—more inner imperative, really, than any sort of formulated thought—was to sound my depths and think things through. This was my first taste of freedom as an adult, and that was how I chose to exercise it. It was as though, suddenly and without explanation, I was taken in for questioning, and I had to play both parts: officer and suspect. *Who was I? What did I know? Why am I here? Do I have an alibi?*

Typically, I'd walk around all day in a semi-trance talking back to the books I'd read, lost in the echo chamber of my head. I read a great deal more those days, again out of an inner imperative, but hardly the assigned work. My self-imposed reading list was a volatile cocktail, unequal parts literature and philosophy, and the discovery of those great contrarians, Wilde and Nietzsche, made my world spin faster.

Unaware of it then, this obsessive reading was in fact teaching me how to write. The rhythms and cadences of my literary and philosophical masters insinuated themselves into my style, just as their stances and daring were persuading me to distrust ready-made ideas and try to formulate better questions.

It was out of these silences and (attendant) solitude that I began writing what would become a book of aphorisms—by transcribing the heady conversations that I was having with myself at the time. My "method" in writing these aphorisms was simply to jot down on a scrap of paper (the back of a napkin, receipt, or whatever else was handy) what I thought was worth quoting from my soul's dialogue with itself. If ever I tried keeping a notebook, the thoughts would hesitate leaving their cave, sensing ambush. So, by night I kept bits of paper and a pencil by my side, just in case. And, when something did occur to me, I feverishly scribbled it down in the dark, without my glasses, out of the same superstitious cautiousness of scaring ideas off.

These aphorisms were to reveal me to myself and served as the biography of my mental, spiritual, and emotional life. I read as I wrote, helplessly, in a state of emergency; in my youthful fanaticism, I was convinced I was squeezing existence for answers, no less. I felt that one should only read on a need-to-know basis, and write discriminatingly, with the sole purpose of intensifying consciousness.

Strangely, during these years of white-hot inspiration, I discovered that when I returned home to Egypt (for the summer, Christmas, and eventually following graduation) I was unable to write aphorisms. No longer the master of my environment, and forced to accommodate the interruptions that make a life, I gradually realized that because I had lost my silences, I had lost my voice. Which is to say, I composed the bulk of the aphorisms in my book, Signposts to Elsewhere, before I turned twenty-two.

It would take me several years to begin writing again and, out of this unsettling and involuntary silence, would be born two new forms: poetry and eventually essays. After a decade or so of aphoristic silence, spurred by the terse wisdom of the Tao the Ching and Sufi teachers, I find myself returning to these brief arts and speaking to myself in sayings, once more, noting how I and the writing are changing.

Birthday Soul-Searching

SOME DAYS, I WILL look up—from the book covers I'm buried in, or computer screen that I'm plastered to—and experience a mild panic. What have I done with my life, I'll wonder, and has the extraordinary gamble of entirely devoting myself to literature (at the expense of all else) been worth it; has it paid off and at what personal cost?

On the eve of turning forty-six years old (which, in turn, is four years short of fifty!) I'm asking myself these questions with renewed urgency. Yet, once the anxious flutter subsides, I'm left with the same answer: I had no choice, really, there could have been no other way. A life of letters—first as voracious reader, then as delirious writer—has been vital and meant so many things for me, it's difficult to begin to untangle them.

On one level, reading and writing is play, serious play, and escapism, from suffering that I was not otherwise equipped to deal with. Which is to say, the literary life is a deeply enjoyable form of self-medication, pursuit of altered consciousness, self-parenting, even. Books—by others and, eventually, my own—were there for me in ways that people were not/could not have been. They revealed me to myself, over time, mentored me, sustained and inspired me—giving me a way to be in this world, but not of it . . .

Strange to say, perhaps, but it was reading and writing that also taught me how to meditate in a fashion—slipping through the bars of self and time—as well as how to bow, give thanks, pray. Whether or not I realized it, from the start, books pointed me in the direction of the long, hard road to transformation, and helped me take the first steps. Admittedly, at times, life as a writer has seemed like a lonely vocation. Yet, in fact, the opposite is closer to the truth. Literature (again, my own and others) has in fact, repeatedly, rescued me from loneliness and connected me to the world. Miraculously, it has gifted me friends across space and time, raising the great dead from previous generations, as well as granting me far-flung readers of my own work that I've connected with, virtually. In the poignant words of Argentine writer, Jorge Luis Borges: "Despite a writer's life being solitary, if they are lucky, they might come to discover they are at the center of a vast circle of invisible friends."

Thank you, readers/friends (visible and invisible) for being part of my literary life, and co-partners in this remarkable adventure (so far). I hope I've not been too self-indulgent and that, at times, my words have mysteriously spoken your silences, the way writers have spoken mine. Here's a dear line, from a discarded version of Rilke's Notebooks of Malte Laurids Brigge that sums up better than I can how I feel about the work that still lies ahead, on the page and off:

> . . . he realized that what was within him was scarcely begun; that,
> if he were to die now, he would not be capable of living in the af-
> terlife; that they would be ashamed, over there, of his rudimentary
> soul, and would hide it away in eternity like a premature baby.

As a companion piece, a short poem of mine that touches on some of these Existential themes:

> My Life is thinking of me, again
> and wondering . . .
> whether I care for it
> what it means to me
> and what I make of it?
>
> It fears that I take it
> for granted
> It worries how I spend it
> or save it
> with whom I share it
>
> It knows I do not know
> all that it knows
> that I forget what I do
> but, it shrugs this off:
> another "lover's quarrel with the world"
>
> For, at heart, it is certain,
> I cherish it as sacrament
> and when we think of one another
> it feels like harmony of the spheres
> or rubbing shoulders with Destiny.

Kneeling in Stages

IT IS A FAIRLY remarkable thing to put out into the world a book of nearly twenty-three years of marveling, questing and helplessly confessing, in verse. Seeing the figures 1993–2015 on the cover of my Balancing Acts: New & Selected Poems is a little like contemplating one's own tombstone. Here lies a life, in Poetry. It is humbling and bewildering to meditate upon over two decades of being and becoming. As Yevgeny Yevtushenko puts it: "A poet's autobiography is his poetry. Anything else is just a footnote."

But, with this metaphorical tombstone, and the closing of a book on several chapters of one's life, comes the liberating and enticing possibility of rebirth. Here is a poem, from my poetry collection, that hints at this new life:

Arrivals

I don't quite know how it occurred
that this great fish has appeared
almost fully formed, it seemed
to crowd out all else in my aquarium

Perhaps, this creature of the depths
always was, just out of sight
secretly feeding on hidden longing
and now demands acknowledging

With the swish of a majestic tail
it's upset my incidental decor—
gone the rubber diver and plastic treasure.
The glass frame itself can't be far behind . . .

Growing up in Egypt, a predominately Muslim culture, I instinctively rebelled against what I perceived as a hypocritical religiosity, and took refuge in what might be described as philosophical literature. This entailed throwing out the luminous baby (faith) with the murky (cultural) bathwater. But worshiping at the altar of the mind, I found I was becoming one of its chew toys and that doubt and cynicism (however clever or seductively presented) were diminishing and, ultimately, a dead end. Fanatically devoted to life of the mind, I came late to a certain type of love poetry: songs of adoration, ecstasy and surrender addressed to the Divine.

Which is to say that, at the end of my fourth decade, a bundle of slim volumes (mostly Persian, treatises and poetry composed several centuries years ago) had begun to work their quiet magic on me. A small window appeared to be opening within, or a veil lifting, onto a vast, previously unimagined vista. And I came to realize, in humility and awe, that after decades of intellectual exploration, I still stood on the shore—before an immeasurable Sea.

I found I was also returning Home, in a sense. For the first time in decades I, a recovering Existentialist, found myself able to slip through the back door of a widely-misunderstood religion I thought I'd left behind, Islam. Led on by abiding longing, I crawled, again and again to Sufism for succor, sustenance, inspiration. To paraphrase Rumi, I let myself be silently drawn by the strange pull of what I love, and it did not lead me astray. In blindly trusting this way, I came to realize that books, persons, circumstances all can be employed as mouths or arms, to address us and draw us closer. Mysticism is a courtship.

Living in the US, at this particular historical moment, when there is mounting suspicion and murderous ignorance in regards to the "Arab/Muslim world," I've grown to feel a responsibility for my writing to serve as a kind of bridge, or peace offering, tending to our shared humanity. Prose can do that, by tackling misconceptions directly, but poetry does it by attempting to "tell all the truth but tell it slant" and bear witness of our spiritual condition. Poetry, as I've come to understand it, as a form of prayer, praising, upward-reaching and glad, within wing's wind of a Great Song . . . "Ah, to be one of them! One of the poets whose song helps close the wound rather than open it!"—Juan Ramón Jiménez

Below, is another poem of mine, from Balancing Acts, that attempts to sing the ineffable:

Embracing, We Let Go

Perhaps, we are negotiating
not just with one, but always two
—who share the same soil, it is true—
one who lives, another who is dying

A shift in balance begins to take place
once a love of silence is confessed
its roots run deep, its shade a world
and her fruits impossible to forget

From the first, we surrender something
and, gradually, consent to be emptied
transfixed by so much soundless music
drunk and sated through lipless mouths

What use to name this silent master
preparing us for dying or the Divine
(I'm not sure there is a difference)
but know in embracing, we let go.

Reborn in the USA

An Immigrant & Poet's Story
(who also happens to be Muslim)

BORN AND RAISED IN Cairo, Egypt I came to realize, at the age of thirty-two, that I could not live, love and create there, any longer. I required new air and it was, finally, time to dare and take a leap . . . I would, later, notify only a handful of family and friends of 'this audacious, purifying, elemental move'—to borrow the words of poet, Philip Larkin, from his *Poetry of Departures*.

But, first, I attempted to articulate this terrifying-liberating position to my boss at the United Nations (UNESCO) where I'd worked for nearly a decade. It's not you, I respectfully suggested, it's me. I need to move on. In turn, I appreciated his gracious unwillingness to immediately accept my resignation, his insistence to think it over, as well as his generous offer for a promotion.

Still I, politely, insisted that I needed to get out while I could and see if I might live differently. I felt I had, at least, a few books within me, fluttering wildly against the bars and, if I did not act, now, I might never be able to set them free. Hard to describe this crucial turning point, in prose. In a poem I wrote, after the fact, I managed to put it this way:

Dawning

There are hours when every thing creaks
when chairs stretch their arms, tables their legs
and closets crack their backs, incautiously

Fed up with the polite fantasy
of having to stay in one place
and stick to their stations

Humans too, at work, or in love
know such aches and growing pains
when inner furnishings defiantly shift

As decisively, and imperceptibly, as a continent
some thing will give, croak or come undone
so that everything else must be reconsidered

One restless dawn, unable to suppress the itch
of wanderlust, with a heavy door left ajar
semi-deliberately, and a new light teasing in

Some piece of immobility will finally quit
suddenly nimble on wooden limbs
as fast as a horse, fleeing the stable.

It *dawned* on me how utterly destabilizing this leap of faith was, and that it meant leaving behind the security of everything I knew: work, family, friends, familiarity. Yet, there was a woman I cared for at the other end (isn't it always a matter of the heart, where seemingly-mad decisions are involved) and I had made up my mind to return to the United States, where I'd gone to college a decade earlier and met said lady friend.

Even though my lawyers, stateside, warned me it was a long shot, less than a year after applying for an artist visa, I was very lucky to be granted one for Aliens of Extraordinary Ability (O1)—which made me feel a little like ET, and that the tip of my index finger might glow when I write. In retrospect I realize how, especially, fortunate I was to be bestowed this honor, considering that I was a young, single, Muslim, Arab male—a combination regarded with increasing suspicion, unfortunately. Counting my blessings, I came to accept that I had also found a new Home and, feeling more confident, I proposed to my college friend within the year, who had patiently, loyally been by my side all along.

Nearly fourteen years have passed since this fateful move. In all this time, I have only mustered the courage to visit Egypt, once, eleven years after 'fleeing the stable'. I watched with my heart in my mouth, from the US, the rise and fall of the Arab Spring, as we collectively struggled for liberation and rebirth. Considering the dashed hopes of Egypt's heroic 2011 people's uprising, from this great distance, I admit that I found it demoralizing to see many of our once fearless freedom-fighters experience revolution-fatigue and allow themselves to become desensitized to the current military propaganda machine.

Over time, I've come to regard my beloved Cairo as a joyous child whose confidence has, profoundly, been shaken by repeated scolding and attempts at molding. We're not quite ourselves at the moment, I tell myself, and are battling for our souls. I remind myself that we're merely experiencing what the French would call, *un mauvais quart d'heure* (a bad quarter of an hour, or a brief unpleasant experience). Something, I suspect, many in Trump's America might relate to.

Our unfortunate present moment does not define us; we're better than this unbecoming fear and loathing. The lengthening shadow that we are witnessing—in the Middle East, in Europe, in the Divided States of America—is just a hiccup in time, viewed in the context of humanity's long illustrious history. When my spirits sag, I am buoyed up by the noble Arabic slogan that circulated following our Egyptian Revolution: 'Despair is betrayal, and Hope a responsibility.'

Examining my own present moment I recognize, with gratitude and wonder, how one seemingly unavoidable shift (from one continent to another) presented me with a new world of unforeseen possibilities. At forty-six, I find myself happily married for twelve years and, no less incredibly, with seven critically-acclaimed books of poetry and prose to my name. Mysterious thing, Art, how if one is faithful to it (and fortunate), in time, it can alter the artist and recreate them in its own image.

Upon further reflection, I am beginning to better appreciate the significance of having been raised in an Egyptian culture—where proverbs were viewed as both common utterance and a sort of magical invocation. I grew up with grandmothers, maternal and paternal who, at times, spoke almost exclusively in pithy sayings: a string of maxims, sing-songy, witty-wise remarks, for every occasion.

Also, being half-Lebanese, meant that Gibran Khalil Gibran, celebrated poet and philosopher, was an early and inescapable influence. I even suspect that matters of literary heritage might have been written in blood, since I was named after my paternal grandfather (Yahia Lababidi), a celebrated musician and poet who passed away long before I was born, yet bequeathed me a love of song, intravenously. When, in my late teens, I found that I could unburden myself in verse and epigrams I felt that, for the first time, I was truly beginning to earn my Name.

These days, I feel another sort of calling, and sense of renewed purpose, in contemplating my momentous immigration to the United States. In this age of short attention spans and shot concentrations, there seems to be in the US, at least, a Renaissance of Aphorisms—something that I would never have imagined when I first started writing these brief arts (anachronistically, I felt) nearly thirty years ago. For example, I had the distinct honor to be featured in the first book of modern American aphorists, Short Flights (Schaffner Press, 2015) alongside some of this country's finest thinkers and poets, as well as being invited to Oxford University (at the end of 2019) to launch my book of aphorisms, Where Epics Fail, and discuss *The Role of Wisdom Literature in Today's Troubled Times*.

Living in America at this historical moment when there is mounting mistrust and murderous ignorance directed towards immigrants and, more specifically, the "Arab/Muslim world," I feel a responsibility for my writing to serve as a form of peace-offering, addressing our shared humanity. One way of doing this is to try and communicate through my brief meditations the edifying beauty found in Sufism, the mystical branch of Islam. I had achieved far more than I imagined, when I made this decisive leap to make a new life in the United States. Now, its dawning on me that everything realized, thus far, is mere apprenticeship and the real work might just be beginning . . .

The Failure of Misanthropy

CZECH WRITER BOHUMIL HRABAL used to say that he drew his worldview from a dry cleaner's slip he came across in Prague, which warned clients that "some stains can only be removed by the destruction of the material itself." If the stains *are* us, what if we were to take this risk?

I look at the darkness of intolerance and violence spreading across our world and wonder, what if Donald Trump might not be the moral crisis we needed to awaken us to the world's suffering and our interconnectedness. The price of a New Chance—past the murderous folly in the Middle East and self-defeating arrogance of the US—is nothing less than surrendering our old, failed, broken ways.

Perhaps President Trump *will* Make America Great, Again, unwittingly, by bringing about a Revaluation of Values. The peaceful, powerful Women's March on Washington, DC, dwarfing in number those who attended Trump's inauguration and echoing throughout the US as well as the world, seems to suggest that it might be safe to hope for change, again. Heartening, too, to witness impassioned rallies in airports throughout the country welcoming immigrants and protesting Trump's unconstitutional executive order or "Muslim Ban." Provoked by his administration's disregard for science and denial of climate change, we also witnessed a Scientists' March (the Facebook group created to support this event had more than 300,000 likes, last I checked).

For my part, as immigrant and writer, I've come to regard my art as a type of literary activism. By way of example, I had the good fortune to play the roles of peacemaker and activist in an important new anthology, Truth to Power: Writers Respond to the Rhetoric of Hate and Fear (*Cutthroat*, 2017) alongside many fine writers such as Rita Dove, Patricia Smith, Martín Espada, Wendell Berry, Patricia Spears Jones, Sam Hamill, and many others.

In *Truth to Power*, writers from diverse cultures / ethnic backgrounds respond in poetry, fiction, and nonfiction to pressing social issues raised by the campaign and election of Trump, including: immigration, women's rights, African American rights, and environmental issues.

Being a dual citizen of the US and Egypt, at this defining historical moment, I see all too clearly how culturally diminished and spiritually impoverished we become when we close our doors to the world and our hearts to Others. I hope that my aphorisms, below, might serve as a reminder of our larger allegiances to one another.

The right to free speech ends where hate speech begins.

The bigot's crime is twofold: not knowing others well enough to love them, and not knowing themselves enough to recognize their own hatred.

We are responsible for our enemies. Compassion is to realize the role we play in their creation.

Our morality is determined by the level of immorality that we can afford to live with.

Unheeded pricks of conscience might return as harpoons of circumstance.

We can lend ideas our breath, but Ideals require our entire lives.

As with all battles, how we fight determines who we become.

Every time we betray our conscience, we strangle an angel.

Yet, it's not certain we are allotted an infinite supply of winged pardons.

Where there are demons, there is something precious worth fighting for.

You can't bury pain and not expect it to grow roots.

How attentive the forces of darkness are, how they rush to answer our ill-conceived wishes.

As you progress to the Light, notice how jealous shadows also redouble their efforts.

How vast the future that it can serve as a bottomless repository of all fears, hopes, and dreams.

Strange, how one hate enables another; how they are like unconscious allies, darkly united in blocking out the Light.

Buoyancy of the human spirit in the face of turbulence is the source of the miraculous.

In serving words, faithfully, we also serve one another.

Like incantations, certain word combinations can set a sentence or soul in motion.

In the deep end, every stroke counts.

Our salvation lies on the other side of our gravest danger.

To sense we are always at a great turning point is a sign of spiritual vitality.

There is a point in unlearning, where we cannot proceed any further—without Transformation.

Heaven save us from tragic seriousness; teach us to play, divinely.

Perhaps crisis is self-induced disaster—a last-ditch effort we gift ourselves to, finally, transform.

Best not flirt with disaster, lest it decide to commit.

We're here to pass around the ball of Light while keeping our fingerprints off it.

The only failures are misanthropes.

Mistrust a person seeking power without a sense of humor—it usually translates into a lack of mercy.

A lesson to bullies, big and small: controlling others is a spiritual impossibility; those who try must exist in a state of existential insecurity.

Mercy is to cover the nakedness of others and stand beside them—naked, yourself.

The Pornification of Popular Culture

A Rant

It's DIFFICULT AT TIMES not to suspect that American popular culture aspires to the condition of pornography. Either that, or it's got a serious crush on smut. Turn on the television, if you dare, and you're assaulted by all varieties of obscenities, delivered by persons publicly misbehaving, in different stages of undress. From the shores of New Jersey to Miami, whether they're infamous nonentities in their twenties, desperate housewives, guests on daytime talk shows or hormone-maddened teens on vacation, it seems *everyone's gone wild*. Of course, to say this in our unflappable age of cynicism and mass distraction is to sound like a relic, or worse, a prude. But I'm neither. I'm a middle-aged artist who believes in Art and Culture in a Big Way, yet find myself wondering, time and again, *What's going on?*

I understand there's always been a place for unedifying noise. But the top of the charts is not that place. Enter a bookstore, if there are any still around and drop to your knees in despair. Once upon a time, books were written by writers who had something to say and the talent to say it well. Now it's all celebrity memoirs. It's *nice* that celebrities can write, or be ghost-written, and that more and more people feel their stories are worth sharing with the world. But when did books become hardcover tabloids? What life lessons, for example, can we take away from the memoir of a teen pop star? Don't you have to have lived a long, rich, remarkable life first? And if it's not bubblegum musicians, it's another brash talk show host writing of her sex-capades (with not one but two of her books simultaneously on the New York Times bestseller list).

Question: When exactly did it become socially acceptable to launch your career with a "leaked" sex tape? Answer: when narcissism and shamelessness became qualities to celebrate as well as try to emulate. When celebrity ceased to be about celebrating extraordinary achievement and became instead a celebration of itself. Hard to distinguish the shiny women's magazines at the checkout dispensing racy how-to advice from the dodgy men's magazines at adult stores. With porn and prostitution glamorized and de-stigmatized, it's not uncommon to hear of ordinary college girls turning to either to supplement their incomes.

Check out a random selection of music videos or episodes of so-called *reality TV* shows and it appears the stripper is the new cultural icon. (Why else, of all the ways to get fit, would pole dancing become a fad?) In the exhibitionistic world of pop music, adept at concealing depths while revealing surfaces, there's an incorrigible figure who best personifies this vulgar, sexually aggressive New Woman. Refusing to cover up, despite being over sixty (and dating a string of men less than half her age) this one-trick pony has spawned a legion of pantless imitators.

Out the window are complexity, ambiguity, restraint, subtlety or sensitivity. In their place, the crotch in your face. The younger starlets take after their pop mother, schooled in the art of cheap provocation or minimum effort and maximum effect. Nothing is sacred for this new crass class of loud-mouthed attention-grabbers. They court controversy at any price, pimping serious issues—Freedom, Love, Religion, Revolution, Tolerance, you name it—all in the name of further self-promotion and exposure.

Dispiriting stuff. Speaking of commodifying ideals, there's a bunch of popular (once-called) *dating shows*, where ordinary-seeming folks go about finding "the loves of their lives" while a nation of voyeurs drools. Heavy words are lightly thrown, girls are kissed, fondled, discarded, and, boys, too, toyed with and broken-hearted. Strange business, this amusing ourselves with the real emotions of strangers. But one mustn't wag the moral finger too sternly. Nothing is personal anymore; inner life is an oxymoron and we must share, Share, SHARE within an inch of our lives. Besides, it's all entertainment, the way news in the United States is entertainment, and vice versa (entertainment is news). By way of example, shortly after the young female hostages in the Ohio kidnapping were released, one of the rescuers was swiftly turned into a caricature for mass consumption, his TV interview transformed into an inescapably catchy tune.

But back to the pornification of culture. What happens when sex sells . . . *out*? When no one bats an eye when ads for major American clothes lines seem to be peddling—how to put this, delicately—kiddy porn? Or at the other end of the spectrum, mommy porn? When the erotic novel that captures the public's imagination is kinky sex for the middle aged, bored housewife? Mercifully, I had the discipline *not* to read Fifty Shades of Perversity, but even squinting across the room at its so-so prose, it's fairly surprising to consider it was embraced by the mainstream.

Sure, there have always been intrepid adventurers at the fringe, the *avant-garde*—artists, activists and rebels of all stripes fall under this class. But what happens when the extreme *becomes* the mainstream; can the center still hold when it folds upon itself? If we are all at the transgressive forefront, how do we know when we've gone too far? Isn't part of the real danger of being on the margins the fact that one might fall off the cliff, altogether? What happens if we're all following, blindly, unshocked, unshockable, when we face a real abyss?

In the midst of this madness, a TV show aired that gave me pause for thought. It was light-hearted and jokey, in a nervously sophomoric way. Only in this post-shame age, it's not sex it was jittery about, but the G-word. You see, the premise of this unlikely comedy, *Save Me*, is that a vocally *un*religious woman discovers that she's become a prophet of sorts and receives divine messages.

Unsurprisingly, our awkward TV visionary did not fare well within this current, conflicted culture, for whom belief is *the love that dare not speak its name*, and was promptly taken off the air. Even within the context of the show itself, the treatment of the heroine seemed embattled as to whether she was authentic or psychotic. But what is the significance that such a show materialized on primetime, albeit briefly, in the first place? Could it be that this fast-food culture of disposable entertainment, quick fixes and gurus-to-go is sounding some sort of alarm, and in need of *Saving*?

Virtual World
Life-Enhancing Versus Soul-Destroying

I HELD OUT AS long as I could before signing up for an email account. At the time, I viewed the idea of electronic mail as invasive, and unnecessary; by far preferring the romance and torture of letter-writing which took days or weeks to compose and send. But at the repeated entreaties of a dear friend (and early adopter of new technologies) I caved in. I remember pressing the "send" button on that first email felt like diving off a cliff—as terrifying, as exhilarating. My threatened, and admittedly precious, terms of agreement in those heady days were that I would *not* report on my outer life, or any daily activities, but rather share glimpses of my mental diary.

For more or less the same reasons (perhaps, out of a writerly fear of being consumed?) I never owned a mobile phone, until I moved to the US, over a decade ago. Why willingly carry a tracer, I thought, shrilly interrupting my inner dialogue at any moment? If someone needed to contact me, urgently, they could reach me at home or work. But, the rest of the time was mine: to dream, to escape, to slip between the gaps. Now, I shamefully confess, my iphone serves as a sort of life-support machine, and I suspect I am not alone. I'm still not overly fond of *speaking* on it, but think of texting as a kind of telepathy. I've even come to share, through the pores, bit of my life on Facebook and Twitter (after, you guessed it, also fighting them off for as long as I could, in hopes that social media would go away).

Instead, what does seem to be going away to my dismay, and those of my ilk, is the so-called *real world*, specifically the print world. As a writer, it fills me with dread to see independent publishers endangered, actual bookstores going out of business, book review sections in esteemed newspapers folding and, subsequently, the newspapers and magazines themselves struggling to maintain a physical presence.

As I put it in a short poem "Shuttered Windows": "To speak of the smell and feel / of books, the erotics of the text, / has begun to sound perverse. / One by one, the old places of worship/ become quaint and are vacated / In their stead a gleaming, ambitious screen."

Yet, I am also beginning to see the error of my ways, and realize the patent folly in being a self-defeating Luddite. I don't read on Kindle, but five of my books are available, electronically, and I hope that *others* do! I do read, rabidly, articles, essays, reviews, you name it, on my smart phone and computer, and even wrote my first i-phone poem—when forced to check in my bag at New York's MET museum, and left with only "a gleaming, ambitious screen" to record my impressions.

Which is to say that, as I gingerly enter my fifth decade, I am making a kind of peace with the virtual world. It's all just wrapping paper, I tell myself, whether paperback or electronic. What matters is the gift inside, the words themselves; namely, that they are read and connect with people.

So, it seems that the world itself is now migrating online. Fine, I'll work with it. Not just for survival's sake must we stoop to engage with this brave new world, but also because it's spiritually foolish to condescend. I have friends, writer friends only slightly older than myself, who regard things like Twitter and Facebook as infra dig, insisting that they "mean us harm." I get it, or a part of me does. But, the other part, doesn't. It might be virtual, but it's still *real* people in *real* time. Managed judiciously, it's simply too great a learning experience to pass up.

Wherever people congregate, *en masse*, for sustenance—such as the great communal wells of social media—we must pay attention. Real friendships are forged in these virtual communities, vital news shared, and that most elusive thing of all, inspiration, sparked from so many souls colliding in wonder and thirst for human contact. Yes, I remain aware of the many serious dangers: the regrettable narcissism networking engenders, the cluttering of our inner spaces, the real and paradoxical isolation that results from so much online "socializing" as well as the attendant erosion of social skills and, no less importantly, the damage to our attention spans and loss of privacy.

Particularly, in regards to how the Internet can detrimentally affect our concentration, meaning our capacity for immersive reading/critical thinking, I remember being set alight by an *Atlantic* magazine article (which the author, Nicholas Carr, developed into a fine book). The title of the piece encapsulated all my misgivings, "*Is Google Making Us Stupid?: What the internet is doing to our brains.*" Shortly after this seminal, but somewhat alarmist, piece appeared, a slew of articles, backed by scientific studies, were keen to make a counter argument: Google and the Internet might be making us smarter. True, multi-tasking stands to render our memory worse, they suggested, but certain types of memory are improving as search engines reroute our brains.

"Abundance of books makes men less studious" stated a critic of the printing press, Hieronimo Squarciafico, as early as the 15th century. This might well be the case today, too, with the wealth of unsorted, uneven information available at our fingertips. Yet, perhaps this truth also speaks to our innate laziness as a species, rather than the evils of abundance. For those with discipline and curiosity to sift through the buried treasures (as well as the sanity not to entirely *live* online), the Internet need not be a soul-destroying monster but can serve as (I shudder to state the obvious) a life-enhancing tool.

The Slow, Public Death of a Musical Hero

Morrissey

It's disheartening to see the once intelligent and articulate lead singer of The Smiths, Morrissey, smearing his legacy with hateful and ignorant statements: downplaying sexual abuse, blaming the victims, while ranting against Muslims and immigration: "Everyone sleeps with minors. What are we supposed to do, throw them all in jail?" is one unfortunate quote. "If you try to make everything multicultural" says the Irish immigrant, "you will not have any culture in the end."

Remarkable the contradictions that can exist in one human heart. Morrissey enjoys a massive Latino/Mexican following and, throughout his long career, has aligned himself with outsiders. Yet, there's something ugly in the air—fear, hatred, ignorance—and it seems he was not smart enough to avoid catching it . . .

The singer continues making such uninformed pronouncements: "I'm sad that Berlin has become the rape capital . . . because of the open borders." For what it's worth, regarding Berlin, according to statistics, sexual crime is actually on the decline in the city, while the overall number of reports across Germany has remained lower than the UK, Sweden and the US. It's distressing to hear this once-refined artist beginning to sound as coarse, and dangerous, as the far-right, anti-Islam party, For Britain, which he supports—while suggesting that Nigel Farage "would make a good prime minister."

Words matter and Morrissey, who sings about 'living for the written word' should know better. As an example of hate speech leading to physical violence, court documents reveal that the Canadian gunman who killed six Muslim men in a Quebec mosque was an avid follower of alt-right figures, while authorities also found a photo of him in a MAGA (Make America Great Again) hat.

While Morrissey is no stranger to controversy throughout his decades-long musical career, it becomes increasingly difficult for people of conscience to appreciate his art as he continues to spew such divisive and mean-spirited sentiments, including these vile, and ignorant remarks, posted on his website: '*Halal* meat requires certification that can only be given by supporters of ISIS.'

A cursory listen to his album, Low in High School, suggests that Morrissey has found lust in Tel Aviv while taking leave of the rest of his mind and good taste. Critics of Israel's actions—say, the bulldozing of Palestinian homes in the occupied territories—are 'jealous' according to his bewildering, simplistic assessment. Further, in an inflammatory (self?) interview on his site, he offers this fresh provocation and weirdly willful nonsense:

> As far as racism goes, the modern loony left seem to forget that Hitler was leftwing. When someone calls you racist, what they are saying is: hmm, you actually have a point, and I don't know how to answer it, so perhaps if I distract you by calling you a bigot we'll both forget how enlightened your comment was.

Never mind that Hitler, actually, banned unions, workers' strikes and abortions; or that his regime persecuted homosexuals, despised immigrants, was anti-gun control for the majority of Germans, pro-Nationalism and pro-militarism. There is no reasoning with a mind and a heart, stubbornly closed.

Yes, throughout history, there have been far too many examples of artists acting badly. The question is: where do we draw the line, and withhold our support: when it infects the art? when it affects our core values? After all, what we are willing to overlook or pardon often says a lot about our own priorities.

Of course , the near perfect art is one thing, the flawed man, another. But, it becomes harder to make this moral distinction when the artist in question is known as a *lyricist*, not merely a singer, or a musician. In the case of Morrissey, we're listening to the poetry of his words and his clever word play, more than we pay attention to the music itself.

Vocally, Morrissey remains in fine form (considering he is approaching sixty) but it is near impossible to separate the man from the art, when his ugly views find their way into the songs and in his own words, he insists that they are one and the same.

This was something I wrestled with, to some extent, being an admirer of Woody Allen's films. Wagner's music is, more or less, banned in Israel (having been tainted by association with Hitler). Similarly, there are many readers who, on principle, will *not* read great poets like Ezra Pound for being a vocal anti-Semite, or philosopher Heidegger, a pro-Nazi. Again, where does one draw the line?

Pity that an artist of Morrissey's caliber and heightened sensitivity should allow such steel to have crept into his blood (admittedly, over the years). Is this what occurs when one leads an isolated, self-absorbed life, feeding off negativity and quick to lash out in spite? Has the solitary cynic, finally, become an embittered, older man with little love left for the world?

Who knows. But the horror is that he is not alone. At times such as ours, it seems apt to meditate on these cautionary words, below, from someone who knew far more than my fallen idol the price of silence and speaking out. Martin Niemöller (1892–1984) was a prominent Lutheran pastor in Germany best remembered for this oft-quoted postwar piece of wisdom:

> First they came for the socialists, and I did not speak out—because I was not a socialist.
> Then they came for the trade unionists, and I did not speak out—because I was not a trade unionist.
> Then they came for the Jews, and I did not speak out—because I was not a Jew.
> Then they came for me—and there was no one left to speak for me.

Irish Singer, Sinead O'Connor, Converts to Islam

THE ARTIST-FORMERLY-KNOWN-AS SINEAD O'CONNOR shocked the world by announcing that she had renounced Christianity and embraced Islam. Here, she is, in her own words:

> This is to announce that I am proud to have become a Muslim. This is the natural conclusion of any intelligent theologian's journey. All scripture study leads to Islam. Which makes all other scriptures redundant. I will be given (another) new name. It will be *Shuhada'*.

I received this news with mixed feelings. She was a music idol from my youth that I still admired and, few years earlier, I'd even had the good fortune to correspond with her, briefly. At the time and since then, my impressions were that she was a suffering soul, desperately, in need of good friends and people she could trust in her life.

I, also, recognized that she is a genuine seeker; in 1999, she became an ordained priest, by a breakaway church in Lourdes (although not recognized by the Catholic Church, which does not permit women to become priests). But, as some will recall from her controversial Saturday Night Live appearance in 1992, when she ripped up a photograph of the Pope live on US television, hers was a bitterly conflicted relationship with the Catholic faith.

Obviously, I wish *Shuhada'* (which means 'martyrs', in Arabic) peace and healing. That said, it's disheartening to see the incredulity and contempt that are already being heaped upon her. Some point out, not so nicely, that she's been searching for a sense of belonging for several decades, going from one group to another. As if there was anything wrong with that, especially, considering her history of abuse (at the hands of her mother) and struggles with mental illness. Others, cynically, suggest that making this announcement is some sort of stunt, and that she is sharing it to gain more media attention.

This makes me wince. I feel that when one falls in love (which is what faith is) it's natural to wish to declare it from the rooftops. Further, she's long been a champion of the underdog, and it's really helpful to have an ally like Shuhada', during these unfortunate days of rampant Islamophobia. Only time will tell, of course; but I also know that it's in the spirit of Islam (and all faith) to think well of others and try to give them the benefit of the doubt.

Unfortunately, fear and loathing of Islam have become so widespread that, often times, people do not even recognize they are engaging in it. So, I'm well aware, she has her work cut out on her journey ahead and wish her safe harbor. The heart is full of mysteries and wants what it wants—callings, particularly, are inscrutable, miraculous things. As French theologian, Pascal, memorably put it: *Le cœur a ses raisons que la raison ne connaît point* ("the heart has its reasons, which reason knows nothing of").

Review of *The Teeth of the Comb &*
Other Stories

AT HIS VERY FINEST, Osama Alomar is heir to Kahlil Gibran, whom he greatly admires, by way of the Surrealists. Despite their apparent playful wit, Alomar's deceptively slight short stories have teeth and bite. In spare, accessible prose, one encounters the painful and bitter poetry of exile running like a blood-red thread through this slim, but dense collection of flash fiction—an allegorical literary form that, in the Arab world, dates back more than a millennium. This keening is to be expected, since Alomar is a Syrian refugee and author with a growing reputation in the world he left behind. "Censorship is the mother of metaphor," Jorge Luis Borges shrewdly noted; and it is true that literature under restrictive regimes tends to develop a flair for allegory, confessing in code. One can't help but wonder, reading this richly imaginative collection, to what extent such circumstances might contribute to the author's facility with metaphor and gift for symbolism.

After immigrating to the United Sates, Alomar drove a cab for a living as he struggled to carve a creative space for his epic miniatures. In one of the touching fables found in The Teeth of the Comb, money talks and the paper bills say to one another: "We are like nations that have been sold, imprinted with thousands of fingerprints and crammed into thousands of pockets until they are in tatters." In another, poignant two-line story: "The feather said to the wind in a slain voice: 'what's this tyranny?' The wind answered her: 'what's this weakness?'" Throughout Alomar's quietly Stoic, hallucinatory fiction of ideas, everything communicates—animate and inanimate—in order to hold up a mirror to the human condition with all its self-deceptive, hypocritical and, at times, destructive ways.

Amid these shape-shifting characters and their fluid perspectives, the author tells the truth, indirectly, about the pity of wars, the violence of oppression, privation, loss, longing, and societal ills common to Third World and First World, alike. By making it strange, the fabulist delivers the news in disguise, in an attempt to awaken us to common sense. In the shock of recognition that follows, we are better able to examine our false assumptions and suffering world with more compassion and thought.

Rarely sliding into bathos, at times grim and often light-hearted, these aphorisms, parables and riddles are not, however, literary snacks to be consumed hastily. Alomar is a writer worth knowing, who gives voice to a wide scope of personal insight and a magnitude of public pain that we can hardly fathom by perusing newspapers, alone. The edifying tales this creative artist offers (ranging from one-line short to several pages long) are brief political, psychological, philosophical and moral meditations to ruminate over, carefully—sometimes with a smile, sometimes, a sigh and, sometimes, both.

Review of *By Fire*
Writings on the Arab Spring

WHERE DOES ONE BEGIN to speak of the Arab Spring, after all that has been expended in dreams, analysis, and lives? In By Fire, Tahar Ben Jelloun, Moroccan intellectual and one of the most acclaimed novelists writing in French today, attempts to creatively rescue from the ashes Mohamed Bouazizi, the self-immolating fruit vendor credited with igniting the Tunisian revolt.

This slim novella, the first fictional account to tackle the subject, was initially published in 2011 at the height of the protests. Gracefully translated, with an illuminating and exhaustive introduction, by Rita S. Nezami, By Fire is a work of imaginative empathy and real compassion. Upon reading the work of fiction in one sitting, Nezami spontaneously combusted into translation: "There are urgent stories out there that need to be told in as many languages as possible and made available to world readers."

Ben Jelloun, for his part, trusts in the power of literature to enflesh a symbol, lend voice to silent masses, and get to the heart of a human drama more powerfully than any news report might. "I focused on Mohamed's story," he says in an interview. "I closed my eyes, I saw it, and I wrote it. Beyond the specific situation in Tunisia, Mohamed Bouazizi became a valuable symbol for all cultures and all countries in pursuit of dignity."

Also collected in this slender volume are Ben Jelloun's nonfiction accounts of the political back-story, The Spark. Here, he categorically condemns dictatorship and police brutality in Tunisia and throughout the Arab world, contrasting their cruelty and corruption to the living poem of an oppressed people rising up in peaceful resistance (specifically, in Tunisia and Egypt).

All first-rate poetry is occupied with morality, according to T. S. Eliot; and By Fire, in its quietly lyrical way, is above all a moral book. Reading it is meant to prick our conscience and disturb us—as we consider the pitiable conditions and institutionalized injustice that push a human being to use their body as a last site of protest, to die in order to be heard. Together, the nonfiction and fiction sections complement one another in telling the humiliating life story of our desperate protagonist, from the inside and out, in plainspoken, urgent prose.

"Despair is betrayal" was one of the slogans of the Egyptian Revolution, urging people not to lose hope in change. In that sense, this is not a despairing work but a reminder of what was once possible and what is still at stake if—through ignorance, apathy, or worse—we turn the other way when confronted with the suffering of millions of innocent others.

Daring to Care

Notes on the Egyptian Revolution

THE FOLLOWING WAS WRITTEN merely hours after Mubarak's frankly contemptuous last speech, and several hours before the exhilarating news of a Free Egypt, the next evening. Everyone was crest-fallen that the President, who once boasted he had 'a PhD in stubbornness' had not announced his resignation, and rumors were circulating that things were going to turn vicious the following day. It was even suggested this was all part of the regime's cynical strategy: to raise hopes, and frustrate them, until demonstrators lose patience and turn violent. Then, those in power would have the excuse to fire on them, Tiananmen Square-style. I was not convinced. I believed with all my being that Love—for life and Egypt—would prevail and the peace, civility, and tenacity that marked this People's Uprising would triumph. And so I wrote this piece . . .

Overheard in Tahrir Square, a Muslim brotherhood man speaking to a secular woman: 'There was a curtain between us that made us fear each other and misunderstand each other. After spending these days here, fighting together, eating together, and bearing the cold I can see that we are not different and that we may have different ideas but we can easily communicate and respect each other.'

I know I'm not alone when I say my heart has been, and remains, full-to-bursting with the remarkable series of events taking place back Home. The mark, and success, of a true revolution is not merely overthrowing an old regime, but ushering in new ways of thinking and being. Which is why it's truly uplifting to see so many of the false barriers being toppled: say, between men and women, whom we saw out at the protests, chanting for equality, in unison, and even praying side by side in the streets; or Muslims and Christians, who came together as Egyptians, respectfully, and protected one another. As Egyptian writer Ahdaf Souief says: 'They said we were divided, extreme, ignorant, fanatic—well here we are: diverse, inclusive, hospitable, generous, sophisticated, creative and witty.'

UNLEASHING A PENT-UP CREATIVITY

With the promise of freedom in the air, we witnessed a renewed vitality in the streets of Egypt and a sort of cultural revolution, or the unleashing of previously pent-up creativity. From the start, Egyptians' playful spirit and irrepressible wit were on full display during the 25 January People's Uprising. 'Please, leave, my hand is hurting me,' read one banner; 'you must leave because I need to cut my hair,' read another. Mubarak's paltry concessions were answered with pithy ridicule: a banner depicting a computer and the message 'cannot install freedom, please remove Mubarak and try again'. Our fabled love of language was a constant throughout. Al Jazeera reported poetry readings at Tahrir Square. Egyptians heartily sang the punchy poems of Fu'ad Nigm, who in his verse uses puns and colloquial speech to critique the state and mock its corrupt leaders.

As they recited poetry, people were admirably organized and generally festive—singing, dancing and staging improv-theatre—showing us all that a revolution could be a work of art, and a way of life, even. Demonstrators not only camped out in the square, dubbed Liberation City, they set up open-air clinics, barber shops, hosted a wedding, shared food, jokes, news, and frisked one another for concealed weapons.

To the naysayers, who insisted that the uneducated masses were not ready for democracy, the Egyptian uprising, which has been referred to as a *Dignity Revolution*, demonstrated that civilized behavior was not the monopoly of the educated. On the contrary, our illiterate were educators in courtesy and a kind of natural elegance. Speaking of the awe-inspiring scenes in Tahrir Square, another acclaimed Egyptian writer, Alaa Al Aswany, summed it up thus: "Revolution makes everyone more beautiful, it's like love."

Clever, and often bitingly funny, the street verse that proliferated was spontaneous and does not really survive translation. But, to anyone listening, it was obvious that these were a people for whom poetry matters and, considering the immense personal risk involved in protesting, that words were also actions. To offer just a flavor of this ephemera, here are a couple examples, which rhyme in Arabic: *'Shurtat Masr, yâ shurtat Masr, intû ba'aytû kilâb al-'asr'* ('Egypt's Police, Egypt's Police, You've become nothing but Palace dogs'); or the more blunt *'Yâ Mubârak! Yâ Mubârak! Is-Sa'ûdiyya fi-ntizârak!'* ('Mubarak, O Mabarak, Saudi Arabia awaits!')

OVERTHROWING OLD FEARS

On a psychological note, I think it fair to say that fear has ultimately been at the heart of these past decades of state-sponsored psychological warfare. Which is to say, this People's Uprising has really been about, finally, overthrowing the tyranny of our old fears—Mubarak and his henchmen representing just a particularly stubborn symbol of these—no more, no less.

It is not without significance, then, that the youth should have led the way in the revolt of the insulted and injured masses. After all, it is the nature of youth to be fearless, and laugh in the face of danger; just as it is the nature of each successive generation, through subtle rotations, to act as a corrective to the previous generation. (With around sixty per cent of the Egyptian population under the age of twenty-five, we had a lot of youth to count on.) First, the young held our heads still to show us a new vision of Egypt, and then they gently took our hands and showed us how to achieve it. That the youth helped us realize our dream is because, against all odds, they *dared to care*.

On 25 January 2011, we surprised ourselves as much as the rest of the world. Our passivity is legendary, and it has been said that the Sphinx is more likely to lose its temper, before the Egyptian people revolt. Yes, our resignation ran deep and, moreover, was justified by an equally entrenched fatalism. Yet, suddenly, unburdened of our obstinate insecurities (or 'mind-forged manacles' in the formulation of Blake) people came together with a newfound sense of their own possibilities, and discovered the invincibility of unity.

One of the many arresting images that emerged from this revolution is a photo-shopped close-up of a man's chest, mid-costume change a-la-Superman. Except, underneath his unbuttoned shirt is not the iconic S (for Superman) but rather a luminous image of the million-strong demonstration in Tahrir square. This is how we all become heroes, by drawing on our considerable strength in numbers or transcendent power of The People.

THE WHOLE IS GREATER. . .

Nor has it been a weakness that this has been a leaderless revolution, since people seem to have intuitively grasped, early on, that here the whole is greater than the sum of its parts. Wael Ghonim, a key figure in sparking the revolution online, wisely shirked this mantle and underscored the point in his address. Before a surging sea of demonstrators gathered in Tahrir Square (which earned back its name, Liberation Square) to grant the recently released activist a hero's welcome, an emotional Ghonim spoke briefly and from the heart:

> This is not the time for individuals, or parties, or movements. It's
> a time for all of us to say just one thing. *Egypt above all.* At which
> point he and the crowd chanted those three words several times:
> *Egypt Above All. Egypt Above All. Egypt Above All!*

Those, like myself, who watched from faraway parts of the world
(where we thought we were building new lives) suddenly felt distances col-
lapsing and were sucked into the vortex. It took an (inner) quake like this
for us to realize that maybe 'you can never go home, again' but you can
never leave home, either. After having nearly lost hope in the possibility of
change, I'm now beyond proud of all those gallant Egyptians cleaning our
streets, literally and metaphorically, and paving the way for a Free Egypt
(soon, now) where we may live with liberty and dignity.

Considering how many people were involved, it is remarkable how
little blood was shed, and how it seemed to unfold, naturally. The nonviolent
protests in Ukraine came to be known as the Orange Revolution, the peace-
ful regime change in Czechoslovakia, which overthrew the communist gov-
ernment, was referred to as the Velvet Revolution (or Gentle Revolution).
Fairly early on, and fittingly, the almost flower-like people's uprising in
Egypt was given an evocative name: The Lotus Revolution—the lotus being
a flower that was highly appreciated by Ancient Egyptians.

RETURN OF THE REPRESSED

Somehow, I am reminded of Freud's 'return of the repressed.' The Egyp-
tians have not quite been themselves, lately, and now they've decided to take
back their country and their lives. This is who they *always* were: tolerant,
patient, honorable and free. Despite the corrosive apathy of recent years,
this incredibly peaceful, civilized revolution is how they are now proving, to
themselves and the world, that they are heirs to greatness.

Religious extremism and chaos, the bogeymen cited by East and West
alike to justify an unfree Egypt for far too long now, can only grow in condi-
tions of oppression and hopelessness. There is no reason to believe that is
any longer the case. Egyptians marching towards the horizon of their hopes,
with pride and ownership of their country have a different agenda, and
we've seen evidence to support this. As a case in point, a flyer from Tahrir
Square reads:

> This country is your country. Do not litter. Don't drive through
> traffic lights. Don't bribe. Don't forge paperwork . . . Don't harass

women. Don't say, "It's not my problem." Consider God in all
your work. We have no excuses anymore.

Despite the drawn-out stalemate, I believe that every day Egypt is clos-
er to climbing out of the dark hole that it's been in, and blinking in the light
of a New Dawn of its own making. What a difference a couple weeks have
made! The Uprising truly has been the ultimate antidote to impotence or
despair. If there's one thing this has taught us—from Tunis to Egypt, to the
Middle East and the world entire—it is that you never know when enough
is too much, and also that one (Tunisian) man and one gesture (burning) is
all it takes to get a Revolution in motion!

Kafka writes: "There is a point of no return. This point has to be
reached." I believe that point of no return has been reached, and crossed (in
our hearts, at least). Or, to put it in other words, also overheard in Libera-
tion Square: 'Whatever happens next, things will never be the same.' Even
amidst all the tense anticipation, there was no denying this shy, nascent
sense of moral victory.

Words—such as *Hope, Will, Change, The People, Freedom, Dreams,
Future*—after having been corrupted and nearly losing their meaning in our
public discourse in Egypt are, now, charged with so much lived idealism
and practiced heroism they have become incandescent. Poetry is suddenly
the domain of the average person in the streets, and everyone seems to have
awakened from a long slumber, more alive, with senses tingling brightly. In
this struggle for the soul of Egypt, its personal and political destiny, between
the power-lust of an eighty-two year old tyrant versus the longing of eighty-
two million souls, I never wavered which side I was betting on.

From Tahrir Square to New York Square
Justice for All

WITH OCCUPY WALL STREET fighting for its life, by supporting each other, Egyptian and American protesters can make the impossible possible.

Egyptians, as I've known them and grown up among them, have always been able to differentiate between governments and people—their own and others. This is true of Egyptians BR and PR (Before Revolution and After Revolution). They may be illiterate, but they are also shrewd. They may be uneducated, but they are not uninformed. Of course, the Revolution accelerated this and served as a crash course in political awareness because, suddenly, people discovered they could actually *do* something and participate in their own governance/destiny.

Growing up in Egypt, it was not uncommon to see a group of people gathered at a coffee shop to chat, or smoke or play backgammon while listening to the news on television. Instinctively, they filtered the truth from the propaganda as they sipped their teas, or took a drag on their water pipes. 'Transparency', a term much abused, elicited knowing smiles; 'Freedom' in any context—of the press, speech and, especially, elections—was always considered a bad joke.

When I made the US my home, in my early thirties, I was surprised to discover the extent to which most people in America appeared confounded with their government and its policies. Despite Americans, generally, being better educated and enjoying comparative liberties, to question the powers-that-be seemed a kind of sacrilege. I suppose this is one of the paradoxes of Democracy: because you are represented, you don't actually need to participate. In the end, despite the considerable differences in their circumstances,

Egyptians and Americans came to share one similar response: apathy. Mercifully, this is no longer so.

Even before the mass protest known as Occupy Wall Street began to spread from one state to another, Americans were looking to the Middle East Revolutions for inspiration. In those first exhilarating days when the Egyptian uprising was unfolding powerfully and peacefully, it was strangely heartening to see protesters, in Madison, Wisconsin, carrying signs referring to Governor Scott Walker as 'Mubarak of the Midwest' or 'Hosni Walker'. Opponents of the Governor's stance on unions viewed him as dictator, and 'Mubarak' had become shorthand for a bully who threatens violence.

With Egyptians experiencing a form of revolution-fatigue, and unable to place their full trust in military rule to secure the way ahead, it is equally touching to see protesters in Egypt returning the favor by holding up signs declaring 'From: Tahrir Square To: New York Square Justice for all. We are the 99%.' It's at times like this that it becomes inescapably clear how people are people, everywhere, and that we take courage from one another. Injustice is antithetical to human nature and courage is catching. The way that the fire from a burning man, in Tunisia, seemed to set an entire region aflame.

With the world, increasingly, becoming a smaller place, the US protest movement and Middle East upheaval seem to be converging. Just days before the NYPD swept in and evicted them, Occupy Wall Street approved $29,000 to send 20 observers to monitor Egypt's upcoming parliamentary elections. This, in response to an invitation sent to the New York occupation, from a representative of a coalition of Egyptian civil society monitors, requesting their assistance. Here's the exchange, on Twitter:

> @LibertySqGA: Dear #OWS, we are very moved by the warm welcome we received from you when we visited New York svrl wks ago. #nycga #ows

> @ LibertySqGA: Egyptians are vry proud to have bn the inspiration for yr movement and wish you the best in achieving yr goals. #nycga #ows

> @LibertySqGA: In the spirit of international solidarity, request we go visit & observe their parliamentary elections! Also tht we send invite to networks.

Granted, the significance of this gesture is a symbolic one, but the 'OWS Ambassadors' also suggest that their participation will "work to protect and support the civilian monitoring efforts of Egyptian activists on the ground and constitutes a concrete stand against the use of American weapons against peaceful demonstrators." Who is to say what will actually come of this but, in my humble view, the effects of such acts of solidarity are incalculable. As we are seeing again and again in the Middle East and beyond, when people come together in this way to safeguard their collective values and hopes, anything is possible. Liberty Square is, after all, not only the name of a square in Egypt . . .

Egypt
The Unraveling

Whoever fights monsters should see to it that in the process he does not become a monster.

—NIETZSCHE

IT SEEMS THAT EVERY time I sit down to write about Egypt, after our revolution, I am under slept and overwhelmed. Following the horrific Rabaa massacre of August 2013, and if the Egyptian Ministries are to be trusted (always a big IF) the death toll stands at 638—about as many people as were killed during the historic eighteen days it took to oust Mubarak—and a staggering 3,994 injured. This is to say nothing of the uncounted bodies still waiting to be *officially* processed, or numerous reports of families being pressured to sign statements saying the causes of death were suicide, in order for them to claim the bodies of their loved ones.

Sickening, in this context, to hear Prime Minister El-Beblawi praising the police for "self restraint"—which is, of course, not to excuse the pro-Morsi supporters/Muslim Brotherhood of the dreadful havoc they've wreaked. Frankly, I've had neither the heart nor stomach to watch any of the gruesome videos circulating, but on the basis alone of the dozens of churches they have burned, they have forgone the moral right to speak of "legitimacy" ever again.

Yet, because I dared to share on social media news of Mohamed El Baradei's principled stepping down as interim prime minister, I have been drawn into exhausting virtual battles by "friends" for supporting this traitor, and told by otherwise gentle-seeming folks (cultured, liberal, even Sufi-admiring) that the army's use of violence is completely justified, that the Muslim Brotherhood are "cockroaches," "a cancer," basically inhuman, and therefore deserve to die, unmourned.

Here are El Baradei's closing words from his resignation statement:

> I am afraid I cannot afford to bear the responsibility of a single drop of blood before God, and before my conscience and the citizens of Egypt. Unfortunately, the beneficiaries of today's events are the advocates of violence and terrorism.

To my ears, these are words of sanity, posing ethical questions we should all be asking ourselves. What becomes of us when we condone the excessive use of violence and mass murder? Are we not accomplices? And how is it that we are able to put our blind trust in the army after we've suffered their abuses of power in the not-too-distant past (the Maspero massacre, "virginity tests," and so forth). Yes, I am one of many relieved, after the gross and dangerous ineptitude of Morsi's leadership, for Egypt to have another chance at real freedom. But might we also imagine that post the people-endorsed coup, the army might have its own cynical agenda in mind (read more power)?

Those who pit us against each other, or set churches on fire and terrorize us, are not our friends. This is not why the long-suffering Egyptians dared to dream of revolution in the first place; Egypt deserves better than having her hopes tossed between the devil and the deep blue sea. To be sure, we've other 'devils' besides six decades of military rule or the perils of the Muslim Brotherhood to contend with. Lack of education is certainly one, and in the words of Aristotle, "Poverty is the parent of revolution and crime." We would do better, then, to address these serious societal ills than allow ourselves to be distracted and deceived into more tragic battles.

Certainly, there were other ways to "clear the sit-in" besides mass extermination of the protestors. Violence is always a failure of imagination and compassion, and it begets violence; just as fighting hate with hate only escalates it. This is the unraveling we are witnessing now. This is how we ended up in this choice-less mess, in the first place (between the Military and Muslim Brotherhood stalemate).

Understandably, emotions are running high, and patience is wearing thin in the face of so much daily chaos, so many disappointments and seemingly no hope in sight. But, in the midst of all this, we must not lose sight of each other's humanity, since how we respond to these soul-trying challenges will determine who we become.

Hard as it may appear at times to see past the divisiveness, hurt and fatigue, it is worth trying even harder to remember the noble goals of our peaceful revolution. We were stronger when we united around common goals, and focused instead on what we love: Freedom, Dignity, Egypt. All human life is sacred and equal; we should see to it in fighting the monsters of injustice, ignorance and oppression that we do not become monsters ourselves.

Bassem Sabry

Voice of the Egyptian Revolution (1982—2014)

THE EGYPTIAN JOURNALIST, BASSEM Sabry, embodied the best of us: commitment, compassion and profound optimism. Even as he witnessed the noble ideals of our Egyptian ('Dignity') Revolution being betrayed, and the country becoming bitterly divided, he dared to continue caring and upheld his code of honor. Sabry's voice never descended into the fray of mounting cynicism, apathy, or worse: condoning violence. We mourn him so deeply, and widely, because he kept our conscience alive, reminding us of our larger allegiances towards one another and, through his inspiring example, that how we fight for our freedom determines who we ultimately become. Bassem (meaning 'smiling' in Arabic) employed gentle humor instead of the unfortunate, spiteful contempt now prevalent in the public discourse. In the midst of all the chaos and mayhem, he did not permit himself, or us, to lose sight of the humanity of all Egyptians, even as many allowed themselves to become desensitized by the military propaganda machine. This is why, irrespective of political leanings, he was the go-to-blogger, civil rights activist and media analyst for anyone trying to understand the unraveling in what was once referred to as the Cradle of Civilization.

That Bassem is dead, of an unconfirmed accident at the devastatingly young age of thirty-one, is almost too much to fathom. He leaves a gaping hole in our psyche and, as Egyptians, we must redouble our efforts to live with decency and integrity, without him there to nudge us in the right direction. Yet again, we can be buoyed by his wise, undying words. You can read his thoughtful, spiritually alert and emotionally generous reflections, upon turning 30, "Eleutheria—(Almost Everything I Have Learned In My Life)" on anarabcitizen.blogspot.com.

July 4
New Independence Day for Egypt?

EGYPT IS NOT HAVING a second revolution. We're still wrapping up our first one. Until the end, ousted Egyptian president, Mohamed Morsi, continued to fatally miscalculate the extent of the people's fed-up-ness (enough was too much, two years ago) and squander the goodwill extended him a year ago. With his defiant speech, Morsi effectively sealed his political death, echoing Mubarak's contemptuous last effusions by way of Qaddafi's hallucinations. As with fools past and toppled, Morsi appeared oblivious of the *vox populi*: record millions who took to the streets, many of whom had voted for him and were now calling for his ouster at his one-year anniversary. The concessions he offered were appalling, another case of Mubarak's far-too-little, far-too-late, and were delivered in a similar tone: patronizing, delusional, full of denials, and blaming everyone but himself for the mess. The masses were incredulous and devastated afterwards. As with Mubarak's disastrous last address, rumors immediately began circulating that things were going to turn vicious the following day.

Pity the Egyptians that they must turn, once again, to their abusers and rapists, the army which gave Morsi a forty-eight hour ultimatum to sort things out. But this is not a case of Stockholm Syndrome. We've not quite yet forgotten, or forgiven, the Maspero Massacre, the so-called "virginity tests" and the army's ghastly abuses of power and intimidation. We just need a breather, to figure out what we don't want. We rushed into "choosing" Morsi, as an act of defiance and desperation, finding ourselves between a rock (old regime) and a hard place (military rule). At last, the Muslim Brotherhood illusion is exploded and we finally see them for what they are, more bullies and bad politicians—which is to say, more corrupt hypocrites, only this time hiding behind a holy beard. If we hadn't fully realized it, Morsi's response to the historic (and remarkably bloodless) June 30th protests, spelled it out for us: a leader who pushes his people to the brink of a civil war cares more for himself than for the welfare of the country or its citizens. Despite his ludicrous repetition of *his legitimacy, his legitimacy, his legitimacy* throughout his unfortunate speech, the graffito on the presidential palace walls says it all, 'The legitimacy of your ballot box / Is cancelled by our martyrs' coffins'. What's next remains a mystery. But there's no doubt that—despite the tremendous economic deprivations, divisive politics and spiritual provocations Egyptians endure on a regular basis—two years later, we still dream of justice and freedom, enough to risk life (and to do so in a largely peaceful manner). There's little chance of us repeating the same mistakes, and it appears that the army doesn't want the job/headache this time round, as talks are underway with opposition spokesman (and Nobel Prize winner) Mohammed El Baradei. "Hope is the last thing that dies . . . "

Egypt
Bread and Social Justice

EVEN THOUGH I WAS born and raised in Egypt (not far from the now-famous Tahrir Square) after several bewildering years away from Home, I can finally say: *I don't know what Egyptians want.* I am not an admirer of either the Muslim Brotherhood, or Morsi, yet wept the day he was "elected." Why? Because, watching a sea of Egyptians flooding The Square, I was overcome by the joyful noise of these long-suffering people who felt that, for the first time in decades, they had been heard and their human dignity, somehow, restored. Of course, the other choice, old regime and military rule, was no choice at all, merely more oppression with impunity. Still, I hoped, this was a step towards discovering what they did not want; give him enough rope and this Morsi will, eventually, hang himself. Well before the recent uprising, he had been making outrageous, and paternalistic, remarks eerily reminiscent of his predecessor: "police never attack citizens; up to 90% of the people support him, and, no, Christians have not been fleeing the country." In view of such provocations, the new *Time* magazine with his mug on the cover and the headline: The Most Important Man in the Middle East was regarded by many as in poor taste or, worse, an insult (another US-backed-dictator-in-the-grooming). Mercifully, Egyptians did not wait three more decades to stand up to their new "Pharaoh" (as he has been dubbed). With his latest power grab Morsi, fatally, miscalculated both the intelligence and mood of his subjects. [The learning curve is steep, this time around; mass protests came less than two weeks after the presidential decree issued by Morsi granting him powers above judiciary review.]

Living under Emergency Law since 1967 (except for an 18-month break, in 1980) Egyptians had, psychologically, crossed a point of no return during the January 25 Revolution in 2011. Taking their cue from the Tunisian uprising before them, and courage from one another, they cleared a fear barrier and deep-seated apathy by taking to the streets, *en masse*. Since then, protesting has become a way of life and, after decades of feeling disenfranchised, Egyptians are keen to engage in the decision-making process and self-determination. Yes, there is confusion and exhaustion, but as a popular mantra has it, which was demonstrated in practice: *The Revolution Continues*. While Egyptians continue to battle for their soul and figure out who they want to be and whom to trust, they do know what they will *not* tolerate any longer. Anything that smells of dictatorship is flat-out unacceptable. So, when riot police fired tear gas on peaceful demonstrators, bitter jokes circulated about Egyptians having become immune to tear gas, and left with no more tears to shed. The cry of hundreds of thousands of demonstrators, from all walks of life, that converged on the presidential *palace* and drove Morsi into hiding was simple enough for anyone to understand: *Hurreyya* (Freedom). Meanwhile, throughout the rest of the country echoed another fairly blunt chant, made popular during the ouster of Mubarak: "the people call for the downfall of the regime."

To Kill a Mocking Girl
An Artist in Kuwait

THE ARAB SPRING HAS only just begun. As Eliot pointed out, mixing memory and desire is a cruel business, and the winter (of passivity) kept us warm. But to cite another literary and seasonal reference, this time by Anais Nin: "the day came when the risk to remain tight in a bud was more painful than the risk it took to blossom." In this sense, one can safely say that revolutions of the minds in the Middle East are still blossoming—and being witnessed on many frontiers. One need not be a feminist or even an activist to agree that, alongside the political, religious, and economic challenges, there remains a sexual one. Which is to say that, within patriarchal societies, gender equality as a basic human right is a critical element in any successful revolutions.

Kuwaiti/Syrian artist, Shurooq Amin, is such a freedom-fighter. A self-confessed 'creative thorn in their sides', Amin, who is also a poet and a professor at Kuwait University, is a natural-born provocateur and fearless in addressing sexual politics through her art. Her arresting canvases typically mirror socio-political ills and hypocrisies; for example, female oppression—veiled faces, child brides, gagged mouths, and bound hands—or the contradictions of Western influence (technology, culture, fashion). This is the artist as activist, shedding light on social injustices while illustrating the perversions of pleasure, or what happens when needs are denied a natural outlet, and grow sick. While respected in Kuwait, and internationally recognized, Amin's daring has not gone without censure at home. Her series *It's a Man's World* (March 7, 2012) was shut down by local Kuwait authorities, after only three hours, on the premise that the artworks were "pornographic" and "Anti-Islamic," accusations she contests. (The controversy worked in her favor, was covered widely, and she even trended on Twitter.) Not one to back down, Amin's following collection (at the Ayyam Gallery) showed how censorship is the mother of creativity. Evocatively titled *Popcornographic,* she continues to poke where it hurts, examining sensitive subjects such as religious taboos in the Arab world.

Coming to America

The Remake

I THOUGHT I HAD it, ages ago. Attending American schools, K-12 (albeit in Kuwait and Egypt) meant I was familiar with the lingo. Even though I spoke some Arabic at home, I never formally studied it at school, which translated into reading, writing, and dreaming, in *English*. What's more, I had gone to college in the States, so there really shouldn't have been any sort of culture shock for me when I made the US my home.

But, my college years (in Washington, DC) were a kind of reactionary blur where I'd spent most of the time with my nose buried in a book, experimenting with things like philosophy and silent fasts instead of taking in the New World around me. Seasons came and passed without my noticing, and I would return home anyway at the end of each semester. So, when I decided to move to the US I was, for all practical purposes, living in America for the first time—the same way they say that you never know someone till you *live* with them.

Thus, in spite of my early Americanization, landing in the States in early 2006 I felt like an untitled, and near penniless, version of Eddie Murphy's African prince character in his 1988 hit comedy, *Coming to America*. A series of cultural confusions during my first year of orientation, featuring my soon-to-become wife, convinced me that I was "off the boat" and that Project Integration was still underway.

America had changed, and I had too, since those college years (this was the tail end of the Bush Years, and pre-financial crisis) but, somehow, I had not wrapped my mind around the basics last time I was here, like: the credit system. So, when my fiancée disclosed to me the amount of her mortgage, I was genuinely scandalized. After I candidly told her I thought such debt was criminal and she should do time for it, I gave her another piece of my overwhelmed mind. "In Egypt, we have a saying" I volunteered "extend your legs only to the extent of your blanket." Meaning if your blanket/means are limited, no need to stretch/splurge. She heard me out patiently, brushed the whole thing off (deciding not to tell me either about her student or car loan) and assured me I was over-reacting.

As a fledgling poet, I sent out countless packets of my work to magazines across the country, like quivering arrows, in hopes a lucky few might hit their target. One day, my wife brought back an envelope to me. "You need to include the state *and* zip code," she said. "I filled it out, correctly" I replied. "No, you *didn't*," she continued matter-of-factly, "you *just* wrote Portland." "Oh no," I shot back, rather smugly. "I read that one very closely. It said Portland *or* the zip code; and the 'or' was written in caps." Very slowly, as though speaking to a small child, she let me know that OR stood for Oregon.

Meantime, I was looking for work and without much success, when I came across what seemed like a plum position. I could not contain my excitement. "Diana," I nearly hyper-ventilated into the phone "come over, at once, and check out this job! I'm prepared to sell my soul to the devil and then retire after two years." She tumbled into the room, also breathless, like a happy puppy; "Where, where, let me see . . . " I cautioned: "You're going to need to sit down for this," presenting her with the job description. As she scanned the form, I volunteered: "I know, I know, it's a military job . . . but I'll temporarily swallow my principles [I'm a die-hard pacifist] for a salary like that . . . "

"You have the skills . . . " she ventured, cautiously. "Keep reading, please," I responded. She continued, "Okay, you get the typical benefits: health, dental, 401k . . . " I bounded across the room and mouthed it like a miracle. "Can you *imagine*, for an editorial job? Heck, I'll do it for a couple years, then quit! Plus, they can keep that extra thousand dollars . . . " She gave me an incredulous look and burst out in a fit of uncontrollable laughter.

*For non-Americans, a 401(k) is a standard type of retirement savings account in the United States, and has absolutely nothing to do with my fantasies of fortune and early retirement.

If You Want To Know the Real Meaning of Pity

IF YOU WANT YOUR heart to break open, visit an old people's home. Walk down the corridors of the abandoned and try not to avoid the eyes of the elders, haunted or vacant, but mostly hungry, starved for human affection. *Is it me you've come for?* one will ask desperately. *Help me, help me!* another shouts, face contorted in terror and pain, as she slips off her bed. So, you stop and help, naturally, only to have the nurse smile at you, knowingly, and tell you that the apparently imperiled elder is fine and behaves this way for attention . . .

Before you make it to see the unfortunate you are here to visit, first pass by rows upon rows of these pitiful, heart-rending souls, wandering in hallways, lost in some inner space, stacked in rooms like some broken pieces of furniture or parked outdoors like malfunctioning machines that sputter back to life, in fits and starts . . .

I was there, on this day, to visit my ninety-year-old neighbor, Mr. Crosby. We'd become friends over the years and, returning from a long trip away, I was saddened to learn he'd been moved into a nursing home. I've known him, on and off, for less than a decade and, even when he enjoyed his full faculties, Mr. Crosby was not the easiest person to get along with. A ship man, he was happiest at sea, and when they finally let him go at work, just a few years earlier, he confessed to me, plaintively, *Whatever am I going to do on land?*

I didn't have an answer but, when he was up for it, I'd pay him a visit and we might grab a coffee or lunch, together. Perhaps, we'd watch a little television or I could listen to his stories (never quite sure, with the deterioration of his mind, of their veracity). After a recent stroke, he began to come undone more rapidly, mistaking his remote control for his telephone, and cursing like the sailor he once was, more and more frequently, as his life became an unmanageable knot of frustrations.

Mr. Crosby no longer listened to classical music, which had previously given him some solace, and his physical ailments became the only company he kept. If he was not by himself in the lobby of the apartment building, he was out lurching in the streets, like a storm-tossed ship. Frequently, he stopped traffic on his short outings around the neighborhood. I was not the only one in our building who feared for his safety. Yet, when I asked, I was told by our building management that Mr. Crosby has undergone testing and he was not found eligible for government assistance.

My solitary neighbor had never married. There were a few kind souls from his cruise ship days who checked in on him, from time to time, and managed his financial affairs. But, apart from them, there was no one else in his life, really, or family that he could count upon. As the loneliness and dementia tightened their grip he'd sob, in horror and self-pity, and repeat that he was dying.

He wished to end his journey in Cape Cod where, as a younger man, he had serviced the boats of the Kennedy family (a story I *did* believe, on account of the details that he provided). More than once in his reduced state, Mr. Crosby had asked if I'd help him sail back home, from South Florida where we lived. He'd even gone so far as to fill up a couple of gas canisters, in his bathtub, for this longed-for homecoming trip. Alas, I had no sailing experience and he was in no condition to act as captain. I declined, but suspected I might not see him, again, when I took my last trip out-of-town . . .

Now, he's in a nursing home, nearly Home, bewildered and winded. Seeing him, he offers his frail hand and a wan smile, grateful for the visit, but also embarrassed. He apologizes that he is not good company and, after taking a couple of excited gulps from the smoothie brought him, keeps shivering and nodding off. *Very good to see you*, he offers his hand, again, less than a half hour later, grimacing, and asks if he could take a nap. Of course, of course, I say, and let him be.

Here's a short meditation of mine on Time:

Mourning Stroll

An old man, hobbling down the pavement
supported by crutches, pauses
before a noisy schoolyard
— children frolic in the sun

Through thick glasses and heavy hearing aid
he strains to see and hear, what . . .
but his own golden boyhood?
The eyes well up with easy tears.

Tribulations of Publishing

To PUBLISH A BOOK is *not* impossible—provided you have the patience of Job, armadillo-thick skin, and staggering confidence in your work. There are exceptions, of course, but I can only share my experience.

In my late teens, unconsciously, I began working on my first book, Signposts to Elsewhere, by scribbling in the margins of books by my literary masters, at the time (aphorists like Gibran, Wilde, Nietzsche, Blake, Kafka, etc . . .). This was nearly thirty years ago and, even though I grew up in a culture where many people spoke in proverbs, hardly anyone knew what an *aphorism* actually was.

I carried this manuscript of my one-liners for years, revising it and hardly showing it to a soul. It was a near-archaic form, who would care anyway? It would take me a full decade to get it published, after completing the bulk of it by my early twenties. The first kind hand extended to me at the time was by Alain de Botton, popular philosopher, who generously shared with me his agents' contacts to help me get my manuscript into print.

Yet, it was not to be. Market considerations and such. A succession of other established writers, with a penchant for wisdom literature or poetry took me under their wings. Invariably, they suggested that I publish excerpts of my work in magazines, first (online or in print) to establish a publishing record, before a press might consider taking a chance on an unknown writer, especially, one writing in such a "difficult" genre.

I did manage to place some of my writing in magazines, in Egypt, where I was working as an editor for the United Nations, as well as abroad (UK, USA, etc . . .). Yet, in between my slender successes, I received a barrage of rejection letters from publishers, telling me that my work was too philosophical for a poetry publisher, or too poetic for a philosophy publisher, etc . . .

I despaired and rallied. Inspired by my countless rejections, I wrote a poem:

Rejections

Rejections I receive, regularly
from the best and rest of them:

We have considered your proposal, but
decided not to accept it for publication.

Thank you for your submission,
sorry, we cannot make an offer.

We are unable to use your poetry
it is not quite appropriate for us.

We do appreciate your interest
good luck better luck best of luck.

Still I continue to draw and send forth
quivering arrows from this aching bow

Emboldened by Becket's wry quip
"Try again, fail again, fail better."

Citing Nietzsche's modest abundance
"an artist does not know what is finest in their garden"

As I arrange yet another bouquet
always, with Baudelaire, in search of the New.

Within six months of my arriving in my new home, the US, my luck changed, dramatically. James Geary, former editor of *Time* magazine (Europe) and an aphorism aficionado, invited me to submit to his encyclopedia of The World's Great Aphorists—alongside giants like Confucius, Voltaire, Twain, Shakespeare, and Emily Dickinson! I could hardly believe my good fortune when, shortly afterwards, my first book ("Signposts") was accepted for publication.

Since then, I've gone on to publish six more books (with six different publishers) including my latest collection of aphorisms, Where Epics Fail, from Unbound (UK) in collaboration with Penguin Random House. While the rewards have been deep and abiding—participating in international festivals, reaching students and readers in far-flung corners of the world, award nominations—they've, largely, *not* been financial.

With the exception of very few big name publishers, with bottomless purses for marketing, authors are, increasingly, relied upon to get the word out before, during and after book publication (through social media, book signings, word of mouth). It can be faintly exhausting, for a wallflower. But, such is the irony of being a writer, or a private person in a public profession.

Which is why, finally, getting a book out into the world can feel like (to borrow an old-fashioned, somewhat machismo expression from my parent's generation) like marrying off one of your daughters. Proud papa can earn some hard-won relaxation, and not have to worry as much about her welfare. Unless of course, said daughter (the difficult to marry one, who took a decade to find a suitable suitor) should return home.

That is how I felt, one morning, when I learned a book of mine was no longer available for sale. Or, if I might be permitted a mixed metaphor, it seemed like I was receiving a 'break-up' letter when I checked my mail to find a note from the publisher of my first book ('Signposts') notifying me that she was *out of the book selling business* and my book, along with many others, would no longer be available through her!

So, I spent the better portion of that morning in something of a minor panic, reaching out to nearly a hundred contacts in the literary/publishing world to explore my options for this, now, homeless book. Do I take back my single-again offspring, as some friends suggested, and try to self-publish in these trying times for the publishing industry? It's an option, and my ever-resourceful wife seemed up for it. But, I simply didn't have the heart or brain-space or *oomph* to go through all that—especially, with a new book of mine forthcoming in a few months, requiring me to conserve my finite energy.

Mercifully, I didn't have to consider this option as I, eventually, acquired a literary agent (my first) who soon notified me that Hay House (the publishers of Deepak Chopra) accepted to re-issue *Signposts*. This was something of a minor miracle, I was told by other authors who warned me that, despite receiving glowing reviews and many awards, they've not had luck reprinting their work, for decades! So, I'm counting my blessings and breathing easier. I'm also turning to a quote by Roman playwright, Terence, for sustenance: "Books, too, have their destinies."

What will be, will be and who knew that this temporary setback was meant to result in a bigger, better opportunity!

So, You Published a Book—
Now, What?

I RECEIVED THE FOLLOWING note from a reader, and soon-to-be-published
author:

> I have been carrying around manuscripts for a while, and have
> my first book coming out with a small but respectable publish-
> ing house in one month, after having given up hope several
> times . . . It's a philosophy book [in Dutch] for a general audi-
> ence, so will have to think of how to reach people. I'm very bad
> at networking & marketing, rather spend my time writing . . .
> Looking forward if you would write about how to approach that
> . . . the hurdle after finding the publisher so to speak ;)

This piece is dedicated to her, and all aspiring writers. I realize that
what to do *after* publication might seem like a stretch for writers who are
still getting started. But, with the publishing world in a state of transition,
it's never too early to start preparing and modifying expectations. For non-
writers reading this, I think it might be of interest in demystifying the writ-
erly life and, perhaps, bursting some myths along the way about books and
writers.

PARENTING TIPS FOR THE NEW AUTHOR

Imagine, after years of carrying a living, pulsing dream (aka manuscript)
finally, a publisher says *Yes*, I will help you deliver it into the world. Euphoria
ensues, huge relief, validation, and an urge to broadcast your extraordinary
good news and celebrate, once you still your beating heart! At last, you can

put your feet up and earn some hard-won rest, basking in a sense of accomplishment, as your book finds its way to readers. Maybe, occasionally, you'll rise to answer the phone if it's a reporter looking to interview you or the postman beating at your door to deliver a royalty check. Otherwise, the work is work; fame and fortune are yours.

No. Unless you are the lucky 0.000000001 percent to have your book made into a blockbuster film or Oprah declaring your genius at the top of her lungs or, more rare still, a critically-acclaimed, bestseller championed by the New York Times. Rather, think of publishing as parenting. Do your responsibilities end with having a baby? No, they begin. Here's how I described this arduous task in a poem of mine, *How to Make a Name for Yourself* (then, I promise, I'll try to break it down, in prose).

A Name

To have a name and make a name is not the same
True, both are spun of love and will and dreams
But one is blindly granted as we blink in the light,
The other we must forge from our innermost

Nameless, once more, we are reborn into the world
From the soul's furnace, we strive to stake our claim
Hotly hammering desires, giving shape to longing
And setting it to cool, approximating an ideal

Then again, we must teach this babe to crawl ahead
Mothering it with care, fathering it with courage
So that, one day, it can freely live apart from us
And find its place in our clamoring times and after.

Book signings, even for fearless exhibitionists (which the majority of writers are *not*) can be daunting affairs. In addition to summoning the bravery to share your (oftentimes, intimate) thoughts before a room full of strangers, you must brace yourself for the fact that, in most cases, said room will *not* be full. Accept the empty chairs, overlook the yawning, texting, etc . . . and pardon the many who will walk out before purchasing a book. The ones who *do*, and take time to engage in meaningful conversation with you afterwards, will make it all worthwhile.

I have to back up for a moment. As part of your book publishing preparation, try and secure an endorsement or two from an established author—these will make a difference in your book's reception and audience turnout at signings. Again, this is not easy to do, but if your writing is strong and you, politely, approach an author who works in the same genre, it's well worth your time and effort.

Remember, you're new in this town, nobody knows your name, and there are countless others vying for readers' limited attention. Before readers can give you a chance, it helps if someone higher up the chain gives you their stamp of approval, signaling that you're worth the time. As in life, not just *what* you know, but *who* you know counts; so begin networking, and try to do so with elegance and grace.

Before blogging on Steemit, I virtually lived on Facebook and Twitter. With a combined following of around twelve thousand, I relied on this community for much: emotional support and critical feedback, publishing and literary leads, even crowd-funding my last book. If I read an interesting article or book (and the author was still alive) I would see if I could follow them, online. That way, I could hear from the horse's mouth about the ins and outs of the industry—including what journals, magazines, blogs featured the type of work they did (and that I was interested in): philosophy, poetry, spirituality, or culture.

It was through Twitter, for example, that I learned of NPR's call for "micro poetry" and, as a result, had two of my 140-character-poems featured on their Tell Me More show: *Bodies Are Like Poems* and *A Word-Shaped Web*. Later, I had the good fortune of being invited to the NPR studios for a full-length interview, to discuss my latest book and An Artist's Story of the Arab Spring [included in the Conversations section of this book].

To those unfamiliar with National Public Radio (NPR) it's worth mentioning that NPR reaches 30.2 million weekly listeners through more than 1,000 public radio stations. Online, NPR.org attracts a growing audience of 36.9 million unique monthly users. Needless to say, this is far more potential readers than any book signing can promise. Also, it is worth adding that getting on the radio is not the easiest thing to do, either. Yes, luck plays a big factor, yet podcasts, now, abound.

The other time-tested route to share your book news is through reviews. Again, your chances increase, online, with all the new outlets available; do your research and find the best match. Unfortunately, book review sections in major newspapers are caving in (as, regrettably, are bookstores themselves) so if you discourage too easily, this business is not for you.

Still, it doesn't hurt to try your small(er) city paper or magazine, as they are more likely to consider sharing news of a local that did good. Haunt libraries (yes, they still exist) for tips and find out if they are hosting any cultural events or if you could join a group reading or donate your book—*if* they will not consider ordering it, directly, from your publisher. Meantime, continue writing, not another book, but shorter pieces that you can place in current publications. Your byline, featuring news of your new book, becomes your banner, your personal book ad embedded wherever you publish your writing.

Of course, always, rely on the support of others, near and far: biased family members and cheerleading friends spreading the word, but also enthusiastic readers, and kindred spirits you meet along the way. I hope this might be of some use or interest to readers and writers. I've never quite put all this in writing, although I've been asked many times in person, or via email, by readers, students and aspiring writers. In the future, I will direct them to this article.

The Hell of Complaining

WE ALL KNOW THE type and have been them, at times: The Chronically Dissatisfied. Short-changed by life at every turn, or so they believe, they adopt a scorched-earth mentality. Each time they unbutton their lips, it's to tear down, belittle, bemoan: the weather, the news, their colleagues, the world. At the very least, to satisfy their disgruntled hearts, they will emit a long and windy sigh.

We learn, over time, to avoid such persons, or minimize our interactions—and not ask them how they are doing, or about their work, or their weekends, for fear of the deluge. Sometimes, they might overhear themselves and, in turn, they will complain about how difficult it is being them.

There is no age limit to this misbehavior, of course, and growing older does not mean growing up. But maturity and, certainly, evolving does mean complaining less—since, we cannot complain and truly learn, at the same time. Rumi says this best in a handful of words: "If you are irritated by every rub, how will your mirror be polished?"

Which is to say, those so-called 'irritants'—obstacles, hurdles, challenges, disappointments, delayed gratifications, even heartache—they are all there to help us grow, and polish the mirror of our heart. But, first, we must perceive them in this light, and try to work *with* them, not against them.

Patience, of course, is key. Another Sufi teacher, Idries Shah, puts it this way: "The impatient man is his own enemy; he slams the door on his own progress." Because my mind works in quotations I am, now, reminded of yet another. In this case, it was Christian counsel on a wooden plaque at the entrance of our childhood home (even though we were not raised as Christians). Known as the "Serenity Prayer" and written by the American theologian, Reinhold Niebuhr, it read:

Lord, grant me the serenity to accept the things I cannot change,
Courage to change the things I can,
And wisdom to know the difference.

To recognize that all is not within our hands, and act on what is, this is wisdom in practice. Generally speaking, I've found that patience, acceptance and gratitude are effective antidotes to complaining. Asking *how can I best use these testing circumstances* is a better approach than knee-jerk resistance, and negativity.

Because we also live, virtually, on social media platforms where other suffering souls visit our feed/communal well in search of something to refresh them, it's worthwhile to try to balance our tendency to vent with some uplift. Otherwise, without recognizing it, we might find one day that we have become like those persons we avoid: The Incorrigible Complainers. C.S. Lewis eloquently sums up this unfortunate predicament:

Hell begins with a grumbling mood, always complaining, always blaming others. . . but you are still distinct from it. You may even criticize it in yourself and wish you could stop it. But there may come a day when you can no longer. Then there will be no you left to criticize the mood or even to enjoy it, but just the grumble itself, going on forever like a machine. It is not a question of God "sending us" to hell. In each of us there is something growing, which will BE hell unless it is nipped in the bud.

The Many Bullies in our Lives

I'M THINKING OF THE many bullies—big and small— from the playground variety to internet trolls, partners, parents, presidents, dictators, etc . . . Of course, public and private tyrants are as old as humanity itself. It's an ancient spiritual truth that those who cannot master themselves are hell bent on controlling others—exacting revenge for their personal inadequacies, even on the world stage.

Yet, do these bullies see themselves this way? Most likely, not. It's a perversion of human nature that bullies (and, you can test this against those in your own life) tend to play the role of victims. Part of the danger of such damaged persons is that they cannot imagine the harm and pain they inflict upon others, so wrapped up are they in their own story. There is an Egyptian saying that addresses this paradox: "The tyrant is only the slave turned inside out."

Think about it, whether in the world of politics, or in the private sphere: the jailer is never free. What is true of nations is also true of personal human relations; keeping others down always robs us of our liberation. Since we are born to be free, controlling others is a spiritual impossibility. Those who try to do so, are doomed to live in a state of agitated insecurity. This, alone, ought to be a lesson to bullies; but it's not.

Look at the contortions, for example, that corrupt leaders go through, just to remain in power, or psychological abusers. The antidote to this, and all other maladies of the spirit, is self-knowledge and seeking freedom. Here is another quote, this time by Russian writer, Anton Chekhov, that illumines the great inner work required of all of us in order to be free of suffering and, in turn, not make those around us suffer, as well: "Write about this man who, drop by drop, squeezes the slave's blood out of himself until he wakes one day to find the blood of a real human being—not a slave's—coursing through his veins."

Writing Without Words

The Strange Case of Sam Roxas-Chua

UPON THE RECOMMENDATION OF Orison Books, a fine literary press focused on the life of the spirit, I acquired a rather unusual book—writing that is not writing. From time to time, I get word-weary. Acutely aware of the inadequacy of letters I, sometimes, long for images, or music, or silence. This book of asemic writing, the writing-which-is-not, curiously, struck me as a combination of all of the above.

Echolalia in Script: a collection of asemic writing by Sam Roxas-Chua was the first I heard of this evocative art form. Somehow, it reminded me of Arabic calligraphy (only minus the intelligible letters)! What is interesting about this unusual form is that it thwarts one of our basic needs, as meaning-hungry creatures, yet rewards another, namely, our intuitive appreciation of beauty.

If, as Oscar Wilde once quipped, "to define is to limit" then asemic writing is open-ended, and collaborative. Like abstract art, it invites the reader/viewer to participate and bring their own story to the page. More and more, I find that I am drawn to such poetry of the ineffable, or art's attempt to express what is unutterable.

This genre-bending 'writing' seems strangely meditative, able to access regions of our soul otherwise difficult to reach by words or painting, alone. It is the hum in between letters and images that Roxas-Chua, marvelously, captures on the page. Here, is the poet and visual artist, who has since become a friend and collaborator, describing his own work: "There are some words I believe we will never have words for. That's asemic to me. A made-up script that is alive, an inner frequency."

When I received my copy of this remarkable work of (he)art, it was quite difficult to describe to the artist my appreciation of his work, using words, since his visual poetry communicates what words cannot. Shortly after, these wise words by Rilke came to my rescue: "Things aren't so tangible and sayable as people would usually have us believe; most experiences are unsayable, they happen in a space that no word has ever entered."

What the Migraine Said

THESE ARE THE WINCING days: walking around shading eyes with hands, ice-pack atop head and, vampire-like, avoiding light, seeking quiet and dark spaces. For weeks—nearly a month —I've been experiencing a fairly persistent migraine. It subsides just long enough for me to read or write a little, but makes itself known if I stare overlong at The Screens, big or small (television, computer and iphone). This has limited my concentration and has me staggering around in a kind of haze during waking hours.

Alarmed by its persistence, I visited the emergency room, where I spent twelve hours (from 7pm-7am) between waiting to be seen and being seen. Mercifully, catscan and bloodwork came back clean. I feel bad complaining, in comparison to the major tragedies I witnessed in the waiting room: relatives howling in pain, writhing on the ground, having just learned of the death of their loved ones, domestic abuse, shootings, all variety of life's walking wounded.

I've been taking medication to control the pain, and gotten an eye exam since, but still feel out of it, dizzy and nauseous even as I type this, versus the acute pain I felt weeks earlier. If the new glasses/prescription don't help, I'm meant to visit a neurologist, next. This experience served as inspiration for the poem, below.

What the Migraine Said

As I lie, here, half in and out of consciousness
I imagine my migraine as a world migraine
my cluster headache as a cluster of world aches
that we must tip toe around like a sleeping tiger

The sleep of reason produces monsters—
this we know from art and the news:
murder and sham leaders shooting themselves
in one foot and chewing on the other.

But, the sleep of reason produces angels, also
like Love, which is no whimsical thing,
a love like bull, bullfighter and bloody cape,
billowing in the wind, like an open heart

Beckett said this best, truth in paradox:
The mystics . . . I like . . . their burning illogicality
— the flame . . . Which consumes all our filthy logic . . .
Where there are demons there is something precious

Once we know this, the rest is silence.
The master is not permitted
the same mistakes of a novice.

Remembering a Legendary Egyptian Actor: *Omar Sharif*

I T ' S EXCITING TO WAKE up and see the familiar face of Omar Sharif staring back at me from that day's Google doodle—featured in forty-eight countries. Despite our fabled, illustrious past, we seem to have precious little to be proud of in modern day Egypt (Egyptian soccer star, Mohamed Salah, being one of our few exceptions).

Yet, beyond Ancient Egyptian civilization, believe it or not, Egypt used to be the cultural capital of the Arab world, not too long ago. You know the song, *New York, New York* well, substitute Cairo just a few decades ago, and the famous lyric still works: "If I can make it there, I'll make it anywhere . . . "

Once upon a time, in the near past, celebrated writers, thinkers, actors, singers, dancers, you name it, were born and raised on Egyptian soil. If not, they came there from neighboring countries to find a culturally-sophisticated audience and attempt to launch their careers.

July 10, 2015, the Egyptian actor best-known for his roles in Lawrence of Arabia (1962) and Doctor Zhivago (1965) died of a heart attack, at the age of eighty-three. Born in Alexandria, to Lebanese and Syrian parents, the young "Michel Demitri Shalhoub" (his birth name) was raised a Roman Catholic. He represented another time in Egypt—more cosmopolitan, more tolerant and, thus, more interesting. The roles he played, in Hollywood, reflected his global citizenship: Arab, Russian, Jewish, Italian.

Before making his English-language film debut with *Lawrence of Arabia*, for which he earned a Best Supporting Actor Academy Award nomination and international fame, Sharif was already a star in Egyptian cinema. I did not know him, personally, though family friends did, but I was captivated by his charm (along with countless others) and when he passed away, it felt that one of youth's emblems had fallen.

Strange how the loss of a public figure can affect us, intimately . . . Yes, as Egyptians, we were especially proud of him for capturing the hearts and imaginations of an international audience, being our cultural ambassador. Because actors are so closely associated with their most important roles, I wonder whether we feel the loss of the person or the gallery of characters that he depicted? I guess both. Sharif played so many rich personalities: Lovers, Adventurers, Clowns, Tricksters, Aristocrats . . . (he was, in fact, hailed by many as 'The Noble'). Perhaps, at heart, he was all of them.

Beyond, his debonair air, it's worth mentioning that Sharif cared enough about Egypt/ians to take us to task when our showy, close-minded, violent religiosity overshadowed our deeper humanity. Which is to say, in his art, he did not shy from tackling difficult subjects (as an actor-activist). He used his art as a platform to help us examine ourselves and reminded us of our renowned hospitality and historic tolerance.

Who will replace this Egyptian icon? Some, from my part of the world, blame Hollywood for not allowing room for another Omar Sharif (only big, bad terrorists). But, I don't. I blame us for the current lack of another like him on the silver screen and world stage. Sharif represented a bygone era, when Egyptians were naturally more sophisticated, cosmopolitan, cultured and confident enough not to be threatened by difference or contradictions—our own or others.

Meditating further, I see it as the difference between the ancient, glorious center of learning in Egypt, the Library of Alexandria, and the current one. It was the prevailing culture that made the former great, the library was a natural extension and reflection of that greatness. Similarly, with our artistic/cultural exports. Omar Sharif was a symbol of our former glory, and rich diversity, which I miss, and want back . . .

Once, we rediscover our *inner* Omar Sharifs—with their effortless ease, elegance and wit—then, perhaps, Hollywood's more diverse casting calls will follow suit. Good night, sweet prince, and may our time-honored Egyptian character and culture be resurrected, in the not-too-distant future!

Frankenstein

Society-Spawned Humane Monsters and Monstrous Humans

INITIALLY, MY AVERSION TO supernatural stories kept me from reading Frankenstein—coupled with the cartoonish depiction of the monster as jolly green giant's evil twin, with bolts protruding from his temples, a tabletop for a head and eternally outstretched arms. I was convinced that the novel would be as dull and lifeless as the countless films modeled after it, and that this was one "classic" I need not rush to know.

After reading Frankenstein, however, I was pleasantly surprised to realize that I had been sadly mistaken. Like all great texts in literature, this one is a complex work, capable of lending itself to a multitude of interpretations, yet not limited to any single one of them.

To begin with, there is no use in ignoring the subtitle of the book, i.e. Frankenstein; or, 'The Modern Prometheus', suggesting that Dr. Victor Frankenstein is the modern Prometheus: a Titan in Greek myth who stole fire from Olympus and gave it to humankind in defiance of Zeus, only to be chained to a rock where an eagle tore at his liver, until he was finally released by Hercules. In this instance, Frankenstein, the modern Prometheus 'steals' Knowledge, attempts to play God and his gift to humankind doubles up as his punishment.

Consider the opening epigraph of novel: "Did I request thee, Maker, from my clay / To mould me man? Did I solicit thee / From darkness to promote me?" The quote is from Milton's Paradise Lost, X. 743-4 5, from which Mary Shelley extensively quotes. It expresses an existentialist angst which echoes throughout the entire text. As in Milton's great epic poem, it is unclear in Shelley's novel who the hero is; both Victor Frankenstein and the nameless creature (or monster, to some) are heroes in their own right. On the surface level, Victor is the hero of the story because he is the creator of the creature. For better or worse, however, Victor has done what no other man has done, he has taken a giant, superhuman step and tread in the footsteps of gods—becoming a demigod, himself—and creating another.

In addition to his superior knowledge and achievements, Victor seems an idealized person: clever and compassionate, etc . . . But, it is as facile to say that Frankenstein is the hero as it is obvious. Instead, it might be the so-called monster who must be perceived as the hero (tragic, of course, since there is little else in this story save for tragedy). Gentle, kind, and sensitive to the subtlest beauties of nature, and human nature alike, the creature contents himself with eating berries and wandering the woods. An autodidact, he teaches himself to speak and read by watching a neighboring family do so from the safety of his home, and later by reading 'the classics.'

Such is the extent of his humanity. Yet, for every loving act he commits, he is met with inhuman cruelty. When he is discovered in the home of an otherwise kind family, DeLacey's, he is senselessly beaten with a stick; when he saves a girl from drowning, he is shot at by her father; and at all other times he is reviled by all those he comes in contact with. Nonetheless, the revulsion of all others does not compare to that of his creator, the one who abandoned him (and here's where the existentialist angle comes into play, again). The creature confronts his creator for the first time, reminding him of his duties:

> I ought to be thy Adam; but I am rather the fallen angel, whom thou drivest from joy for no misdeed . . . Believe me, Frankenstein: I was benevolent; my soul glowed with love and humanity: but am I not alone, miserably alone? You, my creator, abhor me; what hope can I gather from fellow creatures, who owe me nothing?

Later, in the course of telling his tale, the *monster* cries out: "Unfeeling, heartless creator! You had endowed me with perceptions and passions, and then cast me abroad an object for the scorn and horror of mankind."

Finally, he ends his soliloquy with this pitiful request: "I am alone, and miserable; man will not associate with me; but one as deformed and horrible as myself would not deny herself to me. My companion must be of the same species, and have the same defects. This being you must create."

Every angst-ridden, doubting teenager can relate to this outburst—questioning the existence of one's Creator on the one hand, and the wrestling with it on the other (while holding on with tenacity to a life they feel there is little if any reason to hold onto). Or as the *monster* puts it, "Life, although it may only be an accumulation of anguish, is dear to me, and I will defend it."

Only in this instance, the creator in question is a sub-God. For this reason, I view the creature/monster as the tragic hero of this tale: alienated and alienating, at once, abandoned by his creator, and with heightened sensitivity to heighten his misery. Yet, as if matters aren't already complicated, they are made even more so by the interrelatedness of the three central characters of Frankenstein, the novel.

The similarities shared amongst the three narrators: Robert Walton, the explorer, Victor Frankenstein, the scientist, and the unnamed monster are too many to be unintentional. Like Frankenstein, Walton wishes to go where no man has been (in his case it is the North Pole, in Frankenstein's it's on Godly Grounds). Both characters speak of the importance of a sense of purpose. "Nothing contributes so much to tranquilize the mind as a steady purpose—a point on which the soul may fix its intellectual eye'" says Walton at the beginning of his voyage. Towards the end of the voyage, Frankenstein echoes this sentiment, in trying to dissuade the men from turning back, saying: "Be steady to your purposes, and firm as a rock."

The similarities between man and monster, can be illustrated to be almost verbatim, their means of expressing their despair virtually identical, even where their thoughts are concerned. In one of many fits of melancholic reflection, Frankenstein thinks to himself:

> Alas! Why does man boast of sensibilities superior to those apparent in the brute; it only renders them more necessary beings. If our impulses were confined to hunger, thirst, and desire, we might be nearly free; but now we are moved by every wind that blows, and a chance word or scene that that word may convey to us.

The monster mirrors the man's angst moments later, lamenting:

> I cannot describe to you the agony that these reflections inflicted upon me; I tried to dispel them, but sorrow only increased with knowledge. Oh, that I had for ever remained in my native wood, nor known or felt beyond the sensations of hunger, thirst, and heat!

More importantly, all three narrators are creatures obsessed with a quest, single-minded to the exclusion of all else, so that when the monster speaks of "a frightful selfishness" which hurried him on during his retaliation, it might as well be Walton speaking of his voyage, or Frankenstein of his creation to which, like the monster's revenge, "(he) was the slave, not the master of an impulse, which (he) detested, yet could not disobey."

So, what does all this mean? In this particular instance, it's a commentary on the misery of reflection and knowledge, versus the comparative comfort of a simple life. Also, interestingly, while the story seems to condemn *hubris* (pride that precedes the fall) along with ambition, Frankenstein does not repent, whereas the monster does. One would think it safe to assume that the moral of the story, is to caution against overweening aspiration, *playing god*.

From the reference to Prometheus on the opening page, almost until the last, the text is littered with such warnings. "Learn from me" says Frankenstein to Walton " . . . how much happier that man is who believes his native town to be the world, than he who aspires to become greater than his nature will allow." Frankenstein seems to advocate a sense of proportion; he seems to repent, so to speak, against his ungodly creation.

Yet, despite his ruin and supposed realization, Frankenstein does not seem to have learned the very lesson he proposes to teach. No more is this contradiction more apparent than in his last dying words. After he has, passionately, spoken to ship men to pursue their voyage, no matter the odds, he reflects one last time on his actions. "During these last days I have been occupied in examining my past conduct; nor do I find it blamable" he says. "Farewell, Walton! Seek happiness in tranquility, and avoid ambition" he continues, inexplicably.

Can Frankenstein have forgotten the despair and destruction his 'blameless' conduct has caused to those dearest to him, and himself? Is he in a state of delirium as he says those words? Or has he always been in a state of delirium? In stark contrast, whatever the case against the *monster* and his crimes, it crumbles in comparison when one learns that he regretted his actions and lived a life of self-loathing for their sake. Unlike his creator the creature, at least, offers the reader the satisfaction of his dissatisfaction, remorse.

Not that he will forgive himself, even if we chose to forgive his horrendous actions. Nonetheless, the *monster*'s actions can be understood sooner than those of Frankenstein—if one views them as reactions to culture, or culture-created. After all, Frankenstein created the creature, abandonment and cruelty created the real monster. For abandonment, his creator is responsible, but for cruelty culture, too, is accountable: Romantic Culture.

Just as the contemporary ideas of atheism can be seen to inform the creation of the creature, the collapse of the social contract and/or the corrupting nature of society can be considered responsible for the transformation of creature to monster and his subsequent moral deterioration. What is it about early nineteenth century culture that calls for such intolerance towards the society-spawned monster, and how can Frankenstein be seen as "a contribution to the effective dominant culture" as Williams says in his essay: *Base and Superstructure?*

One concrete example of seeing the monster in terms of a cultural studies analysis would be to say that the monster represents the horrors of a dawning/emergent culture where, for example, formative research in electricity is in practice. (After all, it was electricity that brought the monster to life). But, perhaps this analysis is too concrete—in my eyes, at least—which is why I'd rather view the making of the monster in terms of two key concepts: Aesthetics and Literature, or looks and books.

From the moment of his conception, it is sadly the case that the creature is deserted by his creator solely on account of his appearance, "the horror of that countenance." Subsequently, each and every person who encounters the creature who, initially, is blissfully unaware of his own outward appearance judges him, accordingly.

It is very telling, and a scathing commentary on the superficiality of society, that the only civilized audience the creature is granted is with one who does not have the prejudice of vision to discriminate, nor the brutality of youth to intimidate: Delacey, an old blind man. Never does anyone 'pardon his outward form', as he says, and love the unfortunate creature for his good soul and high thoughts. Instead, he is always seen as hideous, abhorred, ghastly, loathsome, distorted, wretched. The list of negative adjectives is long, and they appear almost as often as the incessant appraisals of nature, in sharp contrast—a view which even the monster subscribes to.

Yet another view to which the monster subscribes to is the importance of books, or high culture. In that sense, the oppressiveness of literature, is the monster which Frankenstein's monster mirrors at a society that cannot stand to see its own reflection. That books define each of the narrators cannot be denied. For, just as the fantastic scientific readings of Frankenstein are fatal, so are the 'classics' to his creature (particularly Paradise Lost, to which he confesses: "excited different and far deeper emotions" than his other readings). Ultimately, it is telling that both man and beast end up comparing themselves to Satan: "All my speculations and hopes are as nothing; like the archangel who aspired to omnipotence, I am chained in an eternal hell."

Can an Editor Get Too "Creative"?

A Writer's Quandary

IT'S A TOUGH (SOMETIMES, thankless) task being an editor. You're meant to make the writer look good, while not drawing too much attention to yourself—rescuing the fire from the smoke sort of thing. Good editors know what a writer is trying to say and how they wish to achieve it; they do their magic, backstage, allowing the writer to bask in the spotlight. Fine, humble writers, in turn, know to give credit to their editors and fully realize that the task of selection and omission is in itself an art.

But, sometimes, an editor (misreading the intentions of a writer, or asserting their own) might overstep their boundaries and trample on a writer's fragile ego. *How dare they presume to take such liberties with my work?* the scandalized writer gasps, incandescent with righteous indignation. A milder version of this occurred to me as a result of a rather unusual experience.

Upon the request of an editor to submit work, I sent in a batch of new aphorisms. This was the response I received: "I really like what you are up to and where your spirit goes. What you sent won't really work for me on its own. To that end, I've taken the liberty of selecting particular lines to make a more condensed piece."

Over the years, I've grown accustomed to rejections, due to differing tastes, etc . . . but, this was a first. Said intrepid editor had, actually, selected some stand-alone aphorisms of mine and woven them into a 'poem'! I did not wish to rush to judgment, but admit to feeling conflicted about the results of our uninvited collaboration.

The words, below, are mine—minus the connective tissue, such as: *for*, *that* or *and*. But the sequence, the line breaks, the "poetry" . . . I don't know that I can call my own. On one level, I'm flattered (strangely moved, even) that an editor would take the time and care to engage in this manner. But, writing is such an *intimate* matter, and rearranging the words of another is akin to shuffling their thoughts and emotions. The aphorisms I submitted were conceived as independent meditations and, even though some naturally cluster together and share common concerns, this editor's presentation somehow felt alien to my spirit. In the end, I had to trust my instincts and declined publication.

We are the guardians of our dreams
We're here to pass around the ball of light, while trying
to keep our fingerprints off it. We are here
to remind
each other that we do not choose our work,
we merely consent to it.

Heaven save us from tragic seriousness; teach us
to play, divinely, for no matter how
we dream or scheme,
being born is always a surprise.

Poor rational mind, it would sooner accept a believable lie
than an incredible truth. Certain silences
are more damning than words; they are actions.

As with any wild animal, it's unwise
to turn our back to life. Those who speak ill of life
only smear their own names.

Said a poem to a poet: can I trust you? Is your heart pure
to carry me; are your hands clean to pass me on?
For a poem arrives like a hand in the dark
and carries the native tongue of hysterics—adolescents and mystics,
alike.

We steal from ourselves when we share an idea,
or a feeling—before it has ripened.
When in doubt, meditate upon your wound.

Art is the love we make by ourselves,
says the ego. Art is the love we make with an invisible other,
replies the spirit.

Strange, how our weaknesses can be strengths
in disguise, and vice versa.
Treat life as seriously as you would a dress rehearsal.

For each time we betray our conscience, we strangle an angel.
And, yet,
it's not certain we are allotted an infinite supply
of winged pardons.

As a Man Loves a Woman

IN EARLY 2014, I found a bird egg in a flower pot on my balcony and, shortly after, went bird mad: raising generations of wild pigeons and bonding with their young. One incident, in particular, revealed to me how dearly I loved these winged beings that I was borrowing from the sky . . .

I awoke one morning to see, out of the corner of my eye, a falcon swoop down into our tenth-floor balcony to carry mama pigeon away from the eggs which she was sitting on. This happened in an instant; the sky seemed to darken, momentarily, and the predator was off with his fast food.

Outside, everywhere, were signs of a pitiable struggle: scattered feathers and two unattended eggs, a day or so shy of hatching. Instinctively, I brought the unhatched eggs in, not quite sure how to keep them warm. Only moments later, a terribly beautiful (young) falcon returned, presumably, hunting for those precious eggs, all piercing golden eyes and fierce talons on display.

The falcon and I stared one another down for a short eternity, with a mix of hostility and respect, only a thin screen between us—until the predator, perched on the balcony railing, leaned into the sky and, gracefully, soared away. In that instant, I realized how protective I was of my feathered friends, which I'd gotten to know over the past month or two, and felt responsible for (as well as guilty that I'd let them down).

I've heard it said pigeons don't mourn, that it's all about instinct—if they lose a mate or an egg, they'll just go find/make another. Or that wild birds don't bond, it's all about food. Well, the remaining member of my feral pigeon family (poppa) was listless after this incident, mourning all morning, slow moving and out of it, over the loss of his mate.

I knew, for sure, something was wrong when poppa turned down his favorite snack (unsalted, raw peanuts) and simply sat on the balcony floor, at the opposite end of his abandoned nest. He just sat there staring ahead and, occasionally, stood up, facing me and cooed . . .

It was devastating and I didn't know what to do. I tried putting the eggs on a hot water bottle, but they were deserted all night. Poppa pigeon seemed spooked by the site of the crime (flower pot/nest) and hurried away from there.

Tentatively, he ate a bit when he saw me eating and, eventually, he found the energy to perch on the balcony railing, so he could better scan the sky. Meantime, I whispered assurances to him like a madman: 'That's it,' I said, to say something of use. 'Keep looking out and about. You'll find a new mate and have more eggs.'

Then, miracle of miracles, momma returns, having survived the vicious falcon attack! And, I realized, in the striking words of inventor Nikola Tesla: "I loved that *pigeon* as a man loves a *woman.*" Below, an ode of mine:

What the Sunset Said

Something happened as the light was dying
it wasn't just post-coital exhalation
where the once-possessed body is used up
and all that remains is bodiless trance

Rather, it seemed they were mirroring
a preternatural stillness,
two spiritual sentinels
transfixed and somehow *Other*

Science calls it "twilight calibrated magnetic compass"
yet it appeared beyond mere direction-finding
more a kind of existential orientation
consolidating all they knew, and listening

with their entire being, participating
silently, in a universal hymn
until they were pulled, as out of a viscous substance,
by the hungry cry of their nearby young

to become two feral pigeons, again
with this-world considerations
parenting, foraging, keeping alive
and, dazed, they consented to their stations.

Conversations & Fictions

Questions & Aphorisms

Idries Shah Foundation

1. *What do you hope people take away from your work?*

Broadly speaking, thanksgiving and awakening. I hope that my body of work—essays, poems, aphorisms and conversations—encourages readers to question received wisdom, moving past the false idols of popular culture and beginning the difficult work of heart purification.

2. *You have chosen to write aphorisms. Is that connected to a Sufi-informed view of the world?*

'The best words are those that are few and to the point,' Rumi says in his discourses, *Fihi Ma Fihi* (It Is What It Is). In that sense, aphorisms are connected to wisdom literature, in general and, yes, Sufism in particular. Ibn Ata Illah, an important Sufi saint and sage of 13th century Egypt, bequeathed us his treasured *Kitab al Hikam* (Book of Wisdom) composed of aphoristic writing.

   I do not feel I have so much chosen to write aphorisms, but rather that I have been chosen to communicate in this form, one I've been drawn to since I was a teenager.

3. *What are your poetic influences?*

As a young man, I began with literature that was at the intersection of spirituality, such as: Gibran and Eliot. This, eventually, lead to the prayerful work of Rilke, which I still revisit for its great longing and numinous quality. Lately, I try to occupy myself with Sufi voices, primarily.

4. *Can you explain a little how the aphorisms form, or come to you? Do they need much editing?*

I define aphorisms as 'what is worth quoting from the soul's dialogue with itself'. Which is to say that, out of the ongoing conversation I have with myself, occasionally, I'll overhear a line that I think is good enough to stand alone and represent the subject I've been musing on.

These aphorisms might begin as talking back to an author, in the book margins, or be triggered by an observation or incident in my daily life. More mysteriously, they might arise unbidden as a kind of summation of a matter I've been preoccupied with for years.

As with poetry, the better the aphorisms, the less of a need to edit them. Also, like poetry, I cannot compose an aphorism on command and, if I find myself struggling too much with phrasing, I sense they are not ready, yet.

My hope in sharing these aphorisms is that the reader, too, might somehow partake in these states of revelation.

5. *What is the importance of Idries Shah's work in the world today?*

Past the great mystic poets of Persia (Sanai, Attar, Hafiz) Idries Shah was my first proper introduction to the foundation of Sufism—not merely as an art form, but as an art of living. From there, I graduated to Al-Hujwiri's remarkable *Kashf al-Mahjub* (The Revelation of the Veiled), one of the earliest Persian treatises on Sufism. What Shah, Hujwiri and other Sufi guides do is to offer us glimpses into secrets available to all who peer behind reality's persistent illusions—partly accounts of the lives of saints, partly practical guide books to self-transformation.

At a time of unfortunate and widespread Islamophobia, it is important to have teachers like Shah who invite us to consider the beauty and peace that can be found in Islam and its mystical branch, Sufism.

A selection from Lababidi's hundreds of aphorisms:

> There's freedom is not needing to have an opinion on everything.

> We are captive to what we create.

> The divided self is spiritually immature. Divine union begins with self unity.

> All the unmet promises that we make, to ourselves and others, will return to taunt us.

> A cluttered mind makes for a poor mirror.

> Poor rational mind, it would sooner accept a believable lie than an incredible truth.

> The contemplative life is not a passive one.

As with any wild animal, it's unwise to turn our back to life.

Does the contemporary prevalence of 'life coaches' mean Life can no longer be relied upon to do her job?

Our eagerness to arrive at our destination—and impatience with ourselves and life along the way—echoes childhood's mantra: Are we there yet?

Educated is schooled in the ways of the heart; literate is versed in the alphabet of emotions.

Be wary of persons reluctant to assume blame, but eager to accept credit.

The more closely we listen to ourselves, the more likely we are to over-hear others.

See the sun, how it shifts the light of its attention, gradually, from one thing to the next. Be like it—don't fixate.

In life's exams, it's no use straining to copy the answers of another, since we are assigned different questions.

Mysticism and occultism might appear similar; the difference is that the latter does not ask whence the Vision is issued from.

Airplane wisdom: 'Make sure your oxygen mask is well-adjusted, before helping others.'

Part of forgiving is, eventually, forgetting.

Unchecked insecurities become vices.

Patience is not just waiting; it's also doing while we wait.

The only real borders are those of our compassion.

There are many ways to touch the depths; lightheartedness is one of the most profound.

Unstuck . . .

with Brian Chappell

YAHIA LABABIDI REMEMBERS LATE nights in his dorm room at George Washington University, tossing in bed as the voices of Wilde, Rilke and Kafka reverberated around him. Words or phrases, even the tiniest snippets of philosophy, would teem, pulse and swirl to a boiling point, until he could no longer resist formulating his own response, entering the conversation. "They were literally bouncing off the walls," he told me, "I would go to bed with a stack of napkins or receipts, and I would never put my glasses on because if I put my glasses on it would scare the thought away. The fox would not leave its hole if the hunter was outside."

But he persisted, and his haphazard notes, over time, became numerous and provocative enough that multiple professors and mentors encouraged him to compile and try to publish them. The result was Signposts to Elsewhere (first published in 2008) containing his meditations, in the form of a long list of aphorisms, on what he sees as the central human questions: "We've always been wrestling with the same things . . . It's still a human being, in a body, trying to deal with other human beings, in a society. It hasn't changed that much . . . I'm more interested in those who can distill the matter to its essence." Just such a project begins in *Signposts*, where Lababidi liberates the essence of these ideas from the shackles of cliché, which, he believes, are truths that have "lost the initial shock of revelation." The aphorism is "not just an aesthetic thing, but an edifying thing. They are truths that we stumble across and, hopefully, try to live up to some of the time." Not greeting card rhetoric, but, actually, "we think in aphorisms. If we quote the outcome of our thoughts, they are aphorisms." Consider the following, from *Signposts*:

> The thoughts we choose to act upon define us to others, the ones we do not, define us to ourselves.

Opposites attract. Similarities last.

Time heals old wounds because there are new wounds to attend to.

With enigmatic clarity, Life gives us a different answer each time we ask her the same question.

The primary challenge for creators is surviving themselves.

A good listener is one who helps us overhear ourselves.

Previous iterations of these ideas have probably occurred to us, but the delicacy of Lababidi's aphorisms resides in the fact that, as James Richardson asserts in his foreword to the book:

> Unlike the poet, [the aphorist] doesn't worry whether we've heard his exact words millions of times. Nor does he have the Philosopher's care for consistency. He doesn't mind that today he warns 'Time is money' and tomorrow contradicts that with 'Stop and smell the roses.' He has neither the ambition nor the naïveté of the systematizer, and his truth, though stated generally, is applied locally. When he says 'Like father like son,' he doesn't expect anyone to object, 'Wait, I know a son who's not like his father.' He means that right here, right now, a particular son has behaved just as his father might have.

This dialogic interplay between the universal and the local provide the aphorism its applicability (and popularity). It has a special quality of speaking to the particulars of life while remaining unstuck from time and space.

After Signposts to Elsewhere, Lababidi turned to poetry, for which he is now more widely known. He has published in *World Literature Today, Cimarron Review, Agni, Hotel Amerika* and many others. Two poems are, currently, up for a Pushcart Prize. Recently, however, Lababidi has returned to the figures who originally inspired him. Evoking Azar Nafisi, he asserts, "It was these 'dead white men' that really did a number on me. It wasn't a matter of influence, but of initiation. They are closer to me than my own blood." Lovers of literature have had similar moments. Mine was weeping over the end of The Brothers Karamazov, under a dim desk lamp, with my college roommate sleeping nearby. As budding thinkers, we want to let our copious thoughts, despite whoever else may have already had them and articulated them much better, out into the open. In short, to write. Lababidi remembers how his notes in the margin became journal entries, which became essays, which, we now see, became a book.

Trial by Ink: From Nietzsche to Bellydancing (2010) is the type of book critics want to write. It is an intellectual memoir, a sharing of one's own personal engagement with those who have had a dramatic impact. In the spirit of Susan Sontag (who receives an entire chapter), Lababidi replaces systematizing and arguing with a Montaignian approach (whose idea of the *essai* opens the Preface and serves as inspiration for the title of the book) of figuring things out as we go along. "I'm always in a state of discovery and beginning," he told me, "what I think I know, I'm trying to communicate. You have to get out of your system whatever is yours, whatever speaks to you." This, for him, is a refreshing departure from the work of academics, who too often "go to the same well to drink, excluding the regular people who perhaps may be more curious. If you give it to me in a way that is forbidding, I'm not interested."

Trial by Ink, therefore, strives for the opposite. He stresses as much in the Preface:

> This . . . is a subjective work where I attempt to evaluate what I care for and, generally, test my responsiveness to literature and culture. In the course of such investigations particular judgments emerge, expressions of taste and values. They are my *trials*, where I am simultaneously scratching my head and pen across the page, to determine what I think about a given subject . . . In turn, what you have before you is a catalogue of interests, possessions, exorcisms and even passing enthusiasms, derived from what I was thinking, reading, watching, dreaming, and living over a seven-year period.

I envy the intellectual freedom, which Lababidi takes up here, to, say, write about Dostoevsky, without the requisite knowledge of Russian language or history, simply because I love him so much. Lababidi has such a relationship with Nietzsche, Wilde, Rilke, Baudelaire, Kafka and many others. He reminded me, though, that to do this, one must always come from a place of relative authority. "Not to dismiss blogs," he says, "but they are not essays." They don't partake of the type of "deep and continuous mining" and "literary soul-gazing" that are the rudiments of a trial, of an essay.

I agree with this. The first of three parts of *Trial by Ink*, titled "Literary Profiles and Reviews," exhibits his mastery of and, frankly, unique and refreshing insights into his masters. He works most provocatively when he puts figures, who, on the surface, don't seem to have much to do with each other, into an intricate dialogue with each other. Just this occurs with Nietzsche and Wilde. Chapter 3, "The Great Contrarians," is a lengthy comparison of the two, on the levels of style, their affinity for and belief in the

importance of appearances, and their threshold for pain and suffering, espe-
cially since they each met with similar types of struggles, including certain
levels of moral degradation, which have had occasionally negative effects on
their legacies. One need only, as Lababidi does, compare the content of their
aphorisms (they were both virtuosos of the form) to begin suddenly to see
uncanny similarities:

> What fire does not destroy it hardens.—Wilde
> What does not kill me makes me stronger.—Nietzsche
>
> The simple truth, is that not a double lie?—Nietzsche
> The truth is rarely ever pure and never simple.—Wilde
>
> Public opinion exists only where there are no ideas.—Wilde
> To say it again, public opinions, private laziness.—Nietzsche
>
> We possess art lest we perish of the truth.—Nietzsche
> The telling of beautiful untrue things is the proper aim of art.—Wilde
>
> Conscience and cowardice are really the same things.—Wilde
> Not to perpetrate cowardice against one's own acts . . .
> The bite of conscience is indecent.—Nietzsche
>
> Discontent is the first step in the progress of a man or nation.—Wilde
> Every great progress must be preceded by a partial weakening.
> —Nietzsche

This type of analysis occurs across the first part of the book. Whereas
it might not be critically expedient to place Nietzsche, Wilde, and Susan
Sontag into a dialogue, this is nonetheless how they speak to Lababidi. And
that's all he's worried about. Consequently, "I was told not to write this book,
in the sense that it was 'unpublishable.' Who *didn't* tell me that? Academic
publishers thought it was too literary. Literary publishers thought it was too
academic. I was stuck." Perhaps. But, ultimately, Lababidi's book occupies a
space of dialogic freedom in which the personal and the critical mesh with
refreshing enjoyment.

The cultural dialogue continues in the second and third parts ("Studies
in Pop Culture" and "Middle Eastern Musings," respectively). While Part
II contains interesting ruminations on Michael Jackson, Leonard Cohen,
Morrissey, serial killers, and the values of silence, Part III was particularly
illuminating. Here, Lababidi returns to his Muslim heritage in Egypt and
Lebanon (where he spent a good amount of time growing up). His discus-
sion juxtaposes the repugnant effects of draconian sexual repression in

Egypt (especially, contrasted with ritual belly dancing) with the Lebanese's zest for life in the face of seemingly constant and imminent death, in a way that can enlighten a Western reader to the diversity of the "Muslim World," a term Dr. Nafisi derided at the Aspen Institute's Cultural Diplomacy Forum, for obvious reasons.

Lababidi was at the forum as well, and was intrigued by Nafisi. When I reached out to him to discuss *Trial by Ink*, he responded with the type of enthusiasm Nafisi showed me. "Conversation is very close to me," he asserts, not just the type of conversations he has with the likes of Nietzsche, "who is *very much* alive," but with contemporaries and collaborators. He was generous enough to meet with me about his work, and about this type of work in general. At the end of our discussion, I asked him what was next for him. In addition to more poetry, he says, "I am returning to these conversations in a much more direct way." Namely, he is continuing his conversation about his conversations with Nietzsche, Wilde, Rilke, Baudelaire, Kafka, and others in a strictly dialogic way. Chapter 2 of *Trial by Ink* consists of a back-and-forth with poet and critic Alex Stein about these figures. Like the college-aged Lababidi who refused to put on his glasses so as not to scare away his thoughts, "I will call Alex in the middle of the night, without turning the lights on, and just speak." The result is a series of conversations (I hesitate to call them interviews) between the two that digs deeper, that "mines" for answers.

From my time with Yahia and by reading the early stages of these new dialogues, it is apparent that face-to-face conversation, where one can engage another on more dynamic and intimate levels, suits the type of broader cultural and intellectual dialogue he has spent his career trying to foster. He doesn't mind living like an aphorism, unstuck from time, space and generic classifications, asserting:

> I don't think of myself as an aphorist. I don't think of myself as a poet. I don't think of myself as an essayist, which leaves me with nothing to say, so to speak . . . but I'm clarifying something that I suspect I see. I don't get why from 18 to 22 I chose aphorisms, or aphorisms chose me. It seemed like the most instinctive way to talk, to communicate . . . at some point it shifts to poems . . . words have a life of their own . . . ideas have a life of their own. They decide how to dress themselves . . . the form doesn't matter as much as trying to communicate a territory that on some days I have been privileged to have been shoe-horned into.

This openness has organically led him to the dialogic form as the best (only?) way to convey what he sees as the real essence of all these thinkers:

and this is where I wish that the lights would dim and I could whisper it into your ear so no one can hear. This is about the artist as mystic. If you think it's mad, it's mad. If you think it makes sense to you on a personal level, then it does . . . If it works as literary soul-gazing, take it. If it works as pure fiction, then it does.

The ambition, and the already apparent spiritual depth of this new trial, is titillating, the type of book I want to write. But what happens when the conversation is finished? "Ten years of silence, under a rock somewhere."

Artistry Bordering on Meditation

Discussing The Artist As Mystic with Brian Chappell

THE SETTING, YAHIA REMINDS me more than once, is a little absurd. We meet at McGinty's Irish Pub in Silver Spring, situated in a bustling commercial environment, across from a cineplex and multi-storied shoe store. This wood-paneled simulacrum of authenticity, shutting out as much sunlight as it could, served as our original meeting place, a year and a half ago, to discuss Yahia's book, Trial By Ink. We had sipped beers and discussed his intellectual and spiritual awakenings, my recording device picking up the ambient noise of soccer, classic rock, and the increasing din of patrons. Today, the environment is a little sunnier, and much warmer, but still not exactly conducive to discussing mysticism.

The pub, and Silver Spring itself, very much constitute what Yahia, in The Artist As Mystic, a new book of conversations with fellow aphorist Alex Stein, calls the "here-world": "Silver Spring," he assures me in a way that only subtly hints of irony, "has restaurants, bookstores, cinema, and the general feeling that something is happening. What else can you ask for?" But the artist's often troublesome relationship to the "here-world," the humdrum of taking out the trash, answering the phone, and trying to live each day as a citizen, husband, etc., is a subtext of this book. Its subtitle is "Conversations with Yahia Lababidi," but Yahia calls them a series of "lyric interviews . . . controlled hallucinations," in which he "eavesdrops on [his] dreams," then speaks them out loud to Alex. Alex, through his "creative listening," provides the "music" of their arrangement, turning them into a viable, readable book. Their ruminations address the general topic of art and mysticism, or, the extent to which artists are able to navigate the "here-world" of lived life and the "there-world" of their own dreams.

To speak of this problem Yahia allows himself to be "spoken by" major figures whom he consistently refers to as "these guys": Kafka, Baudelaire, Nietzsche, Rilke, and Kierkegaard (among other minor characters such as Bataille, Eliot, and Ekelund). Just how "Any biographer is one who is clever at confessing through the mask of another . . . They can very discreetly tuck themselves in . . . They're lending it their own breath, their everything," Yahia uses these figures as masks through which he can dramatize his own inner conflicts. But this is the point—he reminds Alex in the introduction that "mortui vivos docent," the dead shall teach the living, that we are always in conversation, and therefore a conversation, he tells me, was the

> optimal form for expressing ideas that are too slippery for other forms . . . We were letting these ideas have play. You are a midwife. You show up with a body, because ghosts need a body to communicate, then as soon as you can get them to hold hands, you can say 'please never mind me.

But, he reminds me, "I don't want to make the artist sound too precious because they are just a metaphor for everybody . . . the artist draws from the same well; he only makes a bigger show of the pulling, prodding, and partaking of its contents." Artists self-consciously display the things that we all inherently struggle with; "[these thinkers] are talking to one another, and we're talking through them."

The conversations with Alex are Yahia's way of demonstrating that "between any two artists there are more similarities than differences," and that the closer you look, the more their affinities arise. Their affinities, Yahia and Alex argue, reside not in the life of the mind. "I was exasperated with the mind aspect," Yahia asserts, "I've arrived at the very edge of my mind and it's thin and flat and I'm not interested in it anymore." For too long "these guys" have been examined and critiqued like specimens, the spiritual urgency of their visions suffocated beneath the trappings of the academic; "we are rescuing dear friends from a stuffy academic party and saying 'come out to play!'" The Artist as Mystic uncovers just how each of these figures "comes out" to touch a level of being beyond the "here-world."

These artists recognized that their existences were "exalted," which means, Yahia affirms in the book's introductory discourse, that they were

> called to service . . . The life of the artist may not be apparently monastic, or holy, but there is the same sense of sacrifice, vocation, of having been entrusted with something greater and dearer than one's own happiness. Imagine! To hold something more dear than one's own happiness. That cannot be a voluntary thing.

Indeed, for some like Baudelaire, it may lead you to become a "neur-asthenic idler," wallowing in the paralysis this condition may bring. It is a lonely condition, which consists, Yahia asserts, quoting Heidegger, of "long-ing [which] is the agony of the nearness of the distant." "That got me," he says, "It seemed that it was right there. It! I could almost brush it with my fingertips. But it wasn't right there." For those who can break free of "neur-asthenia" one concept rings true:

> I kept coming back to the idea of attention. Attention is the art-ist's mode of prayer . . . I think of those times when I fly in my dreams. I think there must be some connection between how I fly in my dreams and this state I sometimes come to in writ-ing when I feel that I am aloft, ecstatic. The thing I want to say: In my dreams, it is blinking that brings me back to the ground . . . When I have fallen, I don't know how to get back into that state. But if there is a formula, I think it must have to do with attention.

In this sense, artistry borders on meditation requires the focused channeling of the whole being. One can see how this might lead an artist to become a bit of a misfit, or even a frail neurasthenic, or worse. So, I ask him, how do you negotiate these two modes of existence? "With extreme difficulty," he says, "I have gross tendencies toward imbalance . . . But you used this great unstuck simile last time. You said I am unstuck from space and time, like an aphorism, scurrying to find some balance, always." As for these guys, and the new book about them, Yahia and Alex agreed that "the balance of light has to outweigh the darkness." Yahia admits that he has his moments where he is "marinated in irreality" and he's able to work with precise uninterrupted attention. But for the most part, he says, especially as we get older, it's harder to find those moments of sustained purity. They are replaced by what he calls "interstices," which resemble dream states, which more or less occur accidentally, appearing like Alice's rabbit hole. But, ultimately, the goal is "to turn an accident into a summer home, where you return with some sort of intentionality and regularity if you're lucky." Spending time with Yahia and, to use his words, "breathing in" his energy, I can see how important the quest for interstices is to him. He elaborates:

> At the risk of sounding completely like a mad person, it's like a dream state, whether it's a daydream or an actual dream. It's a noncommittal state; you're abstracted enough in the world of ideas. It's a diffusion of vision, not an everyday life. You abstract, you see everything around it and beyond it. Solitude helps, silence helps, reading helps, to sort of rev up. Another person

helps, to sort of nudge you there. To be really fair, it's always grasped at, it's not like you show up and say 'It's me, again!' [knocking, now, on the table]. . .The cage seeks the bird. The violin seeks the wood. I'd be flat out lying if I said I'd found a way to go back. If anything I'm trying to find a way not to be denied going back. I know the things I need to do to not be denied from going back. Work is one way of doing it. You do what you need to do throughout the day and you don't expect it.

His candor about spiritual things is refreshing, but most of its resonances in the book are filtered through "these guys." To be with Yahia in conversation is to encounter the full range of his feelings on the subject. I begin to see how the book took shape, over the year plus of dialogue with Stein.

Alex used a phrase to describe the core of these spiritual movements. He calls it a "rage for transformation," which he perceives in each of the figures discussed in the book, centering, for example, on Rilke's *Archaic Torso of Apollo*, with its monumental final line, "You must change your life." "You could have said 'Boo!' and I would not have been more surprised," Yahia confesses. But it's this desire for transformation that drives these artists beyond the "here-world" and into, yes, mysticism. Yahia tells me:

Transformation—yes brother—yeah [clasping his hands together], that's what it's all about. But again that's where the writer is a metaphor for everyone. This is not some academic, esoteric, rarefied project. This is something where everyone is going about it in their own ways, maybe without declaring it as such, but it *is* about transformation. All of these guys, if they have anything in common, that's the ultimate thing. But it doesn't belong to philosophy as it does to mysticism. And that's where we're comfortable talking about the mystic enterprise vs. the spiritual one. Because the mystic is the one who's denounced as heretic, because he's gone too far. There's no measuring stick; maybe they're the ones who have to go too far to make someone else realize what is the way. They have to declare themselves divine and then go mad and then backtrack a little bit and realize that that's an imbalance. All of these guys somehow suspect that they are imbalanced. That's the difference between the balanced spiritual life or the philosophical life that is very rational . . . and the mystic, who is reckless and very keen to arrive at once and risk everything, not caring one bit what's at stake. And these guys interest me now [for] this recklessness, because they didn't hold anything back, and they didn't calculate, or care very much, for what they might lose. Everything might just be enough—it might not be enough—but it might just be enough. When you don't give everything, that space in between might be depression, madness. You're gambling with that.

It is a constant quest without arrival, a pushing to the edges of parameters, "using the mind to overthrow the mind. Using words to overthrow words." "It's a continual clearing of the way," he muses, "You're always mid-leap. That's why you're always aching. That's because you can never relax into a normal sitting position."

Toward the end of our conversation, it became more apparent that Yahia prefers balance to the dangers of approaching the mystical. I asked him, expecting him to reply with one of "these guys" or another like them, if he could only read one person forever, who would it be? Without hesitation, he says:

> At this stage, I'm less interested in these guys than I've ever been. It was very difficult for me to return to them . . . The Book of Tao—it's impersonal enough that I'm not wrestling with one person, especially when I have to return to [these thinkers], but I'm very aware of the all-too-human dimension behind it all. I knew that they shat, or slept, or ate, or betrayed their effervescent persona. They were creatures of their own time and they weren't always aligned to their own version of themselves. Because of that and because of their psychosexual specificity, I'm done with that, because I've got my own psychosexual specificity to deal with. I'm also getting older . . . meaning it's unbecoming for me to be under the sway of anyone. It's not as necessary or valid for me. Something like the Tao is a freer space and something that I don't want to be reading on a daily basis, but every time I return to it—I really think I'd give up all these guys for this one book.

His preference for the Tao seems to indicate a new turn in Yahia's spiritual quest. Replacing the mad searching with a balanced rendering of the scale between "here-world" and "there-world." But will he miss these guys? Ultimately, he finally says, "Writing is a way of looking away from something, so you can look on to something else. It's a way of saying that they are alive and they are relevant. They are worth picking up. But it's also a way of saying a grateful goodbye."

The Artist As Mystic emphasizes this gratitude. It captures the earnestness and urgency of Yahia's discourse, which is really only fully encountered in conversations like these. Since our first encounter, he and I have become friends, and he never ceases to exude a refreshing spiritual energy. He's worth reading for that alone. But this is a viable critical/biographical work of any of these figures—Kafka, Baudelaire, Nietzsche, Rilke, Kierkegaard—for the very reason Stein and Yahia claim. That is, while Yahia breathes knowledge of the life and works of these men, the main aim of the project is one of recovery. It's not a "study" of them as much as a grateful encomium, an example of how spiritually-enriching criticism and biography can be written. Therefore the book is ultimately a way for Yahia to be "spoken by" these guys, to offer his own take on art and mysticism through his formidable interlocutors. I am grateful to be spoken by him, even if for a brief interstice.

"If It Weren't For My Wound..."
with Rob Vollmar

The great whale hunt of the spirit life is also pursued in dreams.

-YAHIA LABABIDI

LABABIDI'S ABILITY TO TRAVERSE cultures, disciplines, and even time itself has garnered him considerable attention and praise. His published works include a collection of aphorisms, Signposts to Elsewhere (Jane Street Press, 2008), a book of essays on a startling array of topics, including literature, popular culture, and the Arab experience, Trial by Ink (Common Ground Publishing, 2010); a book of poems, Fever Dreams (Crisis Chronicles Press, 2011); and, most recently, The Artist as Mystic (One Such Press, 2012), a collaborative conversation with fellow aphorist and writer, Alex Stein.

Rob Vollmar: You grew up in Egypt, and your family is of Lebanese descent. How long have your parents lived in Egypt?

Yahia Lababidi: My father is Lebanese, and my mother is Egyptian. They were based in Lebanon and left around the time I was born. I was born in Egypt. They left because of the civil war. Their house was taken over, and my dad still speaks of how the family photo albums were defaced. Recently we went on a visit. We went by to see this idealized, fantastic place that I grew up with. It was conveyed to me by my father and the stories that he would tell me about how it was the Switzerland of the Arab world. You could go skiing and then drive down and be at the beach. I don't know Lebanon. I only visited it as an adult when I was working with the United Nations, in Egypt. I was sent there on a trip, and that was my first proper understanding of it as an adult. I remember thinking, "Good God, it's so physically beautiful" in comparison to Egypt, which has an austere beauty with the desert. I liked the more relaxed morality of Lebanese culture. The piece I wrote in Trial by Ink ["Dancing on the Graves"] was my love letter to that experience as I was able to acknowledge that side of my background.

RV: I thought the premise of The Artist as Mystic was provocative because it draws a bond between two ideas that both resist easy definition. We're left at the beginning with something of a cypher, like "X=Y," but with only a hazy sense of what data we might use to solve that equation.

YL: That's exactly how the project began. Alex was kind enough . . . and you must remind me to talk about him more as we go along because I wouldn't have been able to do this book without him. He gave me the permission, unlocked something, that allowed this to come out because I was thinking about these things in a way that was too intimate, too shy to venture out– especially a concept like mysticism. I mean, good God, I come from a culture where I was forced to resist this type of thing because it was so loud and clumsy. I thought, "No, this is something private. You keep it to yourself." So when I found that I was having my own thing to say about it, I couldn't imagine saying it in a public way. As a result of this project or experiment that he and I had, it seemed safe to come out.

RV: We normally draw a circle around mysticism as something belonging to spirituality, more broadly, but to religion, more specifically. The majority of the writers that you are taking a look at in these conversations are people who have almost aggressively rejected that but still maintain—and you talk about this with Nietzsche and Kierkegaard—a religious timbre to what they are writing.

YL: Yes! They are denouncing, overthrowing. People who are not so familiar with these writers and who are strictly religious find this to be the height of arrogance that I dare to present these particular guys as mystics.

I think, if I'm allowed to say this, that mystics are rebels. They are certainly the rebels of the religious community. That's why they have been denounced as heretics. Whether they are coming from a philosophic tradition or a mystic tradition, they are going further than orthodoxy permits.

They are saying things like "I am God," but they are not saying it in an irreligious way. They just don't want any intermediary. They don't want any dogma. They don't want any middleman. They are lusting for that contact and the immediacy. The meshing. The union. Nothing less will do. They brandish the faith of the heretic. These are people who found that everything around fell short of their exacting standards.

RV: Every religion has its mystic strain. I think of it, then, that a religious system has space in it for people who want to intersect with its ideas on a number of different levels. Some people may just need it to order their daily lives and give them meaning. It's almost like the way we use the internet. Some people want to use it to keep track of what their cousin is doing in another state. Others may want to use it as a tool for discourse. Rather than saying, "This way is good and this other way is more shallow somehow," instead we can just recognize that this is the richness of the religious experience. It has built into it the nuances that can feed these different hungers.

YL: Yes, and different degrees of hunger, too. The mystic is someone who is interested in interdisciplinary ideas. In the larger sense of the word. Religion is a guidebook or an alphabet, but the mystic is one who scrambles all of that to create new words and new sequences. It becomes a launch pad into a greater unknown. Religion might be the runway and the mystic has taken off. This might sound condescending, but I don't mean it in that way. The mystic is much messier also, but in that messiness he is intensifying what it means to wing it on your own. That's the path of someone who is picking up ideas in an interdisciplinary way here and there versus the security of knowing, "I am here. I major in this and only this, and this represents the truth and this is how it is." There is a security in that, to be sure, and certainly there are values and goodness, too. Once you decide that the open sky is your home, then it becomes trickier to find somewhere to perch and make your nest.

KAFKA AND BAUDELAIRE: THE INVALIDS

RV: In the conversation, Kafka and Baudelaire are grouped together. You refer to them as The Invalids. This took me on an interesting train of thought as I was reminded of shamanic traditions in pre-civilized cultures. The shamans are people who have typically been wounded themselves. In recovering from that experience, they are given the tools to help people who haven't wandered into this territory get back to a place where they can function, even though the shaman may never return to that place where they can function in a traditional societal sense.

YL: What you were saying about the shaman, I think is true for this lot, for this bunch of the wounded. There's a quote from Jung: "It is only the wounded physician that heals." Jung is certainly someone who is susceptible to pre-civilization thinking, as you call it. He is someone who speaks of our "archaic residue."

Whether it's Pascal, who is another great thinker/mystic type, or where Kafka found himself—most of these guys are, for some reason or another [wounded] . . . I mean, Kierkegaard speaks of his wound in a very enigmatic way in his correspondences. "If it weren't for my wound . . ."

Another part of it . . . and maybe this is a simplistic way of saying it but also, I feel, true—is that it accounts for their great sensitivity. We tend to heal —all of us— and part of healing is a kind of deadening to feeling. But to live as an open wound is to always be hypersensitive.

RV: The conversation that you have with Alex about Baudelaire reads like a cautionary tale about what happens to those who are clearly called to this mystic state of being and yet won't or can't surrender themselves to it. A quote from your conversation reads that "before approaching that mystic condition, one must accept the diminution of the constructed self. The dissolution of the personality that comes with honest admiration, that diminution was too high a price. In the end, he would not pay it, not even though the alternative was madness."

YL: That's what drove Alex and me mad about Baudelaire, each in our own way. We both wrestled with him. When it came time to do this piece, to have this conversation about him, in this context, that was the great waste and the great pity. Sartre, for example, has his own take. Who else—who is that French maniac?—Jean Genet has his own take. Everyone has his own take on Baudelaire. They all wanted to claim him, as a philosopher or as something else. For this project, to claim him as a mystic is to realize the great loss which he did not realize if you read him as we read him. One can, of course, read him however one chooses to read him. He is a bit of a cautionary tale because it ends badly. It ends with someone struggling desperately towards the light, asking to be whipped to do good work (a friend of his is the one who whips him). He is speaking to himself at a feverish pitch in his diaries to transform. To, finally, take what Kafka calls the "point of no return," that is, the point that must be reached. In Baudelaire's case, he is cheated of that because of syphilis, the degenerative state he arrives to, He doesn't recognize himself in the mirror anymore. He is basically losing his mind. And to see what sort of a pathetic struggle was taking place, yeah, it is a cautionary tale, but at the same time, who is to say that the struggle itself is not the utmost that a person is capable of? So when you very kindly said he didn't or couldn't make this commitment, maybe he did just by struggling, wholeheartedly. Maybe that's the most that can be asked of him given the circumstances.

NIETZSCHE, RILKE AND EKELUND: THE EXQUISITES

RV: As you move into the next section of the conversation, you begin talking about another group, The Exquisites, beginning with Nietzsche. Structurally, it feels like the conversation moves into another territory. It feels like we are talking about people who more fully inhabit this archetype of the artist as mystic.

YL: I thought it was useful, in this conversation, to regard them as one because of their great affinity. I find these slightly hokey affinities. Oh, these two guys [Wilde and Nietzsche] were born one day apart and died the same year. Oh, they were both Libras. I'm susceptible to this kind of nonsense, too! With Nietzsche, Rilke, and Ekelund, it's quite deep. In Rilke's case, they share a girlfriend [Lou Andreas-Salomé] and it's beyond a girlfriend with these guys. It's beyond a soul mate. It's very deep. Salomé is endlessly fascinating for me, and, in the case of Ekelund, who, in many ways, was not participating with the world at large, he was talking to Nietzsche in a way that you don't necessarily speak to the deceased. Even for a dead relative, you wouldn't necessarily assume that kind of familiarity. There is something about those three, and when I throw myself in the mix, it makes a particular kind of sense. If nothing else, it crystallizes the type that I'm hovering around in trying discuss the artist as a mystic. Ekelund spells it out. He says the real poet is a mystic and no less. RV: It is interesting that with Nietzsche, more so than Rilke or Ekelund, the end of his story is really not that much more uplifting than what we got from Baudelaire. Even though the mechanisms of that dismantling were different. He does spend the last ten years of his life—YL: And it may also be syphilis. We don't know definitively but it may well have been syphilis. It's certainly a humiliating madness if nothing else.

RV: So we look at Nietzsche's progression through his mystical experience. Is that a positive story? Is it another cautionary tale?

YL: With this particular one, yes, it is a cautionary tale, but there seems to be more to it. He took on so very much, or so it seems to me. There are some, like Tolstoy, who just dismiss him as stupid and mad. Just like that. And that's the end of it. There's no more. He's not interested in the nuance. For me, there is something heroic about Nietzsche that is not heroic about Baudelaire. Baudelaire is a terrific poet. Nietzsche was not. Nietzsche was something else. There is something heroic about his spirit even with its nonsense and noise—and there's plenty of both—and that's my difficulty now with him is how he was stuck in a certain rebelliousness even if it meant cutting off his nose to spite his face.

In spite of himself, though, he took on a great deal more, so that you can almost set the person aside. If you were just going in there with your archeologist's brush to excavate this site, there's so much more there that you can take and run with in so many different directions. As people have done. I mean, he's been claimed by everyone of every persuasion possible. Yes, it is a cautionary tale because it ends the way that it ends . . . You were asking me about Baudelaire, if I could sort of take him and rewind him or make another story of him. Nietzsche rewinded or , perhaps, forwarded might have been Rumi. I, really, see that possibility in him. It's odd, I understand, to say this. Whatever that means. Maybe I'm back to my hokey horoscope thing. Maybe it's their similariies as Librans. But, Nietzsche's rich contradictions, radical revaluation of all values, insatiable longing and his life as scholar-become-poet-prophet, even the *Uberman*, is realized in the person of Rumi.

RV: You actually go into much greater depth about Nietzsche in Trial by Ink than in these conversations with Alex. I wonder if you could lay out what you see as the connections between Nietzsche and Rilke?

YL: I did have that monstrous essay, and by monstrous, I mean in terms of the demands that it places on the reader, in Trial by Ink about Nietzsche and Wilde. That was just me getting that out of my system so I didn't feel like I needed to do it again. Nietzsche and Rilke, if I had to sum them up—and I have the mind that, whether or not I like it, always attempts to collapse distances, distill matters into a handful of words—I'd say it's an aesthetic ecstasy and that's what Ekelund shares with them . . . he can tag along for aesthetic ecstasy. He can hitch a ride there. He arrives at the same place taking the same caravan that they ride. For them, beauty is not a skin-deep thing. They arrive at this place which demands transformation.

Nietzsche talks about the Overman as necessary . . . if it wasn't for overcoming, he wouldn't have bothered. This is someone who would have, as he admits it, checked out a long time ago. Transformation is the bait that keeps him going. He believes in it, and he believes in it in a big way. He believes in it through the aesthetic experience—even though he's very conflicted about the aesthetic experience and [thinks of] the artist as inferior to the philosopher because he's sort of stuck on beauty.

He'll never clear that hurdle, but then there's a deeper beauty past the music of the language or particular images that they create. It's this deep belief in beauty as their way out. Their way to mysticism really and nothing less. Their ecstatic experiences are aesthetic ones and vice versa. You have Rilke in a much-quoted poem "Archaic Torso of Apollo" saying that even in admiring a work of art, the art demands that *you must change your life*. If there's one thing—and it goes beyond connective tissue, it's an umbilical cord that snags tight between these two—it's this idea that it's not enough to admire beauty. They were both goners for beauty; the manufacturing of beauty and the observation and distilling of beauty. But once they'd begun that, it had to end with, "You must change your life." That's the higher law of beauty.

KIERKEGAARD

RV: Kierkegaard has an almost messianic quality about him. I was interested in the sections where you talked about how he was so engaging in public and then would have these brooding, intensive periods at home.

YL: That really fascinated me as well. I will say, again since he's not here, Kierkegaard is probably closer for Alex than any of these other fellows. He's the one that Alex has studied the closest and, I think I can say this, that he feels the greatest affinity for. After our conversations, I read Alex's work more closely. I'm reading him now among other things. It's interesting to me, after the fact, to see that he's been talking to them, throughout his books, but in another way, in another language. So Kierkegaard meant a great deal to him. I could tell that he was happy to cover Kierkegaard when I suggested him. I could see that this was one that meant a lot to him. The messianic side is one that he admires him most for.

It was really Alex's conclusion, not mine, when he says, "What a great loss for the pulpit not to have had [Kierkegaard]." I never thought it through to that extent. What would he have looked like, actually, within the system? When Alex wrote that . . . I have to here that the way we work together is, after I talk myself dry in the mouth over the telephone, Alex will send me his *doctored* transcript. I'll print it out and curl up somewhere in the corner of a room, in the dark, and read. Then, re-read. And I imagine what I felt and what he's thinking. In my innate, snooty rebellion, I stopped at that pulpit bit. The apartness of [Kierkegaard's] mysticism and then to imagine him within the system; I'd never gone so far as to do that until I came across this book, this journal, by a cousin of Kierkegaard's that was not meant to be published during his lifetime. For some reason, George Washington University library had a hold of it. It was just good luck that I found it right before my conversation with Alex. In reading it, the way that can happen with books if you read them closely enough, if you really lean into them, the spirit of Soren came to the fore.

As a teenager, I'd read in Kierkegaard's journals how he was the life and soul of the party. Everyone hung on his every word. Witticisms fell from his lips. But then he goes home—and he wants to kill himself. I understood that. I was 18 at the time, and I had this juvenile affinity with the masks we put on. You go out. You're in company. You have fun. You're excited, but you go home and you are existentially alone and brooding and hopeless and the rest of it. It was interesting, though, to see to what extent that he was good company. He took it upon himself to keep his "wound" to himself, so that even those closest to him were very surprised in reading his papers to come across that. He was always available.

Even when he had become a figure of public ridicule (he'd set himself up for this with the local paper by presenting himself in such a manner so they could take him on for his views and caricature him—this negative attention or publicity that he got) even then the street remained a kind of theater for him. He had one of those personalities, extroverted personalities, gregarious personalities, exhibitionist also, that liked to play with people the way that Socrates liked to play with people. The difference was he also had enough of, whatever this was, discipline, self-discipline, compulsion to write it down in his brooding moments. He could have been another one of these people who just took it to the street, just challenged people with these verbal and mental games. He seemed to pretty much live this way. Perfect strangers he would approach and "hook them with a look" as he was fond of saying. He had enough faith in human nature, even if it was a child (because he was very much a child himself) he could find a way into them. Find a point of contact to speak and engage with them. His business, his great existential quandaries were really his business and that's probably why he couldn't share this with Regina Olsen, because once you let someone in, a spouse or a partner or a lover, it's hard to keep yourself from them that way. But he could do it with everyone else.

THE ART OF CONVERSATION

RV: It's tempting as we are drawing the comparison to Socrates to recognize that Socrates didn't write anything down for us. It's entirely possible that he had that same kind of internal dialogue that was very different from his external dialogue. The external dialogue is, perhaps, the symptom by which we can diagnose the internal—

YL: Condition! No, I'm writing this down. The external dialogue is the symptom by which we can diagnose the internal condition. That's a neat little aphorism for me, right there.

In Socrates' case, whatever the internal condition was, you have to think, however gregarious the public figure was, you have to wonder if he didn't believe in language. Even in himself. He believed in the exchange of breath that challenged and, potentially, nourished, but he's also a person who concludes in this very sublime manner by saying, "I go to death and you go to life and who knows which is the better of the two?" That's an enigmatic thing to say. The fact that he didn't write is not for lack of thought. To arrive at that condition means that, for some reason, he must have thought it not worthwhile.

RV: I look at the ancient Greek tradition, between Pythagoras and Socrates, and I find it curious that many of those thinkers found language to be almost too debased. It was untrustworthy. As soon as we fix something into words—

YL: It's lost in translation!

APHORISMS

RV: One of the things that you touch upon in the book and in the format of The Artist as Mystic is that conversation brings out aspects of communication that we don't get through an e-mail interview because you have a certain degree of preparation that you do in advance of an interview in planning, but conversations have a way of evolving.

YL: I'm a huge fan of conversation just because of this spontaneous aspect. Whatever it is that you've been thinking and being, you can put in your mouth at the moment; then it also surprises you because the other person draws out things that you can't get to by yourself. The dead interview is the one that is flat on the page. For me, conversation is a living thing, full of surprises.

RV: Given that both you and Alex are aphorists, what did you discover in your conversations about the essential nature of the aphorism serving as a bridge between poetry and philosophy?

YL: That's a good question. Let me start with Ekelund. The form you choose, or the form that chooses you, the form that presents the idea best, is not incidental. It carries significance. The fact that Ekelund chose to express himself in aphorisms means that not only did he share Nietzsche's way of thinking but . . . the aphorist mistrusts language and self on a deeper level. The aphorism is something that you can rescue from both the deceitful self and unreliable language. This is really the first time I'm saying this, so I'm thinking it through with you. That is what aphorists have in common. It's not like the philosopher's certainty where they sit down and lay out systems. With aphorists, it's open-ended, like we said earlier. It's a case of the person who, even if a thought itself is devastating, would like to tickle it and twist it at the end before sending it out into the world. So there is something of the short story writer there. Because it's so condensed, you have to, of necessity, have also the poet's ear for language. If poetry is considered prose—meaning prose that is considered—then every word has to count in an aphorism as a vehicle for the idea to take off or to be sent out. It has to stand on its own. It really has nothing. There is no introduction to it. Nobody comes in and says, "I'd like you to meet my friend, so-and-so, the aphorism." It just arrives, unannounced, and then leaves unannounced too.

RV: The aphorism doesn't leave you an avenue for argument. You can't go through it and discuss or even dismantle it, structurally. It just walks into the room, makes a statement and then leaves. And it leaves you with yourself.

YL: And leaves you with yourself! It walks in and ruffles the room. Where there was complacency, where there was apathy, where there was disinterest, suddenly you are asking, "What was that?" or "How do I feel about this?"

Lots of times, aphorisms—and certainly epigrams, maxims, whatever you like—are half-truths. They are clever, witty, dressed-up jokes with a mind on them.

They are not absolute truths. They are just enough of a truth that they can, as you say, get you to think for yourself about where you stand in relation to them. If they can stir thought, that's all they really aspire to. The enemy of the aphorism is the cliché, the ready-made idea. That's why aphorisms are, by their nature, slightly subversive. They have that twist. They take received wisdom and flip it on its head. They show the opposite of what you thought was truth, the underside of it.

RV: When I think of the presentation of Socrates that we get from Plato, it's rare when he goes on a diatribe and says, "This is how this thing is." It is more common for him to take something that someone has just said, reformulate it as a question and then hand it right back to them.

YL: It's this open-endedness . . . More and more, I'm finding that it's the rigidity of conclusion that one wants to avoid, especially in the larger conversation. If you want to leave room for others, any others, do leave room for them to participate.

INTERDISCIPLINARITY

RV: I wanted to speak with you about The Artist as Mystic for *Crosstimbers* because I felt like it cut to the core of interdisciplinarity. In specialized education, you are being trained to think as one kind of person. You are one thing or another. Not even literature is immune to this.

YL: I've always been a generalist at heart. Interdisciplinarity is necessary because it saves us from specificity, which is nice but only for a short while. The idea of only one way is no good. It's no good in religion. It's no good in politics. It's no good in literature. It deprives us of a multiplicity of possibilities.

Interdisciplinarity says, "There is truth here and here and also over there." You can make a dense weave of these different strands and bring them into agreement in a larger conversation, a larger sense of possibility. That's something I believe in and I believe in it, deeply. Whether it's literature or beyond, I hope never to have to choose one thing to the exclusion of all else.

The City and the Writer
In Cairo

Can you describe the mood of Cairo as you feel/see it?

Cairo, as I understand it, is a joyous child whose confidence has been shaken by repeated scolding and attempts at molding. We're not quite ourselves at the moment, and appear to be battling for our souls. To find ourselves between a rock (the military) and a hard place (Muslim Brotherhood) is not really a healthy mental space. But, I tell myself, we're just experiencing *un mauvais quart d'heure* (" bad quarter of an hour ")—our unfortunate present moment does not define us; it's just a hiccup caused by indigestion, viewed in the context of our long illustrious history. I hear echoes of our fabled wisdom and indomitable spirit in this noble slogan of ours that circulated following our Revolution: اليأس خيانة والامل أمانة ('Despair is betrayal, and Hope a responsibility').

What is your most heartbreaking memory in this city?

The dashed hopes of 2011's heroic People's Uprising . . . After witnessing millions of desperate Egyptians put their lives on the line to create a New World, then for this heroic, historic mood to begin to curdle. Demoralizing to see some of those same people experiencing Revolution-fatigue and allowing themselves to become desensitized to the military propaganda machine. Truly heartbreaking is losing sight of one another's humanity, and descending into the pit of mounting cynicism, apathy or, worse, condoning violence.

What is the most extraordinary detail, one that goes unnoticed by most, of the city?

Our quick-wittedness. In the Cairo I was born and raised in, one was surrounded by a love of language. So, it came as no surprise to me, for example, when our Revolution erupted that masses of peaceful protesters chose to

174

express their dissent and dreams in poetry, chanted jubilantly from Tahrir Square. Wit and verse were always sport, and a kind of national pastime, during the three decades I lived in Cairo. Never mind the high illiteracy rate; it wasn't about being book-smart. "Knowledge is what's in your head, not in your notebooks," an Egyptian saying shrewdly justified (in Arabic, this rhymes, too: *el 3elm fil rass mish fil korras*).

Besides our excellent sense of humor: the innocent joy we take in dancing. Women, men and children of every shape, age and class love to shimmy and shake with sensual abandon. This is yet another example of how the current ostentatious religiosity is an instance of cutting off our nose to spite our face. When an exuberant city, and its people, that were once open to the world, and celebrated for their effortless wit and (belly) dancing, become censorious and closed, they self-sabotage. Thus, a city/people downplay their natural strengths and exaggerate weaknesses.

What writer(s) from here should we read?

I was fortunate to be raised in a household that hosted a sort of informal literary salon, where literary lights like Yusuf Idris (our Chekhov), Louis Awad (intellectual giant) and Ahmed Ragab (famous satirist) passed through. Celebrated poets, like Farouk Goudah and Abdul Rahman Al Abnoudi were family friends, as well. So, certainly, I recommend all those. Later, as a young man living in downtown Cairo, I had the opportunity to meet Alaa-Al-Aswany (the movie adaptation of his best-selling novel, *Yacubian Building*, was being filmed in my building) as well as up and coming writers, such as Yusuf Rakha. Another Egyptian novelist that I've not met, but would like to and recommend is Son'allah Ibrahim, revered for his work as well as publicly refusing the Arab Novel Award, a prize given by the Egyptian Ministry of Culture, under Hosni Mubarak.

But, perhaps in our stifling patriarchal society it is more helpful to recommend female writers, who (perhaps of necessity) also double up as inspiring activists, such as: Nawal El Saadawi, Ahdaf Soueif and (the recently deceased) Radwa Ashour.

Is there a place here you return to often?

In a review of my new book (in the 'Alexandria Quarterly') the reviewer writes: "Yahia Lababidi dedicates his collection Balancing Acts to his native Egypt. But it's ostensibly not the Egypt of Giza and Tutankhamen . . . nor of sprawling Cairo streets and bustling bazaars. Lababidi. . . seems to have something other, and otherworldly, in mind." Perhaps, they are right. But if so, in my defense, I will say that Cairo easily lends itself to myth and metaphor. While I love all of the lived realities above, which perhaps I do not address, directly, in my work, I carry the real and imaginary Cairo in my heart—and visit it in my daydreams, the way one might visit the drowned continent of their youth. Which is to say, I partially recognize that the care-free innocence and exuberance I ascribe to Cairo has as much to do with my younger self as it does with the inscrutable city.

Is there an iconic literary place we should know?

Besides house parties, where literary life thrives, I recommend downtown Cairo, the cultural belly of the beast. It was in downtown Cairo, where thinkers and dreamers met, that the Revolution sparked , and in Tahrir ("Liberty") Square where protestors continued to gather to voice griev-ances. Pre-revolution, I crossed Tahrir Square, for nearly a decade on my way back home from work (at UNESCO Cairo Office) and entered a kind of enchanted world. It was there, in downtown Cairo, at the iconic Café Riche that, one afternoon, I witnessed the deliciously playful vernacular poet, and national treasure, Ahmed Fouad Negm erupt into a spontaneous call and response performance piece with other literati that were gathered there. The Greek club, across the street, and the Grillon bar further down, are other spaces, downtown, one can go for quickening, intellectual conversation, as well the once vibrant cultural center, Townhouse Gallery, which came up (in 1998) as I was living in downtown, Cairo (which, following a prolonged fight with the state government's censorship bureau, briefly collapsed).

Are there hidden cities within this city that have intrigued or seduced you?

"Moulids," or birthday celebrations of Sufi saints, fascinate me. In the heart of Islamic Cairo, for example, you might encounter a hallucinatory, dream-world you would not have imagined existed: snake charmers, bearded la-dies, crowds ecstatically singing, dancing and chanting, in trances (induced by hashish, Divine love, or both) and much, much else. Attracting millions of souls, seeking spiritual or secular release, it's best to navigate these wild carnivals with a guide so not to get lost or harassed in the press of flesh and overwhelming free-for-all. To the outsider, it is not easy to reconcile such amoral revelry with the city, in its comparatively more sober state. But, several times a year, the scarcely-repressed chaos lets its hair down and ev-erything is permitted in the name (or under the guise) of G_d and his saints. This, too, is part of the hidden, contradictory and mysterious heart of Cairo, and Egypt, at large.

Where does passion live here?

In the chaotic, pulsating street theatre, where nearly twenty million souls jostle for space and negotiate their sanity, in one of the most densely populated capital cities in the world. By extension, passion lives in the coffee shops, where people-watching, coffee or tea-sipping, hooka-smoking, joke-swapping and animated conversations are the best way to pass the day. If you want to escape the heat and (noise) pollution, then the thing to do is hop on a felucca, wooden sailing boat, and let your troubles melt away along the Nile. (Bring a friend, music and food or drink for a more lively ride).

What is the title of one of your works about Cairo and what inspired it exactly?

In my book, Balancing Acts, there are many poems written during the three decades I lived in this great capital of memory; few poems address the decisive act of 'fleeing the stable' as well as *cri de coeur* poems that, helplessly, pine for all that I've left behind. Here is a love letter, inspired by my relocating to the US, where I look back with longing, unable and unwilling to forget . . .

Cairo

I buried your face, someplace
by the side of the new road
so I would not trip over it
every morning or on evening strolls

still, I am helplessly drawn
to the scene of this crime
for fear of forgetting
the sum of your splendor

then, there's also the rain
that loosens the soil
to reveal a bewitching feature
awash with emotion

an eye, perhaps tender or
a pale, becalmed cheek
a mouth, tight with reproach or
lips pursed in a deathless smile

other times you are inscrutable
worse, is when I seem to lose you
and pick at the earth like a scab
frantic, and faithful, like a dog.

Inspired by Levi, "Outside Cairo does an outside exist?"

Cairo is a mad mother who devours her children. No matter how voluntary it may appear, exile is never really a choice. Exiles always feel a little posthumous; and the exile's love is absolute—pining for an Ideal. So, in a sense, there is no outside Cairo, even though, in the devastating phrasing of Kenyan-Somali poet, Warsan Shire, "Home is the mouth of a shark."

Below, are a few more lines from Shire's poem, 'Home', which speak me better than myself:

> no one leaves home until home is a sweaty voice in your ear
> saying-
> leave,
> run away from me now
> i don't know what i've become
> but i know that anywhere
> is safer than here

An Artist's Story of the Arab Spring

UPHEAVAL IN COUNTRIES LIKE Egypt and Syria is often discussed in political terms, but how do artists see it? NPR Guest host Celeste Headlee talks about arts and the Arab Spring with an Egyptian-American poet.

Celeste Headlee: Well, that's a look at the political turmoil in Egypt, but how does a poet see it? Painters, musicians, writers, and poets have all used art to deal with and document this conflict for centuries, and the Arab Spring has been no different. And while art is being used to express what's happening, it's also being used to heal. So let's now hear an artistic perspective on Egypt.

Now living in America, poet Yahia Lababidi uses his words to try to provide insight into what's happening in his homeland of Egypt.

Yahia Lababidi: Thank you for having me.

CH: Yahia, as you watch these events in Egypt from a distance now, what effect has that had on your poetry?

YL: Personally, I'm stunned. I am trying to recognize the Egypt I left, years ago, and to send out something that I think is meaningful and, in some way, perhaps uplifting.

CH: But how does it change your choice of words? When you're speaking to people who are, of course, in conflict—perhaps in fear—how does that change the way that you write?

YL: Without sounding too pretentious, I don't believe that a poet owns themselves. I don't think that we can create at will. So, I try, in my prose, to address issues of the day, which is easier to do because that's thought and that's practical and that's detail oriented. And in the po-etry, when I can, when it's been digested, I try to send out something which, again, reminds us of the goals of our revolution, which I see now as being entirely abandoned.

CH: So, Yahia, you can probably understand what that's like—the catharsis one feels when you get these out.

YL: Yes, yes.

CH: Is it of concern if you can't stop writing about violence?

YL: I do see art as therapy in the sense of it reminding us, also, of our larger allegiances to one another, to life. I mean, if the poet has a role, it is not to instruct because people don't need instruction, but they need reminders. And these reminders are to provide vision, if possible. And I think this is what poetry, at its finest, can do.

CH: Yahia, you've just published your volume of poems, Barely There. It includes this one called *Egypt*, which, I understand, is the last poem in the collection. Would you read it for us?

YL: Yes, ma'am. So this was written in August around the time of the massacre in Raba'a, and also the accompanying, horrendous church burnings. So, I'm not blaming either the military or the Muslim Brotherhood. But it was written at this time, and also reflecting on the last couple of years of madness unraveling.

Egypt

You are the deep fissure in my sleep,
that hard reality underneath
a stack of soft-cushioning illusions.
Self-exiled, even after all these years

I remain your ever-adoring captive
I register as inner tremors
—across oceans and continents—
the flap of your giant wing, struggling
to be free and know I shall not rest until
your glorious metamorphosis is complete.

CH: That's a very hopeful poem.

YL: You have to hope. This is—if you take the whole Mubarak era, it's 30 years—as a hiccup in a civilization that is thousands of years old. I don't recognize what is happening, now. This is growing pains, labor pains, whatever you want to call it. But, this is—this, too, shall pass. I hope.

CH: Well, interesting—I mean, your art itself and your view of history is completely influenced by the fact that you grew up near pyramids reminding you of how ancient your culture is.

YL: It's unmissable. I mean, if you do have a sense of history, and if you do have this continuity, you look at what is happening and you say they have forgotten their ancient wisdom. They've forgotten their modern wit. They've forgotten who they are. If we can do anything, as journalists, as moral watchdogs, as poets—it's to say: this is beneath us. These are not the goals of our revolution. This is not a dignity revolution. This is not unity. This is not freedom.

This is more of what we revolted against. We have the military, now, which look very much to me like what we revolted against—police brutality and oppression. That was the whole point of our revolution. I think reminders are what these poems can serve as.

CH: Yahia Lababidi is a poet. His book of short poems, Barely There, is out now and he was kind enough to come to our studio here in Washington. Thank you so much.

YL: Thanks, again, for having me.

Interview with Poetry Nook

We are honored to interview Yahia Lababidi this month, author of the recently released collection of poems, Barely There, which explore a variety of spiritual, meditative, natural, and other topics, in typically concise and impactful form. In this interview, he expands on the spiritual and philosophical development that led to his collection, as well as the "chrysalis" state of his current growth. We follow the interview with a brief selection of the poems included in his book, which we highly recommend reading.

—Editors

In some poems, such as "What If" and "Embracing, We Let Go," you hint at a spiritual struggle or development. What has been your spiritual evolution over time? How has it influenced you as a person, in the choices you've made in life, and as a poet?

This is a big question, and I'm not sure such deep movements of the soul withstand being discussed, directly, but I'll try. Yes, this new book is a document of a spiritual struggle or development, as you put it. For years, I worshipped at the altar of the mind, and now something stirs that is overthrowing the tyranny of the rational. In one of the poems in Barely There, called *Expedition*, I sum it up this way:

> After decades of exploration,
> discovering I stand at the shore
> of intellectual knowledge
> before an infinite sea
> of the esoteric.

An alternative title for my book of short poems was In Chrysalis to suggest this transitional period that I'm undergoing. Also, there's another poem in this collection, *Kneeling in Stages*, which serves as a kind of resume of my inner life and speaks of me better than I do myself.

So as not to sound needlessly elusive, I will add that I am a cultural Muslim, but was not raised as a practicing one. As a matter of fact, as a young man, I distanced myself from religion as a way of protesting against the type of showy religiosity that prevailed in my part of the world and I, generally, did this through my readings in Existential philosophy. Only very recently, do I find myself fed up with the mind and its chew toys and returning to the mystical branch of Islam (Sufism) by way of Persian poetry and also the lives of (Christian) saints. I cannot really speak further of this evolution, since it is still occurring, but no doubt this force is reflected in my writing, as it is in the process of rewriting my soul.

In "Breath" you seem to find spirituality in nature. How do you think about nature in relation to you, and to humans in general?

There is a Persian mystic, Al-Ghazali, who describes well the spirituality found in nature, saying: "this *visible* world is a trace of that *invisible* one and the former *follows* the latter like a shadow." So, if there is consolation and inspiration in the natural world, it is because it mirrors the invisible world of the spirit, and serves as a portal to access it.

What kind of relationship exists between creativity and spirituality, in your opinion?

Another fine, and vast, question. Creativity, as I understand it, is amoral. It plucks its fruits from everywhere, without asking where they come from and what good they might be. Spirituality, perhaps, is about inhabiting a natural state of creativity, one that is more concerned with our moral development, and the revelation of the hidden relations between things.

Do you think there is a connection between poetry and prayer? How do they affect each other in your life?

I think of poetry as prayer. To write is to bow is to pray; bow so low and you kiss the sky. In fact, prior to this collection, I collaborated with a friend and fellow aphorist, Alex Stein, on a book of conversations called The Artist as Mystic. In this series of dialogues, we examine the spiritual dimension in the lives and work of thinkers and poets, such as Nietzsche, Rilke, Kierkegaard and Baudelaire.

We also see some influence from Eastern thought in "Exchanges," among other poems. How have you integrated different belief systems in your own life, whether religious or philosophical?

Western philosophy, my first love, is slowly being replaced by Eastern mysticism, Nietzsche by Rumi. Perhaps, it's strange to say this but I see in Nietzsche a stunted Rumi. I am drawn to the captivating contradictions in both, the serious play, their radical ecstasy. But I see the example of scholar-become-poet, who then goes on to make of his life a work of art, more fully realized in the figure of Rumi.

In "Egypt," you talk of your "self-exile" yet the inevitability of remaining part of your cultural heritage. What prompted your "exile?" What are some of the ways your Egyptian heritage continues to influence you in daily life and as a poet?

I left Egypt because, quite frankly, I was gasping for air and it felt like something had to give. As it turned out, everyone else felt the same way and that something that gave spelled Revolution. What I did not realize was that, by being away, I was deepening my longing and appreciation for my culture. Also, as a result of the current upheavals, ex-pats such as myself find that we, naturally, gravitate to the role of cultural ambassador or explicator—keen to rescue and communicate the Egypt we know and love—as we sift through the many contortions and distortions that are presented in both foreign and local presses.

What are your thoughts on the changes underway in Egypt?

Difficult times. I maintain that the Revolution was absolutely necessary and recognize, ruefully, the revolution-fatigue I see setting in, where people are settling for the unsavory choices of Muslim brotherhood or military rule: two faces of unfreedom. Yet, neither of these thought-dictators represent our uprising, nor do they offer a vision forward of unity, dignity or peace. I am heart-broken as I see how divided people are becoming and how they rationalize the senseless violence being committed. This is not the Egyptian character I remember and I hope during these trying times, when we are battling for our souls, we remember that *how* we fight for freedom determines *who* we become.

Your poetry does not have a lot of explicit political discussion, but there are some lighthearted reflections on issues like racism in "Skin" and commercialism in "Truth in Advertising." What do you think is the role of the poet in discussing societal and political issues or in keeping the art and the society separate?

I wrestle with this question on a regular basis. I think poorly digested politics makes for bad art. At the same time, I think it unconscionable for the artist to fiddle while Rome burns, so to speak. Striking the right balance has been tricky, but I've found it easier to address issues of the day (politics, culture, etc . . .) in my prose, as I feel that I do not own the poetry.

In "Hothouse" you talk about poets you cannot stand. What are your thoughts on the currents of contemporary poetry? What types do you like and dislike? What are you trying to accomplish as a poet?

I don't read as widely as I should when it comes to contemporary poetry, but the advantage of that is that I am always discovering new poets / poems I admire. (Here's my audio library, on SoundCloud, where I recite some favorites: *https://soundcloud.com/yahia-lababidi*). What I like in poetry is what I like in people: profundity, humor, attention to language. What I dislike in verse, similarly, is what I am not fond of in persons: superficiality, insincerity and, in regards to language, a sort of gimmicky self-consciousness. What am I trying to accomplish as a poet? Goodness . . . to *Be*, more fully, I suppose and, in some way, also, to help others do so.

What do you hope readers take away from your work? Do you aim to teach or to provoke thought in your audience?

I think in order to teach that cannot be your stated aim. But, I do believe in provocation, challenging assumptions and "telling the truth slant." I think it's not easy to speak to ourselves, and that we, often, need to devise ruses. Poetry, at its finest can do this and bring us into contact with a deeper self, a larger reality. Then, if we're lucky, it might help us to transform, as well.

Most of your poems are extremely brief. Do you think a shorter form has more impact? Do you think this is inherent in the concentrated intensity of shorter poems or do you think it reflects the changing tastes of contemporary readers as they have become accustomed to smaller bites of information?

All of the above. To begin with, I'm an aphorist, at heart, and always trying to whittle matters down to their essences. Further, the poems in this book were, to a large extent, inspired by the constraints of social media, specifically Twitter—so, I've found the 140-character limitation an invitation to create poetry in miniature. In this way, the poems in my new book are "barely there" on the page, the way their author is "barely there" off it.

Who are your major poetic influences? We saw a quote from Rumi in your book and a reference to "the Way," which we assume to refer to Daoism. How have mystical poets influenced you? How about other types of poetry?

Yes, Rumi and the Persian poets exert a great influence on my being. Also, Rilke means a great deal to me; as he says "We are the *bees of the invisible*. We wildly collect the honey of the visible, to store it in the great golden hive of the invisible." Otherwise, Eliot was a formative influence and Rimbaud, and I still return to all the usual suspects who set me alight as a teenager. Spiritual tourist that I am, Daoism is also a source of inspiration as is Buddhism. If I had to pick a single book, at the intersection of poetry, philosophy and the sacred, it would be Lao-Tzu's *Tao Te Ching*. I regard it as inexhaustible and am struck, anew, by its fruitful paradoxes with each reading. Simply, I think it gets at the heart of life in ways that little else does.

What are your major non-poetic influences—whether people, other literature, events, etc.?

I think, if we pay attention, everything/everyone has something to teach us. Silence has been one of my greatest teachers; Solitude, too.

What are your plans for future work, whether in poetry or elsewhere in life?

After around a decade or so of aphoristic silence, I'm back to secreting these brief arts through the pores. In fact, I've a book's worth of meditations on art, morality, and spirit [Where Epics Fail] and am taking my time to find the right publisher for such a project. Otherwise, I haven't a clue what comes next. More listening, deep self-diving for pearls.

Before we wrap up, we would like to give you a chance to speak to young poets who grapple with faith and writing. Madeleine L'Engle noted that when one is given a gift, one is obligated to serve that gift. Do you agree with this and do you think young poets should follow the idea that art is a type of service—either to be honest to their own potential, or to use what has been given to them?

Yes, I passionately believe that art is a calling and a life of service. In fact, this is the premise of my conversation with Alex Stein, "The Prayer of Attention" (which we developed into a book, The Artist as Mystic).

My advice to young poets would be that, to honor the gift and be worthy of it, they must give of themselves, whole-heartedly, and hold nothing back. The more deeply you know yourself, the more you are able to truly reach others. The more fearlessly you share of your findings, the more likely you are to make an authentic connection with a stranger—in turn, liberating truths that are not just about you, or me, but Us.

Lastly, I would add that part of knowing ourselves entails working on ourselves, training the self and liberating the soul. So that we can answer *Yes*, when a winged poem approaches us and asks: *Can I trust you? Is your heart pure to carry me, are your hands clean to pass me on?*

Discussing *Fever Dreams*
with Val B. Russell

Opening a volume of poetry is very much like opening a door to the poet's emotional life and internal struggle to understand the human experience. Condensing a million truths into one finite statement called a poem is a blending of the intellect with the spirit that is often contrary the pragmatic approach required in daily life.

When I walked through poet Yahia Lababidi's door with his recently released volume I encountered a richly textured, sardonic and often wry account of moments lived in contemplation amid the chaos of an external world that is often contrary to this striving for the answer to the eternal question of what it means to be alive.

VBR: *Every poet has their own way of entertaining the muse and putting passion on the page. What is the process for you when you write a poem?*

YL: You know, in all honesty, I have no process. Each time I write a poem is a surprise. And, when I'm not writing a poem, I don't feel very much like a poet. What do I do to try to get *there*? Reading helps; silence helps; solitude, too. But, all these are no guarantee that a poem will grace me with its presence. So, I try to watch the worlds unfold (inner and outer) as closely as I can, while stock-piling impressions, until the next time that I'm creatively employed.

VBR: *You have such an extensive and versatile range of subject matter in* Fever Dreams, *that at times the atmosphere of the text was delightfully unpredictable. When you were in the throes of putting together this collection was it intentional to maintain an element of surprise for your reader?*

YL: Thank you. Yes, an element of surprise is a good idea, for reader and author, alike. For all the poems that have gone into Fever Dreams, there are probably just as many that I did not include—because I felt like I was repeating myself, or I'd made my case better, elsewhere. I don't think books can ever quite match life's richness; but I believe that just as one should read widely, they ought to write widely, to better represent the variety of life's experiences.

VBR: *You make some social and political statements in this book that caress the sensibility in such a way as to be almost subliminal in their delivery. This is a delicate dance for any poet but you do it exceptionally well, without sounding the least bit admonishing or preachy. The poems "What is to Give Light," "Dog Ideal," "Air and Sea Show" and "Learning to Pray." Do you feel it is an artist's responsibility to be of their time and to share their observation whether it is politically correct or not?*

YL: This is a very important question, and one I've been torturing myself with since the Arab Spring began. I'm relieved you say I do not come across as admonishing or preachy; this is a horror of mine. Yes, I agree that the artist lives in their time, and is required to act as a witness. But, I also believe that the artist lives outside of their time, belonging just as much to the past as to the future.

VBR: *The poems "In Memoriam" and "Poy" moved me deeply because the imagery was bittersweet and these in particular remained with me afterwards. When you are giving live readings of your work, are there certain poems that are more difficult to articulate because of the intense emotion that inspired them?*

YL: Truthfully, I'm still making peace with the writer's life: the irony of an intensely private person in a public profession. It's one thing to share, in print or online, one's diary with the world, so to speak—out of some deep, inner compulsion as an artist. But, it's another thing, altogether, having to get up in front of a room full of strangers and actually read that "diary" out loud. . .

Which is to say, yes, I do have difficulty with readings, in general. While, I'm always grateful to be asked, I'm still working on the detachment required to share such intimate moments with strangers: heartache, existential doubt, even mourning. Lighter-hearted poems, or prayer-like odes to life, poems of praise, these afford me more distance and leave me feeling less-exposed, it's true.

VBR: *Any people who are new to your work may not be aware that you have a rather extensive and impressive publishing history, having been translated into several languages. In addition to this you are also a seasoned aphorist. When I was preparing for this interview I took a stroll through some of your aphorisms and what struck me was that Yahia is a type of teacher and his readers are in a way pupils. Do you feel this is a calling for you as a poet, to teach or enlighten others in some way?*

YL: You are very kind. The only way that I might accept such a generous compliment is to say that I am still aligning myself with my insights or so-called wisdom (in aphorisms, for example). I say in one aphorism that "our wisdom always mocks us, since it knows more than we can." That said, I do see the role of the artist, broadly-speaking, as being one of edu-tainment: educating while entertaining. The balance of this serious play is key. Too much on one side, and it's pompous; too much on the other and it's frivolous.

VBR: *You are an Arab writer and your cultural fingerprint is all over your poetry and yet you are a sort of chameleon artistically, shedding that culture and being naked in your humanity to make stark statements about the life we live and our struggle to understand ourselves as well as other human beings who share the world we inhabit. When you write does the poem come along of its own accord or do you begin with an intention and build on it from there whether it is cultural in nature or more expansive and universal in reach?*

YL: That's a beautiful way to put it: "shedding culture and being naked in our humanity." I don't think I could say much to improve on that. When I'm writing, poetry especially, it's as though I am semi-conscious. In this dream-like state, I hardly think of myself as an Arab man; at times, I hardly feel human. What I'm concerned with is saying something true, without the least regard for my person or my specific background.

It's a paradox to say this, but the more personal I perceive something to be, the more likely it is to connect with strangers, universally. We belong more to one another, than we do to any nation state. As Shakespeare put it, quite bluntly: "If you prick us, do we not bleed? If you tickle us, do we not laugh?" It's that basic, really.

VBR: *As a poet, I am always enamored of those who can make a transition from intellect to feeling within the same verse because poets often belong to one order of expression or the other. Blending emotion with intellect can be much like oil and water, exclusive of one another and opposed. You manage to weave your emotion through some very heavy intellectual words, specifically in the first poem in* Fever Dreams, *"Words" and "Fanciful Creators." The latter carrying the banner of emotion through the use of critical wit while describing from a detached intellectual vantage point, the flaw in the worship of progress and ease over depth and meaning. Is it more natural for you to approach your poetry from an intellectual basis or is it emotional territory that requires you to sculpt a little to achieve some equality between the two?*

YL: You are a close reader (in between the lines) and it's a pleasure to think out loud with you through these questions! I see what you mean about intellect and feeling; and how hard it is to mix the two in poetry. My background, and primary love perhaps, is philosophy. Yet, philosophy and poetry can be like the marriage of heaven and hell, I know. Still, they're both parts of me, and how I perceive the world: the analytical and emotional side.

I will say this, though, more and more, I'm less enamored of the mind, its tyranny and seductions. What I'm finding is displacing my fascination with the life of the mind, is a deep respect for the life of the Spirit. In this open space, there are no contradictions and everything is possible.

Words

Words are like days:
coloring books or pickpockets,
signposts or scratching posts,
fakirs over hot coals.

Certain words must be earned
just as emotions are suffered
before they can be uttered
—clean as a kept promise.

Words as witnesses
testifying their truths
squalid or rarefied
inevitable, irrefutable.

But, words must not carry
more than they can
it's not good for their backs
or their reputations.

For, whether they dance alone
or with an invisible partner,
every word is a cosmos
dissolving the inarticulate.

The Aphorist in Conversation
with Sholeh Johnston

The best words are those that are few and to the point.

—RUMI

APHORISMS CARRY WISDOM FROM generation to generation with a comforting precision, like arrows shot through time. From the ancient Chinese philosophers and Sufi poets through to present day poets, aphorisms have served as a potent distillation of insight and experience for spiritual seekers in cultures the world over. The truths they transmit have a timeless quality, connecting the ancient to the present with the golden thread of universal oneness.

Yahia Lababidi is an Egyptian-American poet, aphorist and essayist, and the author of seven critically-acclaimed books. He is best known for his aphorisms which have enchanted readers across the English-speaking world. When asked why he thinks this is, Lababidi quotes a Persian proverb:

YL: "'Epigrams succeed where epics fail." I believe we are living at a historical moment when the grand narratives—truth, morality, life of the spirit—seem to be failing to hold our attention or capture our imagination . . . Aphorisms, deceptively slight as they are, do their quiet work by helping readers (young and old) tackle the Big Questions: *how do we live, where are we heading and who we are becoming?*' This existentialism is timeless, and has also never felt more timely.

As a citizen of our increasingly polarized world, I feel called upon to use my art to try and alleviate the mounting fear directed at those of different backgrounds and faith traditions. I hope my aphorisms are more than a series of personal reflections. On one level, they are addressed to general readers or lovers of language, and specifically resonate with those who appreciate pithy sayings. But, on a deeper level, aphorisms offer moral guidance and ask us to change our lives. Good aphorisms, I believe, stir thought and invite readers of sensitivity and conscience to breathe life into them, by living at a higher level of consciousness.

Sholeh Johnston: *What was the first aphorism that moved you?*

YL: Hard to say which was, actually, the very first . . . there were so many. Two of the early ones that moved me to my core were Heidegger's definition of Longing: "the agony of the nearness of the distant" as well as Rumi's "What you are seeking is also seeking you." I found both of these strangely reassuring—a reminder that I was not alone and that the spiritual quest was a sort of dance, between two (albeit One elusive, invisible partner).

Aphorisms are how I speak to myself; they are what's worth quoting from the soul's dialogue with itself. Like tiny maps and signposts, I consult them in times of crises. They are the echoes of my silences, metaphysical expense reports. They are also anesthesia, how I am able to cut deeper and keep my wound clean. Beyond being poetry and philosophy, they are prayer.

SJ: *What led you to use the form in your own writing?*

YL: Being half-Lebanese, Khalil Gibran was an early and inescapable influence. Raised in Egypt, aphorisms (or proverbs) were viewed as common utterance and a sort of magical invocation. It was not uncommon for people in my part of the world (even if they were illiterate) to speak almost exclusively in sayings—a string of sing-songy, witty-wise remarks, for every occasion.

Then, as a teenager, in quick succession I read great aphorists like Wilde, Blake, Kafka, Pascal and Nietzsche who seemed to know me better than I knew myself and served as literary/spiritual guides. Lately, I draw sustenance and inspiration from the gnomic utterances of Sufi saints and mystics: Ibn Ata Illah, for example, an important Sufi saint and sage of thirteenth century Egypt, bequeathed us his treasured Kitab al Hikam (Book of Wisdom) which is composed of moral aphorisms intended to purify our heart and light the way.

SJ: *Your aphorisms are playful and evade categorization in terms of content and opinion—they are often political and yet betray no set position. Even though it's clear you are the author, you never fix yourself to a particular belief or perspective within the body of work. What is it about the form that evades being pinned down, and why is this important?*

YL: Thank you. I think nothing is more serious than play and, as a writer and thinker, am relieved that my work avoids categorization, which is limiting. Aphorisms respect truths by not trying to pin them down. They realize that truth speaks in paradox and what seems like contradictions, at times, and seek to remain flexible and fluid. As I say in my book, Where Epics Fail: "With enigmatic clarity, Life gives us a different answer, each time we ask her the same question."

Also, if I might be permitted another quotation, this time by physicist, Niels Bohr, here's an aphorism of his that gets at what I'm trying to say: "There are trivial truths and there are great truths. The opposite of a trivial truth is plainly false. The opposite of a great truth is also true."

SJ: *Which of your own aphorisms has had the greatest impact on your life?*

YL: It's heartening when I see an aphorism of mine has gone viral online, or is used in a classroom setting and it helps me to better understand what resonates most with people. "Eye contact: how souls catch fire" I don't believe to be my finest aphorisms, but it's fairly astonishing to me how widely it seems to have captured the public's imagination. Personally, the one I return to most, lately, is 'In the deep end, every stroke counts' (which, incidentally, was used as the title of a talk I was invited to have in Oxford University, at the end of 2019). A related aphorism of mine that I seem preoccupied with, nowadays, is: "If our hearts should harden and turn to ice, we must try, at least, not to blame the weather."

SJ: *It seems through your work you are evolving the form of the aphorism — is that true, and if so in what way is this unfolding?*

YL: I don't know if it's quite my place to say so but, thank you, for the compliment. I and the times have changed, since I first began writing aphorisms as a teenager in Egypt, nearly thirty years ago. Moving to America changed me and, in turn, my writing—in that I began responding to the new influences around me. More poetry and less philosophy found its way into my brief arts. Also, I was in conversation with the popular culture around me, while trying to honor my inner life which was, increasingly, seeking some spiritual language and Home (that didn't correspond to my new surroundings).

SJ: *What role do aphorisms play in your spiritual path?*

YL: Aphorisms are connected to wisdom literature in general and, at their finest, I believe are there for our edification. At least, this is how I felt when I first stumbled upon the immortal aphorisms of the Tao te Ching and, later, those of Sufi masters.

The Contemporary Aphorist

A KEEN OBSERVER AND a lover of the written word with an insatiable appetite for knowledge is how I would describe Yahia Lababidi, a Pushcart-nominated Egyptian-American essayist, poet and aphorist. I had the pleasure of reading his book, Trial by Ink, a collection of thought-provoking essays on literature, philosophy, and popular art. This book is divided into three sections, the first is a collection of essays focusing on literary giants, philosophers and lesser-known poets. You truly feel the appreciation and respect Lababidi has for the written word and the artist who is dedicated to his aesthetic. The second section of the book focuses on pop culture and larger-than-life characters. The third section gives you a glimpse of the social/cultural aspects of the Middle East , proving he has a keen eye for observation and a bravery for stating things many people will turn a blind eye to. Trail by Ink is a treasure of a book. It is written for those who like to think, converse and observe.

Here, Yahia talks to us about straddling cultures, what inspires him and he offers wonderful pieces of advice for those wanting to write.

Q. In your chapter about Susan Sontag you say she had a foot in America and foot in Europe, straddling cultures. As an Arab-American you, obviously, straddle cultures as well. Do you feel that you have one foot in the East and one foot in the West? How does this influence your work?

A. Susan Sontag remains a heroine of mine for many reasons, not least for having been an example of a world citizen and an engaged public intellectual. Although I speak Arabic, fluently, I regret to admit that I read with difficulty and do not write it. Like Sontag, my formative influences were European (specifically, German) thinkers and poets. Only recently, am

I seriously returning to the East, by way of Persian mystic poets and Sufi literature.

Otherwise, yes, there is no mistaking the fact that as an Arab American I feel a responsibility to act as an explicator of the Middle East. Broadly-speaking, I do this by best trying to represent my region through my person, offering an alternative to the simplistic and often negative portrayals of Arabs/Muslims in the US media. In that way, I believe Art is the best form of cultural exchange and diplomacy.

I was born and raised in Egypt. When I lived there, I wrote of its idiosyncrasies and wrestled with its contradictions in my writing. (Many of these pieces can be found in my essay collection, Trial by Ink: From Nietzsche to Belly-dancing.) Now, that I am based in the US, I try to engage more with American culture, its high-minded aspirations as well as its shortcomings.

But, of course, I've been moved to address the Arab Spring and the ongoing Egyptian revolution in both my poetry and prose. I even participated in a play "Still Living in Tahrir Square" that was performed in Washington DC, in an effort to promote tolerance and showcase Egypt's religious and cultural diversity.

That said, as an artist, I will say I'm wary of tackling politics, directly, and commenting on every twist and turn in the news.

Q. *You are so young and have accomplished so much. You have penned a number of books that have been translated into several languages and have traveled the world presenting your work. What words of encouragement do you have for young aspiring writers?*

A. Thank you. I have been monomaniacal in my pursuit of literature, and am lucky to publish the books I have. Still, I assure you I've been carrying them, in embryonic form, inside me, for decades. So, I suppose this would be my advice for young writers. Don't glamorize the art of writing, do the work, write. Try, at every turn, to test your responsiveness to the world, as well as the elasticity of the language, early on; treat life's experiences (good and bad) as writing prompts. Prior to writing, and alongside it, read, deeply and widely. Feed your imagination a varied diet: philosophy, psychology, ancient cultures, science, the natural world, mythology, world religions, pop culture, art in all its manifestations.

Read the Masters, see what can be achieved (we're as good as our teachers) and cast an eye at what your contemporaries are doing—even if you don't agree with it, you need to be aware of it. Also, don't decide early on what type of writer you are. Push against the parameters of your creativity, and try your hand at as many genres, and genre-bending, as you can. Meantime, of course, continue to live, attentively, so that you are one of those people upon whom little is wasted. Everything that happens to you when you're awake, even your dreams, is material for your writing. This includes all the places you visit (real or imagined) everyone you love, everything you are and become . . .

Once you find your Voice as a writer, you must commit. None of this nonsense about not having time to write, or energy. It's a matter of priorities. If you have time to breathe and eat, you have time to write. Write as if your life depended upon it because, in a sense, it does. Past word games, readers expect writers to lay their hearts bare, to say what most other people cannot or will not say. So, you need to practice the courage of vulnerability, and the state of emotional and spiritual nakedness in public; it's expected of you.

Also, share your work with writers you respect, if they are willing to take a look at it. Lastly, don't assume that the world is waiting for your work and will embrace it once you decide to release it from your clutches. If you feel you have good work, then it should be able to withstand criticism. Stop fantasizing about your unwritten books-to-be and start doing the hard work of trying to getting your work out there, in print and online journals or magazines. Now, brace yourself for rejection, years of it, or sublime disinterest. If you discourage easily, either develop a thicker skin or, if you can, choose a safer, saner existence.

Q. *How do you feel the Arab world has received your work?*

A. Funny enough, I think I am more connected to the Arab-American literary scene in the US, than I am to the Arab world. Of course, this might have something to do with the fact that I write in English (which is part of the reason why I moved to the US) as well as the reality that there are more literary magazines and outlets here than there.

That said, I am grateful to have a readership among English readers in Egypt and my books are frequently reviewed there in local magazines and newspapers, as well as stocked in bookstores. I was proud to have my first book, Signposts to Elsewhere, translated by a respected publishing house in Egypt, Dar El Shorouq. It might have helped that it was a collection of aphorisms, and Egyptians love to speak in sayings and proverbs.

Lebanon, where my father is from, has largely been disinterested in my work, give or take the odd interview. Otherwise, I was pleased to be invited to take part in a literary festival in the UAE (Sharjah).

Q. *How is an aphorist different from a poet?*

A. Aphorisms are not very different from poems and, in the West at least, several aphorists double up as poets. To be a poet is to weigh each word, carefully, and understand how to distill matters to their essences; obviously, it is the same with aphorisms. Also, aphorisms can read like micro-poetry and my book, Barely There (Wipf & Stock, Resource Publications) is actually a kind of hybrid—often times, aphorisms masquerading as short poems (or vice versa).

I've been writing aphorisms for decades, at this point, but find lately that my poetry, too, is getting shorter, tighter, possibly in response to the constraints of social media (such as Twitter). Lastly, one chief difference between aphorisms and poems is that aphorisms belong to the tradition of wisdom literature, so they are also related to philosophy as well as spirituality.

The Aphorism's Story

4 Questions by M Lynx Qualey

WHEN EGYPTIAN POET, ESSAYIST and aphorist, Yahia Lababidi, first began working with "the brief arts" decades ago, he said, they seemed to be an artistic form from a previous era. Only a few practitioners, like James Richardson, Nassim Nicholas Taleb, and Alfred Corn, worked seriously with aphorisms.

But these days, perhaps because of new social media and perhaps because of a renewed hunger for distilled wisdom, the aphorism is undergoing a revival. [Lababidi wrapped up an appearance at the Neustadt Festival, where, as a judge for the prize, he presented and read.]

> ArabLit: *How do you define them? How are they different from proverbs or maxims? Or poetry? Or cliches? Do you agree with James Geary's "five rules"?*

> Yahia Lababidi: I think of aphorisms as 'what is worth quoting from the soul's dialogue with itself.'

> How are they different from proverbs or maxims? To my mind an aphorism can be a maxim (if it is wise, universal and intended for instruction). A cliche . . . I hope not! Cliches are what's nearest at hand, tired truths that have lost their sheen, vitality and the power to shock us into recognition. Aphorisms reach further, to try and breathe new life into an old truth. An aphorism is a proverb with a name tag (proverbs tend to be nameless).

> Recently, in the US at least, there seems to be a Renaissance of aphorisms, something I would have never dreamed of when I began writing them (anachronistically, I felt) as a teenager. The practitioners of the (American) aphorism tend to be poets, and bring to them a poetic sensibility. I've just discovered that aphorisms are also a serious business

in Romania! Geary is a great collector, and popularizer of the form and I'm indebted to him in many ways . . . But, frankly, I don't care much for rules and think that to define is to limit.

AL: *Do you situate yourself in a history and context of aphorisms? Wikipedia calls the hadith "aphorisms." Do you trace an Arabic-language history of aphorisms? English? Other traditions?*

YL: Well, I think I'm more related to the aphorists I grew up reading than I am to modern ones. That's to say, I began writing aphorisms as a kind of response to my literary masters: Gibran, Wilde, Nietzsche, Blake, Kafka, Pascal, Schopenhauer, La Rochefoucauld, Lichtenberg. These were the ones that formed/deformed my mental landscape and whom I was speaking to in my head. Which, obviously, is not to say my aphorisms are on par with these giants; only that I'm in conversation with them and am mad enough to consider them spiritual ancestors.

The hadith I'm reluctant to comment on—but I would say it is closer to maxims, or wisdom writing, in general, than merely aphorisms. I'd place it alongside inspired utterances by sages, such as Confucius or Solomon, for example. I'm afraid I don't really know the origins of the aphorism. But when in doubt, I tend to attribute such things to the Ancient Greeks—who were responsible for that immortal coupling: *Know thyself.*

AL: *Do professional aphorists make use of Twitter? I have noticed Alain de Botton around, spinning what I would consider to be aphorisms. Do you think Twitter offers an interesting new venue for aphorists, a reason why the art might find new legs?*

YL: Another good and meaty question. I am fairly new to (and ever-so-slightly wary of) Twitter, but yes, there are floating around the Twitter-sphere some very accomplished practitioners of these brief arts. Alain de Botton, whom you mention, is certainly one. I first approached him, in my twenties, with my aphorisms and he mentioned to me that he writes them, too. I must add that he was very encouraging and generous, to the point of sharing with me his agents/ contacts in an effort to help me get my first book of aphorisms published! (Alas, the timing was not right and, my aphorisms took nearly a decae to find their way into the world, when American poet, Douglas Goetsch, published them through his Jane Street Press).

So, yes, there's Alain out there, and there's also a couple recent discoveries (for me): one Bo Fowler, who's an (Englishman) Existentialist type of aphorist and, one of my happiest recent discoveries, George Murray, a Canadian poet and an enviably good aphorist.

Another very strong contemporary aphorist, whom I admire and count as a friend, is American poet James Richardson (to my knowledge, he's not on Twitter though). There's also James Guida, another new discovery for me, and the only aphorist I know younger than myself (so, I'm keeping a close eye on him) but I don't believe that he's on Twitter either.

Now, onto the more challenging part of your question: might Twitter usher in new aphorists? I suspect Bo Fowler might thinks so—he finds it congenial enough and suggests Nietzsche would have loved it!. But, I'm not so sure. Brevity is only part of wit, and you can make people count their letters, but you can't make them think . . . Then again, I think it's good exercise in summarizing, considering, and distilling matters down to their essences. But, as with other forms of writing, you have to have something to say first . . . and talent helps.

AL: *Where do people interested in aphorisms find them? What do you think is the best way to give and receive them? Should they be read aloud in a performance, printed in a book, seen on Twitter amongst all the clutter, printed out and turned into art on the wall?*

YL: Well, of course there are the classic anthologies, put out by Oxford or Penguin. For a contemporary update, James Geary is inescapable, I think. Weekly, he seems to be discovering new/old aphorists on his blog. *Fraglit*, for a while, was also a great online source of aphoristic writing . . . But, they also seem to be cropping up everywhere. lately. For example, *Hotel Amerika*, a respected American journal dedicated an entire issue to them. So, those who seek in earnest, shall find.

As far as delivering them out loud, I'd never dared, until a few weeks ago. I was invited to inaugurate an Arts Festival in Maryland, Hear-Arts, where I read some of my poetry alongside a wonderful Egyptian music ensemble, Insijam (there was even a belly dancer!) When I was done with my poems, I tried out some of my aphorisms and, I daresay, they were quite well-received.

Yes, I love to see aphorisms out in the open. (Even on the page, I think they benefit from space around them, to breathe, and so that we might ruminate and better digest them). On a trip to Greenville, S. Carolina, I was thrilled to find aphorisms on cobblestones in their old-style downtown area and nearly tripped over my feet trying to read these delightfully witty, wise sayings.

Also, I'm happy to see them turned into art on the wall as you put it, on the side of schools or art galleries, and love the idea of the outdoors as a giant, open book and space to think (what aphorisms nudge us to do).

Aphorisms

A Brief Art

In conversation, Yuna Rault-D'Inca finds out about the creative process behind the art of aphorisms.

Yuna Rault-D'Inca: *Please explain to us, what exactly is an aphorism and in what way can they be poetic? And I challenge you to summarize the answers to each question in a suitable aphorism.*

Yahia Lababidi: Aphorisms are complete fragments. As with poetry, they seek to make every word matter and to contain an inbuilt music, so that they might be better remembered.

"Impulses we attempt to strangle only develop stronger muscles."

YRD: *Do you abide by James Geary's five laws to create an aphorism: brief, personal, definitive, philosophical—a certain twist?*

YL: With all due respect, I think aphorisms are laws unto themselves; the good ones surprise the writer as much as the reader. Also, I'm wary of being "definitive" about anything really, and believe rigidity is the need to conclude. I prefer that a thought be open-ended. . .

"Time heals old wounds only because there are new wounds to attend to."

YRD: *What is your own definition of an ideal aphorism and what are "other tailored thoughts"? Can you demonstrate on an example?*

YL: An ideal aphorism continues to work on us long after we've read it. It challenges our self-image, world-view and tenderly incubated biases.

"Spirituality occurs at the boiling point of religion, where dogma evaporates."

YRD: You began to write aphorisms more than twenty years ago. How did you become interested in this literary form which most of us imagine to rather being a preferential way of expression used by wise men with white beards?

YL: I am equally attracted to wit as I am to wisdom in writing, and found both in the great aphorists I grew up reading: Wilde, Nietzsche, Goethe, Blake, La Rochefoucauld, Pascal, Kafka, etc . . . Writing aphorisms was my way of talking back to my heroes. In fact, some time ago, I'm quite proud to say, I published a collection of conversations in collaboration with Alex Stein, called The Artist as Mystic, where I return to my literary masters to explore the sacred dimension of much of this type of writing.

"Miracles are proud creatures; they will only reveal themselves to those who believe."

YRD: Are professional aphorists serious men? Do you need to be drunk to create?

YL: What a strange question. "Serious" can be a dull word, in the sense of "humorless." That said, I do believe in serious play. As far as "drunkenness," I'll let Baudelaire answer this:

Be always drunken.
Nothing else matters
. . .
With wine, with poetry, or with virtue, as you will.
But be drunken.

"Pleasure, not joy, may be snatched from life's clenched fists."

YRD: Can aphorisms be fun? Give us an example of a fun way to express something in an aphorism?

YL: I certainly hope so! Here's a few that I hope might tickle you:

Marrying for looks is like buying books for their pictures—a good idea, if one cannot read.

Like cars in an amusement park, our direction is often determined through collision.

Temptation: seeds we are forbidden to water, that are showered with rain.

"Be yourself," they say. "Which one?" I think.

The problem with being full of yourself is that you cannot fill up with much else.

YRD: *Does one need to be particularly educated to understand the subtle meaning of an aphorism, or even to create one? And are they also suitable as a sort of street poetry?*

YL: I like that you compare them to street poetry. One only needs to be educated in human nature and life to appreciate an aphorism. In fact, growing up in Egypt, where wit was a kind of sport and national pastime, it was quite common to hear illiterate people speaking almost exclusively in sayings and proverbs. We even have a saying, in Arabic, that justifies this and basically translates as: "Knowledge is what is in your head, not what is in your notebooks."

"Take two opposites, connect the dots, and you have a straight line."

YRD: *Why did you translate your aphorisms into German?*

YL: To date, I've been fortunate to have my writing translated into several languages: Arabic, Hebrew, Slovak, Spanish, Italian, Dutch, Swedish and Turkish. But I will say that German was a special treat for me, since I was deeply marked by German philosophy and poetry (Nietzsche and Rilke mean the world to me). Stefan Lenkisch, the German translator, was a gift, recommended by a mutual friend of ours that I met online. It would be great, at this point, to find a German publisher that is willing to print a complete translation of my first book (of aphorisms), Signposts to Elsewhere.

"Eye contact: how souls catch fire."

YRD: *Do you think there is a language which is best suited for aphorisms, because it is more clear, more poetic, or because of its sound?*

YL: I'm not sure about that. Much as I adore language, the more one works with it, the more one realizes its limitations. I'm beginning to believe (and forgive me if this sounds too esoteric) that only a fraction of a poem or an aphorism's power resides in its skin, that is to say words. The rest belongs to the spirit that swims through it. As a Buddhist might put it, language is merely a finger pointing at the moon.

"Only after we have mastered a thing are we beyond it; this is true of bodies, emotions, even words."

YRD: *In what way do you think aphorisms are a literary expression especially suitable for today's means of communication—especially Twitter? Have we reached an age of aphorisms?*

YL: Aphorisms seem to require little of our time or attention, but actually reward patience and careful reading—so, they're deceptive that way. In one sense, yes, they're perfect for this telegraphic age—Twitter especially, where one is forced to compress thinking and practice into an economical style. But, at the same time, they are something more than sound bites, or one-liners and, as quite a few of us know, it is often harder to synthesize or be brief than to be long-winded.

"With enigmatic clarity, Life gives us a different answer, each time we ask her the same question."

YRD: *What do you think is the better form to communicate an aphorism— oral or written?*

YL: Again, hard to say. As a form of poetry or wisdom writing—or even storytelling—aphorisms address themselves to the ear, and so belong to the oral tradition. But, they also benefit greatly from private meditation. Ideally, I'd prefer to read a series of aphorisms on my own, and reflect on them, before they are read out to me.

"The thoughts we choose to act upon define us to others; the ones we do not define us to ourselves."

YRD: *How would you suggest one read a collection of aphorisms—such as your own* Signposts to Elsewhere? *There is no real story. So should we read one a day or all at once, or on a special occasion?*

YL: Thoughtfully, and chewing slowly is probably the best way to consume a collection of aphorisms; otherwise, you may give yourself indigestion. There's a reason there's only a few aphorisms per page (in my book) and that is to give us time and space to unpack them, comparing/contrasting their ideas with our own life experience.

Strange to say, the bulk of "Signposts" was composed when I was quite young, between the ages of eighteen and twenty-one; afterwards, I didn't really write aphorisms for nearly a decade or so. I'm pleased to report that I have since broken this aphoristic silence and begun writing them, again. I suspect my style, and concerns have changed somewhat.

"Self-image: self-deception."

YRD: *Short messages, the futility of the net, poetry slamming rhapsodies in the clubs: do you think "serious" and at times lengthy paper-based literature, as we knew it growing up, still has a future? In this fast moving world, are we more than ever in need of poetry? What is your own vision of the literature of the future?*

YL: Again, that problematic word, "serious." To start at the end of your questions: Yes, we are in need of slowing down, and poetry, aphorisms, or nature can do this for us, by helping us to pause and reflect. But, I do not think the brief arts threaten the longer forms, or that the virtual world need be seen in opposition to the real. There will always be room for books; only they seem to migrate from paper to screens, which is fine.

It seems futile to fight technology and the inevitable changes that come with it in how we think and interact. So, I refuse to panic or lament. I don't consider literature in critical condition or dying, simply because it's vital to our well being as a species. I firmly believe it is just as difficult not to dream by day as it is not to dream by night. Literature, and the impulse to create, will continue to live and change shape as long as we humans do.

"All must pass, if we do not first."

Trial by Ink

A Conversation with Tyler Malone

THE ENGLISH WORD "ESSAY" came from the French word "essai," which means "a trial" or "an attempt." It was first used in the way we define it today (as "a short piece of writing on a particular subject") by Michel de Montaigne, when he penned his *Essais* in the 16th century. He saw these pieces as "attempts" at putting down his thoughts into written form, hence the title.

Yahia Lababidi, an Egypt-born writer, currently living in the United States, has just released his first collection of essays. These are, like those of his predecessor Montaigne, attempts at putting down his thoughts into written form. It is fitting then, that the collection is called Trial by Ink. He writes in his introduction to the book, "These are my *trials* where I am, simultaneously, scratching my head and my pen across paper, to determine what I think about a given subject."

The subjects are admittedly quite varied. To give you a clue at what a diverse set of topics we're talking about here, the subtitle of the collection is "From Nietzsche to Belly Dancing." And that only hints at the breadth of subjects. Everything seems to be up for debate: from Michael Jackson to "Bartleby the Scrivener," from Susan Sontag to Ramadan. Though the topics vary widely, one thing remains constant: Yahia's fascination with the subjects and his depth of insight—both of which serve to make this book a surprisingly quick read, a true page-turner (something collections of essays so rarely are). When you've finished the book, you get the sense you know Yahia. You feel you've had conversations with him, and not specifically about the subjects he directly discusses in his essays, but just in a general sense.

I hadn't had any conversations with him, of course—*I had only read his essays*—but when we did get a chance to chat, I felt like I was talking to an old friend. It was like talking with someone who you don't know much about, because you've been out of touch, but with whom you have some sort of connection. Seeing as this issue is our Global Issue, I thought I'd start by asking about global politics and everything that is going on in and around the country where he was born (Egypt).

Tyler Malone: *I know this is an idiotically broad question, but just to get us started, I may as well ask it as simply and plainly as possible: what are your thoughts on the current political situations going on in the Middle East: in Egypt, in Libya, in Pakistan, in Iraq?*

Yahia Lababidi: More feelings than thoughts, and hard to summarize. At the outset, let me say that, for as far back as I can recall, I've prided myself on being apolitical. I justify this by thinking that an artist, or philosopher, is a citizen of no community and, in my defense, cite Einstein's line about nationalism being 'an infantile disease . . . the measles of mankind.' Yet I will admit that I've never felt more Egyptian than I do now. Time came to an absolute standstill for me during those eighteen historical days of the Egyptian Revolution and I continue to be surprised by how affected I am by what's been called The Arab Spring.

Obviously, as an Egyptian, I am more familiar with the Egyptian situation than say Pakistan, but I think the broad lines are similar. Enough is too much. What is now happening is necessary, and long overdue. People in the region are looking over their shoulders and taking courage from one another. It's about putting an end to injustice and the pursuit of home-made Freedom. I see it as a form of global climate change, and all these dinosaur-dictators are becoming extinct.

Drunk on Freedom, the People finally stood up to confront their bogeymen (Tunisia, Egypt, Libya, Yemen, Syria). Now comes the hangover: everyday hard work of reasserting freshly-minted values and forging a new reality.

I'm NOT fool enough to think change will come immediately or smoothly. But, I maintain it was necessary and overdue . . .

TM: *In the two weeks from when we first discussed this interview to now actually doing it, one major event in global politics has happened: Osama Bin Laden was killed by U.S. Navy Seals. Any thoughts on this?*

YL: Well, to begin with I'm not so sure how major a global event it was. Yes, an indefensible, dangerous man has been . . . *eliminated*. But, do I think the world a safer place and the celebrations in good taste? No. Really, what closure does the death of one man bring, ten years later, and at what cost, morally and politically? Speaking of Osama Bin Laden's death, Chris Hedges goes back to the response to 9/11 and makes a very fine point, I think, when he says: "the tragedy was that if we had the courage to be vulnerable, if we had built on that empathy [from around the world], we would be far safer and more secure today than we are . . . I despair that we as a country, as Nietzsche understood, have become the monster that we are attempting to fight."

Of course, I understand the sense of relief Americans have that a monster has been brought to justice, and I share in it. But, again, *at what cost*? The loss of innocence on the part of America, the erosion of civil liberties, the human cost abroad and at home is too high a price.

Immediately after the news of his death, even while the fist pumping and chest thumping was taking place, the news was bleating that we should be afraid, again, very afraid, of retaliation. *Long, windy sigh.*

It's this culture of suspicion I lament: 'see something, say something . . . even if it's a member of your own family' the talking head qualified. That level of basic mistrust in our human family simply can't be a good thing . . .

TM: *My last global/political question before we get on to specifically discussing your new book: I know it is kind of a broad question, but since in your writings you both discuss American pop culture and Middle Eastern traditions and ways of life, I'm just curious how you see in general the culture clash between the Muslim world and the West?*

YL: Again, wording is key to how we understand things. I don't see there being a "clash" between cultures. If there is misapprehension, I don't think it helpful to set it up between the Muslim world (where is that, who is that?) and the West (by that do you mean the Christian World?). Moderate Muslims, and that describes the vast majority of them in the Arab world and beyond obviously, have denounced acts of terrorism/ terrorists and suffer the consequences more than the West.

Likewise, what does it mean to wage a war on Terror? Again, unequal terms. I better understand the term "invasion" of countries, like what happened in Iraq, for example. But a "war" on terror is *absurd*, and unfortunately such military occupations have done more to engender hatred and acts of terror than anything else. At heart, I believe violence (in thought, feeling, action) is a kind of an emotional cliché: the response that is nearest at hand. We must all try to reach further. Or, as Martin Luther King put it: "Returning hate for hate multiplies hate, adding deeper darkness to a night already devoid of stars. Darkness cannot drive out darkness: only light can do that."

TM: *I couldn't agree more. In the preface to your new book of essays* Trial by Ink, *you speak of Montaigne's* Essais *(a word which in French means "trials"). Can you expound on this concept of essays as "trials by ink"? And explain why you chose that as your title for this collection?*

YL: Well, as Montaigne set out to interrogate and discover himself through his essays/trials, so I am attempting to evaluate what I care for, and generally test my responsiveness to literature and culture throughout this book. I wrote about different matters that interest me, or in which I felt somehow implicated, to figure out what I thought of a given subject. In that sense, the essays are personal trials and a form of mental autobiography. Also I like the double meaning of the word "trial." For, just as I am evaluating what I make of this or that personality or cultural tic, so I am being put on trial myself for what I believe in and stand for.

TM: *You are a poet in addition to an essayist—how do you see the relationship between those two different modes of writing?*

YL: Poetry and essays express different aspects of myself, I suppose. Probably not the most wholesome practice to divide oneself thus, but I think my mind is behind the essays, whereas the poetry is more a matter of the heart (in the sense that my prose is more concerned with the analytical and intellectual, whereas in my poems I tend to more emotional issues). But, of course, it's not so cut and dry, and not entirely of my choosing either. I do believe in the secret life of ideas and words. By this I mean their mysterious ability to choose how to dress themselves—say, in poetry or prose—before they address the world.

TM: *What made you decide to write a book on such diverse topics? Was it a conscious decision to talk about everything "from Nietzsche to Belly Dancing" as the subtitle of your collection says? Including Michael Jackson and Morrissey? And Ramadan? And Susan Sontag? Or did these disparate subjects just happen, organically?*

YL: It just happened, organically. These are the contents of my head, and the disparate parts my world is composed of. What you have before you is a catalogue of interests, obsessions, and even passing enthusiasms, derived from what I was thinking, reading, watching, dreaming and living over a seven-year period. I do feel if one is engaged with the story they're telling, the reader picks up on that sense of involvement and discovery. Whether I happen to be writing about pop culture or spirituality, I feel an intimacy for the subject matter and suspect that I stand to learn something essential about myself.

TM: *Though the subjects seem scattershot, there is some order to their presentation. Part One is "Literary Profiles & Reviews," Part Two is "Studies in Pop Culture" and Part Three is "Middle Eastern Musings." You mentioned earlier that you wrote on topics in which you "felt somehow implicated." Do you feel that these three sections put together define you in some way?*

YL: Yes. Generally-speaking, I think I wrote this book to communicate my enthusiasms, the things I care about in literature and culture, in hopes that others would, too. The third section, on the Middle East, is concerned with contradictions that bristle side by side in the region: sex and celibacy, superstition and tradition, etc. . . I do think Art can be a form of cultural diplomacy, and would like to think that a more careful examination of another culture, from an insider's perspective, might lead to a more sympathetic understanding of it. So, there's also that aspect of it.

Having made the US my home, I find that I am more engaged now with teasing out the truths and contradictions embedded within American culture, trying to inspect the national character at closer range.

But, more than anything else, what informs my work I believe are the books I've read, and most of those are neither Arab nor American, but more likely European (albeit in English translation).

TM: *What are your thoughts on the classic high vs. low culture debate? Obviously you discuss topics from both sides of that argument in this book, so do you see that binary as a false one? Is everything equal? Or is there a hierarchy in art?*

YL: I'm a generalist, I guess, and don't recognize the distinction, really. So that along with my literary heroine, Susan Sontag, I also feel compelled to declare: "I am—for a pluralistic, polymorphous culture . . . If I'd had to choose between the Doors and Dostoyevsky, then—of course—I'd have chosen Dostoyevsky. But did I have to choose?" Thankfully, I did not have to choose, either. In this collection of essays, I am able to share my passion for European thinkers and pop music—collapsing (false) distances and seeking to make connections between cultures—thereby getting to think out loud on everything that captivates me "from Nietzsche to belly-dancing."

So, I think a generalist reader would enjoy a collection like this. Someone like comedian Russell Brand, whom I very much admire, and who seems equally fond of Wilde and Morrissey, for example.

TM: *As a writer, I'd be curious to know who some of your favorite writers are: essayists, poets, novelists?*

YL: A lot of formative influences I discuss in my *Trial*: Nietzsche and Rilke are certainly up there. Contemporary essayists: I hold James Wood in high regard; Camille Paglia I think a kind of heir to Susan Sontag; Adam Gopnik and Daniel Mendelson are a delight. I don't read much contemporary fiction, I confess, but as a novelist, I find John Banville is a marvel, and in a league of his own: poet and essayist rolled into one.

TM: *What is next for you? Are you working on poetry or essays more these days? Ever consider venturing into a longer form, such as the novel?*

YL: I wish I could write a novel, but I'm afraid I don't have the breath (or perhaps the imagination) for that. I fantasize about writing a play one day, maybe even trying to collaborate on one. For now, I'm in the process of readying a poetry collection; you can get a peek at some of the poems included in that book-to-be on my YouTube channel.

Poets Online Talking About Coffee
with Russell Bennetts

Your poems often deal with spirituality. Does coffee have a spiritual dimension?

Sure, sipping, mindfully, can be spiritual. Tasting, too. And becoming more awake, obviously. These are all things that one can do with coffee. So, in that sense, to really savor the flavor of a good cup of coffee can be both a centering and transporting experience. Coming from Egypt, my proper initiation into the caffeinated universe was Turkish coffee. There, how it is prepared, how much sugar to add, when to remove it from the heat, and how to consume it are near sacred ritual.

In coffee shops across the country, possibly with a *hookah* close at hand, 'Kahwa' (coffee, in Arabic) is the impetus for wide-ranging conversations and meditations, from paltry politics to sublime metaphysics. Also, not uncommon, following this centuries-old tradition of drinking Turkish coffee is to submit to having your fortune read. That can be done either casually, or professionally, and involves having your consumed cup of coffee flipped upside down in a saucer, swiveled around a few times and set to cool, before the residual grounds—fateful lines and shapes portentous or auspicious—might be deciphered for divination.

By the time I left Egypt, I might've consumed five or more of these mini cups of 'rocket fuel' to get through a work day. Worse, I was mixing potions, and would often start my day with a shot of home-brewed Italian espresso. All of which might explain why, when I made the US my home, I steered clear of that muddy, candied water sold at Starbucks. After such authentic riches, I could not settle for poor impostors.

Fortunately, I did not have to. As an honorary Colombian citizen (my wife's father is from there) I soon made the rewarding acquaintance of Colombian coffee and was back on good, strong footing, again. Perhaps, it's sacrilegious to admit this (at least, in my family circles) but I also enjoy Brazilian and Cuban brews for similar reasons. Still, with *Prufrock*, I found that I, eventually, had to admit one day:

> I grow old . . . I grow old . . .
> I shall wear the bottoms of my trousers rolled.

Which, prosaically, translates to discovering I was no longer able to hold my coffee (palpitations, insomnia, etc . . .) Addictive, extremist personality that I have, I could not settle for just a cup or two, so I went cold turkey. Well, that's not *entirely* true. Rather, I eased into the world of tea, and gradually, sighed my way into the garden of green tea.

In the interest of full disclosure, a further humiliating confession: I, now, begin my days sipping warm water with lemon. Ah, the indignities of ageing . . . Yet, strange to say, I have come to find another clarity in my decaffeinated daze. Which is to conclude that, even at this stage, coffee still offers me (at least, two) opportunities to practice spirituality: renunciation and longing.

The Nervous Breakdown Self-Interview

Hello there. So, previously, you've composed a book of aphorisms, and then you put out a collection of essays. Why poetry, now?

Good question. I suspect that words have a life of their own and, ultimately, choose the form they wish to greet the world in. I'm just the helpless tailor.

What would you say the themes are in your poetry collection, Balancing Acts?

Hmm, themes? Time, Memory, Longing, Home (in this case, Egypt), Language, Love, Death and the tensions between Body and Spirit. [Laughing] I guess that just about covers everything. More or less the same heavies we all wrestle with, and certainly themes that I'd tackled differently in my previous books of aphorisms and essays.

Would you say that makes your poetry redundant to a reader of your previous work?

Well, just because you can hear echoes of the same concerns doesn't mean that I treat them in a similar manner. Obviously I can say things in a poem in *particular ways* that I cannot quite pull off in an essay, or even an aphorism. But, it's not like I'm exactly free to choose new obsessions.

How about the sequence of poems in your collection, is there any logic behind it?

Yes. Is it rational? No. It's just where the pieces fell in place, I guess, after a bit of pushing and pulling . . . from imperceptible magnets, you could say.

Hmmm . . . more on those magnets, if you please. Can you elaborate a little on the forces that pull your poetry together?

I'm not quite sure, but I can try. Basically, I think the poems gathered around seasons of my being. Does that make any sense? Okay, *literally*, I remember laying all the poems out on a hotel bed, somewhere—could've been New Jersey, could've been San Fran. First, there were Words (which I suppose corresponds to Mind) then came Heart, then Spirit.

What do you hope to achieve with these poems? What do you want your readers to walk away with?

I was afraid of a question like that, so I made sure to have a couple quotes handy. Here's one from my favorite (living) novelist, John Banville. "That is what art should do. It should make the world blush and give up its secrets."

Making the world blush and surrender its secrets . . . that's ambitious, and very seductive. Okay, how about you? What have you gotten out of the experience of writing this book?

You're not letting up, are you? [Smiling, long pause] Well, I can sense something shifting. For as far back as I've thought of myself as being a writer, I've revered the life of the mind, lived for and through it. You see, I'm analytical by nature and so, naturally, was drawn to philosophy. [Shifting in seat quite a bit; then, another long pause] I allowed myself to nearly worship the rational, and language . . . [Trailing off, sheepish smile]

[We sit in silence, for some time. The author gets up and returns with a flask, which he sips silently, thoughtfully. Sighing deeply, he begins again, nearly five unnerving minutes later]

Well, frankly, I'm not quite as enchanted with the power of words, or the tyranny of the mind. I find that I'm more susceptible to intuition and the spirit. [Sharp swig from his flask and, more animated now, he gets up to pronounce, quite gleefully] Even in poetry, I'm beginning to realize only a fraction of a poem's power resides in the words; the remainder belongs to the spirit that swims through them!

[Now, the author, presumably a little *tipsy*, is pacing about the room, restlessly. He steps out into the adjacent garden and, when he returns to his seat shortly, he's more subdued.]

To put it bluntly, something I'm striving for is . . . [pregnant pause] to get words to honor Silence, and echo it. [He flashes a friendly, somewhat maniacal grin] Crazy, self-defeating ambition but, with Rilke, I want to be defeated by greater and greater things.. Mining Silence is a worthy pursuit, I believe, in that it purifies language, asking it to sound such depths and essences.

[Upon the author's request, we relocate to a local bar. No sooner are we seated, he begins]

Slippery territory, I know, I know, but I think this is what Rilke meant when he referred to poems as *experiences*. Or you could call them 'excavations'. Something of such mysticism religious scholar, Karen Armstrong, alludes to in this marvelous quote: "Our theology," she says "should be like poetry . . . A poet spends a great deal of time listening to his unconscious, and slowly calling up a poem word by word, phrase by phrase, until something beautiful is brought forth into the world that changes people's perceptions . . . "

[Much as I'm enjoying these confessions, as interlocutor I feel it is my task to, at least, attempt and reclaim the reins. So, halfway into my first stiff drink, I venture:]"I'm really enjoying this . . . But, as interlocutor, I feel it is my task to, at least, attempt and reclaim the reins . . . "

Please, do. [He nods indulgently, bemused by my words]

Okay, so, let me see if I have this right. Mind is suspect; words, too; and echoing silence is what is sought. What does that leave us? Is Beauty also relegated to a frivolous concern?

On the contrary! [The author is beaming, now, as if I'd told a rather clever joke] I believe that the skin of things, the world of appearances, is of some consequence. I'm actually becoming quite obsessed with Aesthetics, lately. I think Beauty, past a superficial concern is quite important and that contemplating it makes us . . . [He's using his hands, at this point, massaging the air] Contemplating Beauty makes us finer somehow . . . morally . . . spiritually.

[Softly, he adds] Beauty is our gateway to the Eternal and Divine.

[He pulls out a crumpled sheet of paper, crowded with notes, more than a few lines highlighted] Here's a Hafiz 'translation' by Ladinsky that gets at what I'm trying to say: "The heart suffers when it cannot see and touch beauty, but beauty is not shy it is synonymous with existence." [And, with that he gets up, and marches in the direction of the restroom. I order a couple of coffees for the both of us. The author is not the least surprised to find these, upon his return. He adds sugar and cream, liberally, to his cup.]

[I clear my throat and proceed, gingerly] Back to your poetry. The illustrations, in Fever Dreams, *work quite well. Were you afraid, at any stage, that they might detract from the images your poems conjure?*

That's a great compliment, that my poems conjure images for you. It's nice when poems create visuals like that, or have their own in-built music. It means they're being experienced more fully, and are more likely to be remembered, too!

I really lucked out with John Tillson, the illustrator—another passionate student of philosophy. He's quite, how do you put it, sensitive to my hallucinations, I suppose. He basically took a look at the manuscript and spontaneously combusted into the drawings that you see throughout. I've also been fortunate to collaborate with a Belgian filmmaker and composer, Swoon, another (*Fever*) dream-interpreter, you could say!

Two of the short films Swoon made inspired by my poems, 'Clouds' and 'Unentitled' were shown in Festivals, one in the US and another in Croatia. While another video, based on my poem 'Words' was aired on national television, in Belgium, as part of a contest called 'De Canvasminuut'. [The crumpled sheet is out, again, and he breathlessly dictates to me a website] You can find some of these sometimes surreal collaborations on movingpoems.com.

I feel privileged to collaborate with gifted fellow artists, including film maker Tim Pieraccini, whose film for my poem 'If' was shown at an art gallery in Brighton (UK). I really find such collaborations breathe new life into the poetry . . . and they allow my words to visit actual places in the world that I've not been to yet!

[Before I can ask another question, he sighs, and adds, almost wistfully:] You know, I'm an *odd* bird; previously, I didn't really think collaborations were possible. They're quite novel to me, really. I always viewed writing as such a terribly private matter that I never thought I could 'play seriously' with another. But, I'm finding I *can*, with sympathetic souls. By the time they pick my work up, I'm already done. If the basic trust is there, it can be enlightening, for me at any rate, to see how an artist translates my work into another medium.

Well, I'm happy for you, to have that breakthrough. I feel like we covered a lot of ground, here. Looking back, at this stage of your career, what would you say you are most proud of?

Kind of you to ask. One of the highlights of my career is receiving emails from students, in high school and college, who've chosen to do reports or presentation on my work, and approach me with questions, etc . . . Kids are amazing, generally-speaking, and it's pretty remarkable to experience their awakening to literature, those sparks of curiosity, and somehow be able to kindle that flame. For some, obviously it's just an assignment or a fling with language but, for a precious few, it's more: the beginning of a life-long romance!

Funny thing is, the kids don't always 'understand' the poems—again, on a rational, conscious level. Yet these poems still reach them, move them, pre-words or past-words. Something in their own depths stirs . . . That's why I've always liked that Eliot line about not having to understand a poem to appreciate it.

And, while I'm bragging, shamelessly, might I be permitted two more recent highlights?

[I'm ordering the check at this point, and he does not wait for me to answer. I decide to keep the tape recorder running, anyhow, as I see my next appointment has been cancelled]

Another great honor [he continues, beaming proudly] has been having a poem of mine, 'What do animals dreams?' chosen for a widely-used US college textbook, Literature: an Introduction to Reading and Writing.

As a younger person (and until today, really) I regarded books as a kind of life support machine—stretched across space and time. I'm greatly indebted to a band of intimate strangers, writers and poets, who altered my mental/emotional landscape, and feel very grateful to be able to give back, somehow.

More incrediby . . . [Here the author grows solemn] I had the honor of being chosen as a juror for the Neustadt International Prize for Literature. After the Nobel Prize for Literature, the Neustadt is, generally, considered the most prestigious international literary prize. So, it's a tremendous privilege at this stage of my writing career to be one of nine jurors who get to be part of the decision-making process at this level . . .

Congratulations, good for you! Well, I think that's a wrap. Wait; how about forthcoming projects? Maybe, in just a line or two?

Hah! Now that I've shaken a few fruits off my tree, I'm asking myself the same question, what's next? More poetry, I suppose. But, before that, a spot of literary soul-gazing. Into the souls of my literary masters, as a way of saying: Thank you, and goodbye. I mean people like Nietzsche, Rilke, Kafka, Kierkegaard, Baudelaire. The ones who did me in as a late teen and from whom I'm still recovering. So, the idea is to put out a book of conversations with Alex Stein, where we explore the notion of The Artist as Mystic. [Sotto voce] A couple of these mad talks are already out in *Agni*, if you care to take a peek.

I'll be on the lookout. [Getting up and extending my hand.] Thank you for this . . . dizzying conversation! Any last words? [I hold the door open for both of us, and linger]

No, thank *you*, for indulging me, and enduring this artist's metaphysics. [He bows, gravely.]

Underground Revisited

with an introduction by Brian Chappell

INTRODUCTION

IF WE WANT TO call Yahia Lababidi's work since Trial by Ink fiction, we should do it for lack of a more accurate term. Like *Trial*, the following, titled "Underground Revisited," exists between genres. We have an invented speaker and audience, and a steady flow of ideas and verbiage. But we don't have a manageable Aristotelian plot, or any sort of substantial tension between characters (except for the occasional thrown shoe). This is man v. himself. Sounds more like a long poem.

On the surface, "Underground Revisited" is a hardy homage to Dostoevsky, a stylistic parody, in the Hutcheon-esque postmodern (i.e., aesthetically and theoretically productive) sense of the word, that, as a good parody does, reaches beyond mere play with form, that says something about that form via repetition and imitation. Here, Lababidi continues the aim of his major work, namely, that of answering big questions.

As he told me, literature hasn't changed that much. It's still people trying to deal with living in their own skin and among others in a society. That's precisely what's going on here. Notes from Underground is so timeless because it, as Dostoevsky's novels so masterfully tend to do, poses fundamental questions about human existence. Lababidi is up to much of the same.

His speaker, like Dostoevsky's, is self-loathing, but attention-starved, deep-thinking, but obsessed with action. He feels trapped between personal codes of being, imploring his (in this case, literal) audience for advice and understanding. Both stuck and unstuck, he struggles to put one intellectual foot in front of the other. This uncertainty cuts to the core of what it means to participate in a discourse, but, more importantly, of what it means to try to get along in one's own life.

UNDERGROUND REVISITED BY YAHIA LABABIDI

Abominable Ladies and Gentleman, thank me for coming!

Tonight, I empathize with every one of you. I'm overcome by a peculiar affection encompassing all and, almost, myself. I do not lie . . . now! Just how long I shall continue to experience this curious condition, I do not know. There are no constants and there are no certainties. Yes, there are none, certainly. We are merely figures of fun moved by unseen forces, which have no right to make any claims to knowing ourselves. (Nor can we assume any credit for our actions, only blame).

It's important, therefore, that we recognize the notion that we should accept ourselves, fully, for what it truly is: a fallacy. We most certainly should do no such thing. To accept oneself, fully, is to assume responsibility for all that wanders in the wasteland of our heads and, that is a most dangerous thing to do. Instead, one should only judge oneself by their actions, and not for their thoughts. Thought is thwarted action, impotent action, unactualized action; active but not action. The thoughts we choose to act upon define us to others, the ones we don't define us to ourselves.

Only partially, of course, for one can never fully know themselves, nor should they want to. The over examined life is even less worth living than the unexamined one, trust me. A little knowledge is a dangerous thing, true, but a lot is absolutely fatal . . . particularly self-knowledge. It is a wonder that people are able to identify on any level at all with others -family, friends, or lovers—when they are unable to identify with themselves. How they do it, I shall never know. Which is not to say that I should not care to know but, the truth is, I do not care to know. I care much more for extraordinary personalities than I do for ordinary persons; and I shall continue to be consumed by character until the day I live (which must account for my most shameful self-absorption). But, I do hope you don't believe every word I've said, however, even I don't. Or, perhaps, especially I don't. But more likely, affectations aside, I don't entirely. Believe every word I've said, that is. You see, I most certainly do not 'see the world steadily and whole'. Rather, I see it oscillating wildly and fragmented. But, everything is difficult to see when one will not open their eyes. I know that. I'm aware that I am walking around with one eye firmly shut, and the other half open. Don't be alarmed. I'm all too aware that I only say half-truths, and that I've lived even less than what little I've seen, all theory and hardly any practice.

With me, there can only be so very little life in my life for it to be livable; any more life and I could not continue; any more light and I would go blind. Yes, I'm all too aware of that. I am aware. I have the suffering of awareness, though, and not merely the awareness of suffering (which is only its offspring). But, please, don't take me too seriously—it's enough that I do.

I'm sorry if you do not find the program amusing so far; I don't either. Why should I make myself amusing to you when I can't find myself amusing? Why should you be able to enjoy me, when I can't enjoy myself? Don't answer me! An answer would rob me of my uncertainty, and that is all I have left. Without it I am left with nothing. Please, don't answer me. But, believe me, I wasn't always this way. I wasn't always a haunted man. You would not have recognized me then, just as I do not recognize myself, now.

You know, the metamorphosis of others from friends to strangers is not so tragic, even if it occurs overnight. To become a stranger to oneself, until one no longer knows who they are . . . that is. Still, one ought not to be suspicious of change, for it might be the only constant. And if history books are littered with instances of hardened sinners becoming selfless saints, then why can't a clumsy, careless clown exchange his costume for the cloak and crown of a sad, thoughtful philosopher? Just why not? But, it is not proper to discuss such matters with strangers. I can see you're already uneasy. There's no reason why you should not be able to enjoy yourselves.

You sir, the one with the divided nature, can enjoy yourself twice, or thrice, or however many times you are unable to identify with yourself. I, on the other hand, shall continue exploiting my selves. Why? Because I am an entertainer, first and foremost, and I am not to forget that ever again, if ever I hope to become a human being, secondly. What does he mean by that you might ask, if I permit. You see, I am not altogether human. Humane, yes. Human, no. But, how can you see? If you could, then it would not be a curse and, I am cursed. Cursed to find differences where there are none, and to ignore the differences that exist. I am the abominable one. Really, it's a shame. No doubt you came counting on being amused, astounded with witticisms, perhaps, and instead you have been abused by being made to witness this savaging, of one abusing himself. Perhaps I should recite you some sublime passage from one of the unassailables, those immortal untouchables, and charm you with the breadth and width of my learning . . .

I apologize, again. I've merely forgotten my place, that is all. Yes, indeed to forget one's place is most certainly all. It is the single greatest crime one can commit against oneself and one's fellows. And, I have done so, repeatedly. But, trust me, when I say that I do so against my will. I am the victim of a virus which deforms and defiles and destroys. No, I am not that. I am the virus itself. So, lest it prove catching, I ask you all not to listen too closely. My origin is unknown, my destination unavoidable. In a void, able. I am. In a void, I am able. *Inavoidiamable.* There, that's something, at least. If nothing else, I have given you a new word: "inavoidiamable." Now, tell me where have you heard such a thing, before? Nowhere, I am sure, for I have not heard it before. I'm sorry, that is another fault of mine, that I cannot imagine. To assume that you have not heard of a word simply because I have not is arrogant. To not imagine, that is the single greatest crime one can commit against oneself and one's fellows. The fact of the matter is, I have tried to concentrate on the world within to the exclusion of the world without, for some time now. That is why I cannot imagine. But, I have only tried, and failed. All along I was aware of—no, I impatiently awaited—the world without. Even when my vessel began to sink I only waited aboard, bored, not to learn a lesson in survival but so that I might tell a tale later. Not share, but tell a tale, like the sole survivor of a shipwreck. No, like the soul survivor . . .

Honorable ladies and gentleman, I have a confession to make: I have no soul! None whatsoever. It's very likely that, due to disuse, I also stand to lose my body, soon. For, just as Evolution suggests that we lost a tail for which we had no use, I am to lose a body I cannot use. Already, I have witnessed my soul silently slipping away from my body, disgruntled and disgusted, unable to play another (false) part except the one written for it— whose language I was unable, or unwilling, to decipher.

Since then, I have forgotten my place as I said. I have borrowed from other souls, much richer, finer, nobler, than the one I do not possess; and, I continue to do so, even as we speak. In exchange, I have loaned myself, only to realize I was over-drawn and artificially propped up on bounced reality checks. That's why I must stand here, and you must sit over there. I must not allow myself to get any closer to you; it would not be fair to either of us. So, please, do not approach me; do not answer my questions; do not even look my way, lest you pity me. You may however, ask me questions—although I feel obliged to state the obvious: I have far more questions than answers.

Yes, sir, in the front row, in the middle. What? How dare you say you are in my position when we do not inhabit the same imaginative universe? I have accessed regions of my soul you do not possess. I have traveled land-scapes of the mind you cannot fathom. I have had rarified sentiments you are not entitled to. What do you say? You want concrete evidence. With all due respect, sir, I am not a construction worker! I do not deal with the concrete. It is the abstract I traffic in. But, if you must, I will give you clear and irrefutable reason why we are not in the same position.

You, sir, are comfortably seated. I am standing, always, and uncom-fortably at that. What's more, you are in the middle, balanced, moderate. I, my good man, am an extremist. I would sooner be beneath that seat in the farthest corner than exchange places with you. I'm sorry. I've forgotten my oath, to myself really more than anyone else: to empathize. Believe me, I do not mean what I say; if I did, I wouldn't feel the slightest need to say it. It is but an act, though I am not an actor, per se.

I can only act offstage, before close acquaintances or distant friends. Still, I ought to try and act more naturally. Really, it's only that I'm in love with my own voice. I am like the bird that, seduced by her song, cannot stop singing throughout the seasons and catches her death of cold in winter (if not of exhaustion, beforehand). No, I am not in the least like a bird. The bird is as beautiful as its song. I can only offer sparkling *whine*. I apologize; I shall not lapse into such extravagant self-indulgence, again.

Thank you, sir, for throwing your shoe in my face. I don't deserve it. You are far too kind and considerate to throw only one shoe. Really, you show such restraint. Yes, madam. You, without the arms, in the arms of the furry fellow. Well, what about Love? Yes, by all means, I believe in it. What it does not create in us, it compliments. It is perhaps the last of the miracles. Its chief allure is how unrealistic it is, yet how senselessly we pursue it. Then, when we think we've found it, how senselessly we chase it away. What is that you say? Oh, no! No, my good lady. You have entirely misunderstood me, and I'm sure that is a fault of mine—since those who are consistently misunderstood must be to blame, somehow.

No, I do not believe in the possibility of love in my situation. I very much feel I am denied this possibility. Unless, of course, I were to find one who were constructed, and then deconstructed, in a similar vein. Frankly, I don't think that at all possible since I'm doing all I can to avoid looking for, or being found by, such a non-person. I say: I will never fall in love and, I don't. It is a self-fulfilling prophesy. Now, tell me, who says there are no more prophets when there are prophesies? Just as, who says there are no more miracles when there exists even the idea of Love?

I tell you, whoever says anything at all has spoken too soon. They are bound to discover the inverse truth, sometime after, perhaps when it is already too late to benefit from. That's why it's best to say nothing, or else everything, if one possibly can. Personally, I never mean what I say when I say it. I might mean it tomorrow, or yesterday. But, never today. That is why I feel that the only thing I cannot endure more than being misquoted is being quoted at all. It is simply maddening. You can quote me on that.

Actually, please do. It would do me a great deal of good to have my words echoed by strangers. It might even restore my faith in humanity, and bring me to embrace the person who uttered those dear, dear words. Yes, sir, with the broken spirit. What is it? o! My God . . . my goodness! What a startling question. I don't quite know how to respond, or if I ought to at all. It is important to refuse to answer certain questions, on principle, since one can't speak lightly about absolutely everything. But wait. I've already answered your question indirectly, which is the best way to answer any difficult question, anyhow. Your answer is "my God . . . my goodness." The two are interchangeable for me. No, they are not. That is far too simple an answer to such a complex question.

I believe there is injustice and there is imbalance; there is evil and wrong doing; there is sickness and suffering; poverty of the body and spirit. How then can I, or any intelligent, seeing human being say that all is good. If we are created in His image, therefore it should follow that He is capable of greater good, and harm, than we are. We are limited, He is limitless. 'The greatest leap of man's mind is to realize its limitations.'

What's that, sir, you say about heaven and hell? I have not made myself clear on that point? Does that mean I have been clear on all others! Please, see me after this is all over and explain it to me, will you. Yes, heaven and hell, there's no denying them. Only not in the next world, Heaven and hell are here. Every day is Judgment Day. If you go unrewarded in your life, then, you must be good; and that, in and of itself, is your reward (and punishment). Yes, it is all absurd and senseless, particularly for the sensitive few who would like to believe otherwise.

Yes, Miss, with the bookcase on your back. One must think everything and do nothing? Are you suggesting then, learned lady, that thinking is not doing? Now, you must be sounding like me to amuse me. But, believe me; I am not amused to hear you repeat such things when I do not fully believe in them myself. I may amuse myself with such folly, you may not. You dishearten me. I did not think it possible to influence persons before, and I do not still.

We receive only the stations our antennas attract, which is why we should keep our antennas out at all times in the hopes of picking up all our stations. Otherwise, I cannot persuade you of what you do not already believe in the dawning of your knowledge. I cannot awaken in you what is not dormant. I cannot plant a seed where there is not fertile soil. That is why it disheartens me that you should be like me in any way. Not that I feel I have affected you, for if you had not heard my words now, it would have been any incident or accident later that would have stirred you to those words. Yet, I wish it were not my words, and that you had heard them elsewhere.

You are far too clever to join the daily increasing ranks of the overfed and undernourished. That is what it means to be overeducated. But, it is not a fault that cannot be undone (sadly, it takes far longer to 'unlearn' than it does to learn, just as it is nearly impossible to 'unsee' what one has already seen). It can be achieved, however, and I am living proof of it. Although, perhaps "living" is too strong a word. Still, I am proof of it, nevertheless. You must not quote any more of those journals or 'important' authors, however. Or at any rate, if you must, then do so with some feeling. Where is your passion? Without it, you are merely a corpse with a borrowed mouthpiece, an ass carrying a bookcase, that's all. Intellect without sentiment is a cold, concrete structure without either doors or windows. Structurally solid, it is uninhabitable to the occupant, and impenetrable to the passerby.

Yes; the elderly gentleman with the black tears and soil in his hands. No, sir, I could not possibly make light of your grief. What you hold in your hands is the Body of God. Yes, the Body of God is not invisible, it is Nature. How can we be in awe of one and not the other? It is the land, the sea, the air and the Infinite Universe. In which case, Humanity must occupy God's nether regions. I apologize, that was careless of me . . . but not thoughtless. I do see the stars in space as His upper body, which can only mean . . . God is not dead.

Nature is independent of us yet, we are dependent upon it. It goes about its natural cycles as it did before we came to be, and will continue to do so long after we cease. We have not tamed nature, we have only maimed it: with electric blades and metal claws that pierce, tear, torture and spoil the air, earth and waters. Or what we call: travel. Then monstrous machinery that devastates and contaminates its skin and soul. This we call: the cost of living. Next to those weightless clouds, Industry has contributed their own leaden clouds to choke the skies. Yet, we shall pass and It shall remain, majestic and mysterious, mocking us who have named it and so think we have known it.

So, sir, I share your grief. For all our private and public worlds—and the monuments built to honor our accomplishments, thought forms and inventions—we are no more than a passing interference, insignificant in the laughing eyes of Eternal Nature. Yes, to be natural in thought and deed is divine. I, however, cannot be natural even when I sleep, or view nature except with envious eyes in my waking hours. There is no hope for me. But surely you, young man with the clear glass eyes, can see that it is not too late for you to be saved, provided you do not grow any further.

No, please, no! You should not wish to grow like me, mine is a malignant growth. I speak since I am not at peace with my silences. My words are elaborate because my thoughts are unclear. You speak with the simplicity of sincerity. Why you would want to emulate me worries me immeasurably and reminds me of the poisonous charm of words. Please, not another word or I shall expose myself! I must forget all that I am to be happy, you must only remember. There is no use denying that yours' is the superior state. Do not think that because you have the knowledge of happiness, then I must possess the happiness of knowledge.

Happiness and Knowledge are not to be wed in my world. For the feeling person, Ignorance is Happiness; and for the thinking person, Happiness is Ignorance. This I know. Ignorance on the first, simple, and natural level of existence is the prerequisite for Happiness, while on the second, more complex (hyperconscious) level of existence, it is the contrary: Happiness is considered Ignorance. But there exists a third level where Happiness and Knowledge can coexist. The selfless few who arrive at this state are those who 'see the world steadily and see it whole'. But, I've already spoken *ad nauseam* on where I stand in relation this notion. . .

All of a sudden, I realize I am weary with fatigue, and I'm sure you feel the same. Thank you, for your patient audience. What's that? One more question? What a terrific trick that is you are performing, sir! Or, is it madam? What do you say? It is not a trick, it is a talent? A gift from God? No, I beg to differ. Look where you are seated, my dear ma . . . friend. The seats by your side are vacant, though there is a shortage of seats. You are all alone. Lately, I am of the opinion that a talent is both a blessing and curse, not one or the other.

Any remarkable ability, as such, which differentiates one from the herd, that is talent, true. But, as a result of it, you will not be viewed with tenderness and understanding; and perhaps as a result of it, too, you will not be able to view others with tenderness and understanding. You call that a gift? No, I must differ with you. I must be allowed to leave, now. I am too tired to continue this charade any longer. Also, I have already said too much, although to some of you, it might seem like I've said nothing at all. Whatever the case . . . Honorable ladies and gentlemen, thank you for coming.

Wait! Don't go. I do not wish to be alone, anymore. I have nowhere to go. There, I have said it! And I said it with neither trembling lip, nor quivering voice. I said it rather bravely and matter-of-factly. Because, I have enough energy to continue. I have to have enough energy to continue. And, sir, when I am done—when I am truly over and done with, and no longer of any use to anyone—then you may throw your other shoe in my face. In fact, please, do so at once; I cannot stand the suspense. Thank you! Now, where was I before I so rudely interrupted my selves?

Oh yes, the fatal gift of talent . Yes, I'm sorry I stand by that. Forgive me, but I cannot take any more questions. Why? Because for every question of yours I entertain, I ignore one of my own. So, the format shall continue to be question and answer; only I shall be asking the questions and answering them. It shall be better this way for all of us. Trust me. But, please, stay a while longer. I require your presence for inspiration. I'm afraid if you leave, my muse shall, too. Also, if you stay, I promise to be more honest than I have been before, within the confines of the impossibility of honesty, of course.

What then, is the impossibility of honesty? Simply, it is to say that complete honesty with oneself is impossible and, with others improper. What one can do however is to bridge the gulf between what is said and what is done. (Perhaps also between what is thought and what is said). That is the utmost extent of honesty anyone can afford. How very polite of you, sir, to nod so understandingly while I am speaking. Really, manners are everything. Manners and Morals, and all the more so if they are natural (and not the product of some pretentious finishing school). More than anything, manners simultaneously express respect and self-respect; and morals enforce them.

Which brings one to ethics. What of ethics? Can ethics exist outside of society? Absolutely! One is ethical for one's sake. Not only do ethics exist outside society, they exist only outside of society, since the ethics within society are simulated and inauthentic. For God's sake, ethics exist outside of organized religion, as well, which accounts for the irrefutable goodness and non-judgmental stance of some atheists. All that is well and good is not found without, but within, irrespective of whichever club one is a member of. It is important not to lose sight of that in one's lifetime, just as it is important never to lose sight of one's death during one's life.

What do I mean by that? "Death destroys a man: the idea of death saves him." To realize that the day shall come when one will lie beneath the earth they tread upon, and to realize that day might be tomorrow, is very wise indeed. Such a realization either endows one with a sense of urgency or futility. As always, the answer lies not in the middle, but in the continual excursion between either extreme. Yes, the senselessness of life and the senselessness of death, that is what one should preoccupy oneself with. Nothing else matters, other than Art, not Science.

What a bore Science is with its relentless insistence on evidence and proof and, how unrealistic that is. There is no proof, and there are no guarantees! Proofs of purchase and guarantees accompany appliances, not us. Which is all the more reason never, ever, never to lose sight of death or attempt any number of ways of maintaining a firm foothold in the quicksand that is life. Make no mistake, we are sinking, and we shall all soon be submerged. There is no avoiding it. Why the startled look, how could you have thought otherwise? Or had you simply not thought? Still, that's no reason not to live because you must die. There is life to live for, and Art.

What is Art? It depends on whom you ask: the artist, or the public. To the artist, Art is the act of clearing their throat to find a Voice, silencing the voices in their head, and luring from its lair what is secretive or mysterious.

It is the act of dressing the invisible, of giving form to the formless. Only by becoming a slave to Art can the artist ever hope to master Life. To the general public, Art is a beautiful translation of the transition that is Life, rendering it more possible to endure. But, Art is not reserved for artists, alone (and, truth be told, many artists are poor artists at that). There are those rare souls who live, artfully, and make of their lives a work of art. Ultimately, to burn brightly with one's own Art, that is the purpose of life (if indeed there is one).

What then, is the greatest sin one can commit? Desistance. To recognize one's passion and not pursue it: to realize and refuse. To ignore your calling is heresy. In which case, I must be damned . . . But, never mind me. Please, never mind me; I mind me enough as it is. Anxiety-ridden and doubt-driven, I am. I wonder: if one forgets about themselves, will they be forgotten? I don't know. I know I don't know. I also know endless self-scrutiny is fruitless. To concern oneself constantly with the endless possibilities of one's growth, and in which direction is, as sure a way as any, to stunt growth. But what can one do?

We are not free . . . to do anything. We are free up to a point, but not Free in the absolute sense. We suffer from a restricted freedom. We are free, within a cage. Yet we are also given a key—not to the cage, of course, but ourselves. This way, we have the possibility of being free, to surprise others and ourselves. But, the true surprise is how hesitant we are to act. And when we do, just how helpless.

Excuse me, may I ask you a question, sir? What is the difference between you and that horse you are riding? There's no need to take offense, an answer will suffice. No, I mean other than that it is an animal, and that it is mounted, since both of those conditions apply to the human condition. What do you say? There are no differences, then? No, sir, you are mistaken, again. There is one, one chief difference you have overlooked. The difference between you and your horse is that his blinders are removable. What do I mean by that? Just that his blinders are external and can be discarded; whereas ours are not and cannot.

Don't be so surprised. We all wear blinders that determine what we see and don't, and accordingly, what we respond to and how. Some of us only see what is ahead of us, while others only see what is around them. The rest of us are looking at our noses. I do not see anything since my eyes are not in accord. But, I promised not to discuss myself, further . . .

How much time and energy we exhaust discussing ourselves when we are, merely, symbols. Collectively, we are a physical manifestation of the complex character of Creation. Just as Nature is the Body of God, all of Human Nature is His Soul. That, I believe, is why we are here: to act and interact in such a way as to make manifest to Him the possibilities of His Being. But, this is not a solemn sermon—much as it may sound like one—since I am not in the position either to be solemn, or present a sermon. Perhaps, I should speak of something else, then. How about aesthetics and insects? Yes, insects and aesthetics, it is. And, o, what a frightful emphasis in our infinite vanity do we place on aesthetics!

You do not agree? Look at a cockroach. Now, look how you recoil in horror. Look at your lips, upturned in disgust, and how your eyes long to recede to the back of your skull. Now, consider a ladybug, and consider your delight. Watch a fly, then, a butterfly. What is it about appearance that allows us to dismiss creatures so carelessly, and approach others so eagerly? What do we know of the nature of the black beetle that depicts it as any less loveable than the lady bug, or the butterfly? It is not harmful, nor is it lacking in usefulness; it only commits the unpardonable crime of not being pleasing to the eye. Likewise, why am I addressing myself to the attractive members of the audience, the more visually arresting of you? Is it because we assume, somehow, that Beauty is a kind of benediction, while ugliness expresses varying degrees of sin. Or, is it more superficial, but more meaningfully revealing, than that? I don't know. Whatever the case, it is a temptation that must be avoided. No, that's wrong. Can you tell me what is wrong with that sentiment? I'll tell you. Temptation is not to be 'avoided', it is to be resisted. To be present and resist, not to distance yourself and avoid, that is noble. But, I have nothing in common with nobility. I tremble before temptation. I must avoid it, since I'm not strong enough. Okay, sir, you may now throw your other shoe in my face; I am over and done with. You already have? Very well, then, I shall exit, anticlimactically. At least, it is closer to the Truth that way. Thank you again and, please, remember me in your prayers.

Voices

Multiple Philosophies Speak Gently to Us

Idealist: We are gathered here to solve the Mystery of Life, no less!

Nihilist: We are thrown here to discuss Nothing, no more!

Idealist: Then the discussion has already begun.

Nihilist: Long before we arrived, and without our consent.

Idealist: Let us persist, then. Will everyone please state their position in one word?

Nihilist: 'Anti-life'.

Idealist: That's a hyphenated word.

Nihilist: 'Hyphenated' then is my word of choice—divided, neither here nor there: nowhere.

Optimist: I say 'hopeful'.

Pessimist: I 'hopeless'.

Optimist: Can't we discuss something more uplifting?

Pessimist: I thought the reason we're here is to discuss Life.

Nihilist: There's no reason why we're here.

Idealist: Then let us create one!

Pessimist: It's hopeless. We've tried many times before, and only failed.

Optimist: That's no reason not to try again. Life is, after all, only one long trial to overcome.

Pessimist: No. Life is only one long protracted error . . .

A mellifluous Voice is heard from no discernible source:

234

Voice: You are both wrong—just as you are both right. Life is neither trial nor error alone. Need I remind you that none of you are in any position to take any positions against Life?

All: Who are you?

Voice: You don't know? You all speak of me with such confidence, and yet you don't recognize my voice? Have you grown so accustomed to speaking of me behind my back that you don't recognize my face?

Nihilist: Whoever you are, you seem to be forgetting that you were not invited.

Voice: You should not always speak so quickly. It is not for you to invite me. It is you who are *my* guests.

Idealist: You are certainly welcome to join us, as your presence will no doubt make for a richer discussion. And while it is good of you to think of us as your guests, in truth, it is we who are the hosts, here.

Voice: I do not doubt that you think so. But, in fact, your good intentions have done me more harm than the malicious lies of others. Yet, I forgive you, for you know me the least of all.

Idealist: I'm sorry to say that I do not know you. As a matter of principle, I do not pass judgment on those I do not know.

Voice: It is true that you do not know me. Yet, truly, you think you do. As for not passing judgment on those you do not know, you invent far too much to ever know things as they are.

Idealist: What's wrong with aspiring to climb higher?

Voice: Absolutely nothing, provided you realize when you've climbed past the mountain top and are standing on thin air.

Nihilist: Peaks and valleys, they're all the same to me: they do not exist. There's only the thin air. Bitterly cold, thin air, howling through an eternal night.

Voice: How like the Idealist you are—how you exaggerate. Neither of you can avoid substituting part of the truth for the whole. Still, you are the more dangerous. It's true the Idealist does me some harm when he shuts his eyes; but you do me even more when you open yours. What he creates, you destroy. And you do not stop there. You also destroy what already exists. Blind in one eye, you obstinately shut the other and claim to describe what you see with your 'open' eye. But, you only describe shadows, and not the Light that casts them.

Pessimist: Granted the Nihilist exaggerates—but don't the shadows, sometimes, loom larger than those who cast them? And don't gray clouds often blot out the bright light of the sun?

Voice: Yes, 'sometimes', and 'often'.

Optimist: Yet shadows do not occupy space, and clouds come and go. Isn't that enough grounds to dismiss them altogether?

Voice. Yes, if you can dismiss ideas on the same grounds.

Idealist: What are we to do?

Voice: (*musing*) I do not know myself—I change too often. Simple, serious and severe one moment, complex, reckless or even playful the next. (*Exclaiming*) Learn to ride a wild animal, I say! Then you will know what it means to be flexible and firm, simultaneously. And now, I must leave. If ever you wish to summon me, you have only to speak all at once, and you shall hear my voice, once more.

Nihilist: No! You must not leave until you've confessed your most awful secret.

Voice: Now, you want me to stay? Well, you have piqued my curiosity. Tell me, which of my 'most awful' secrets are you referring to?

Nihilist: The secret against whose hardness my most bitter scorn seems as sweet as a child's innocence: Nothingness!

Voice: I confess Nothing.

Idealist: What are you two saying? I hope you're not suggesting that one live without hope?

Nihilist: No, only without illusions.

Idealist: I do not blush before the naked beauty of Universal Truth!

Nihilist: You should! Universal Truth is a worldwide lie. It's a cover-up for Universal Absurdity.

Idealist: That's absurd! What do you propose I do with Nothing?

Voice: Create. You can all create out of Nothing. (*To the Idealist*) Build towering sandcastles, if you must; but be careful that you do not build a Tower of Babble. Build life-size, and with your eyes on the Sea.

Nihilist: And knock down what you've built before the Sea does.

Voice: It's best not to flirt with disaster, lest it decide to commit.

Idealist: But what of enlightenment?

Nihilist: What of it? Of what use is being enlightened in an entirely darkened world?

Optimist: What, then, of the ravishing music of Life? What is there to be suspicious of about that?

Pessimist: The music itself. It's the soundtrack to a game of musical chairs. Always moving from one seat to the next—round and round, up and down, with never a moment's rest. And for what? Only to have the music stop, abruptly, and to find yourself standing alone.

Optimist: Except for the winner. They always remain seated. One can hope—no, pray—to be a winner.

Pessimist: In a game of constant unrest and mistrust there can be no winners. Our only hope, if there is any at all, is to pray for an early release based on good behavior.

Nihilist: You pray, and Chance decides. As for the minority of winners whom Chance favors, what's next for them? Still, Nothingness. Life is too set in her ways to change for anyone. She is indifferent to everything.

Idealist: The Music, the Dance of Life, these are certain. The End, too. But, not the *After*. That must remain an uncertainty to look forward to.

Nihilist: No. The After must remain a too-late uncertainty.

Idealist: Even should you die and go to Heaven?

Nihilist: I don't expect as much. It is enough to die. That to me is Heaven: the end of meaningless suffering, the only ever-lasting peace. Blessed are the unborn, and cursed are the rest.

Optimist: Enough! Where has the Voice gone?

Pessimist: It has left us to ourselves.

Nihilist: Again.

Variations on Feet

THERE ARE, AT LEAST, as many types of feet as there are people (and, of course, no two feet are alike). There are feet harmonious, though differently-abled. Like long-married couples adapted to one another's rhythms, they lean lightly on their partner, adept at side-stepping obstacles and shouldering life's burdens. Then there are obstinate individualists, dissonant, each marching to a different drummer, mutinous, as though wishing to jump ship, altogether.

Within those types, there are worlds of feet. Ones that know their place: unpretentious, down-to-earth, faithful to the soil, fleshy or plump, content to do their work in peace. Or, feet that have forgotten their place: ostentatious, haughty with upturned toes, higher-than-thou arches. Or there are pampered feet accustomed to attention, petulant, and given to perpetual tantrums. Fallen feet, blackened souls, sly, reckless, or irresponsibly sensual. Feet capable of extreme feats—dexterous, artistic, ascetic.

Dear Eighty-Year-Old Self

HAVE YOU FOUND PEACE, yet? Have you relinquished the remaining gifts of youth, gracefully? Are you still enamored of the world of appearances, and the charm of words? Or are you, finally, more at ease with your inner life and sitting still, now?

Tell me, what became of all your noisy spiritual tourism—do you continue to dally with this and that, or have you found the courage to commit to a life-sustaining discipline? Did your literary career turn out quite the way you hoped it would, or did you turn your back on it to save your soul?

Remember when you were younger, full of doubt and self-defeating habits? You could not imagine turning twenty-five, because of all the inner hurdles you had to clear; you suspected you'd sooner self-destruct. Then, turning thirty, you felt old, almost like you were outliving yourself . . .

Well, as you know, something marvelous was set in motion around forty. You began to realize your mortality was not an abstraction and to recognize that your pass, for unconscious-living, was slowly being revoked. You started trying to pay better attention. I wonder, elder-me, how this letter (composed during the tumultuous sea-change of your mid-forties) will sound to your experienced ears?

Imagine a New Religion

IMAGINE A NEW RELIGION where small-minded bickering—say, over whose god was better—was not permitted. Likewise, murderous ignorance, where you might lose your life or liberty because how you lived did not suit the hateful interpretation of a so-called believer. Where self-righteousness was banned, since all your time and energy were consumed sorting yourself out, too busy to accuse, point elsewhere, or wag that finger. What if you were not allowed to utter that Unutterable Name until you'd actually earned it, perhaps, as the last word on your deathbed? What might such a religion look like . . .

This, of course, is the old religion, covered in dust, disinterest and misinterpretation. What if we were to approach it, fresh, with Beauty, Attention, Love and Awe as the pillars of the new-old religion. By, prayerfully, admiring the rose of existence, we would stand to be made finer morally, and spiritually, as we practice the ethics of aesthetics. A holy curiosity and wonder would help us to better appreciate, and experience, Emerson's definition of prayer as: "the soliloquy of a beholding and jubilant soul."

Adherents of this new, Nameless faith would be required, as artist-mystics, to submit their private lives in the service of intensifying consciousness, through fasts, silence and odes to joy. Their entire lives could be carefully arranged around the conditions most conducive to the ripening of gratitude. We might begin to practice the art of living and sanctify our days with a humble walking meditation, such as this:

Try and leave everything in your path in slightly better shape than you found it: the home in disarray, the neglected pet, the lonely neighbor, the homeless person on the bench, the hungry birds in the parking lot, the despondent stranger in the elevator, the overworked elder at the checkout, the trash-littered sidewalk, the overturned shopping carts . . .

Encounter

I STIRRED IN THE small hours of the morning. Sensing a presence, I did not return to sleep, but ventured into the living room, apprehensively. There, by the balcony, sat a familiar figure—cross-legged and reading in the semi-dark, with just the milky moonlight for company.

I do not know how I knew, but I did. I recognized the intruder, at once, with a mixture of dread and affection. "I'm sorry," were the only words to leave my lips. "I'm sorry, too," replied my longed-for-self, with a sigh of infinite kindness and pity.

He did not rise to greet me and, somehow, spoke without words, transmitting what was needed. Catching his glistening eye, the caring made me cry. "You've taken every detour to avoid me," he gently reproached. "For every step I've taken towards you, you've taken back two."

I did not know what to say in my defense (how could I protest against myself?) "I missed you," he said, "and feared you'd forgotten me." His admonishment was tender as a kiss. "I visit from time to time, and hope you'll ask me to stay." I knew what he said was true, and felt that way, too.

"I worried," he continued, "if I postponed this visit, we might never meet, in this life . . . and so I came to sharpen your appetite." He rose and moved towards me. "There's no need to speak, return to sleep. But when you rise, try to remember me. And to keep awake."

The Softer Light of Middle Age

Being 45 is like 4:30 in the afternoon
it's not late, but it's not early, either
You had a fine start, much was achieved
but, now, a wave of drowsiness descends

Certainly, you're not ready to call it a day —
time to look up and take a little break
Cut up a fruit, maybe, some nuts for your heart
while you sip from a cup of mint tea with honey

A sigh escapes as you reflect upon
how best to spend the remaining hours
You might decide to forego that nap
keep awake a little longer, go for a walk

Good idea to clear your head, while taking
in the splendor of the setting sun, soon
You can raise the blinds, before you head out
the softer light won't harm your furniture.

Refugees

Imagine, if we stopped migrating
birds at the border . . .

Said: "No, this stretch of sky,
sea and land are out of order

Can you perch someplace else,
please?
Perhaps, in your native trees?"

The Limits of Love

You're welcome to a small helping
of care, a portion of our concern
Ache, if you like, but don't cry
on our shoulder, for overlong

Please, help yourself and move on
or you may find yourself, abruptly
at the outskirts of compassion
by the fence, where barbed wire begins

There is a sign that you can't miss:
Keep out, it reads, in blood red
"Private territory, trespassers
will be shot with indifference."

For Millennials

Young Narcissus
contemplating your beauty
in a lake of selfies

I, too, am enraptured
by your shifting reflections
updated, regularly

Please, look away —
lest we both stumble and fall,
drowning in our vanity.

The Deranged Snowman

Marooned on foreign land, his heart had turned to ice
and the snowed upon man could only blame the weather
Immigrant, militant, belligerent . . . they cried
when he tried to blend in with other snowmen

The children pelted him with snowballs, hard as hate
while their shameless pets treated him like a frozen fire hydrant
Worst of all, were the month-long Christmas carols—
an incessant din that kept him from sinking into thinking

He felt like a preposterous imposter
feigning passions that were not his own
Instead of the forced hilarity and dreaded sentimentality of this holiday season
the estranged iceman pined for the solitary melancholy of his desert home

Rather than further endure his lamentable predicament:
insufferable scarf, clownish carrot nose and unseeing button eyes
He longed to feel burning sand beneath his naked feet
and lusted after the sun's hot kiss on his bare face

Deeper still, he was haunted by hermit dreams,
with the mystical words of Rumi echoing in his ears:
"Be melting snow
Wash yourself of yourself."

The Hazards of Shaving
A Study in Vanity

THIS EVENING THERE WOULD be a larger, more discerning crowd than last and it was imperative that he look his best. He was immaculately dressed and coiffed. All that remained was to shave before he left. Entering the bathroom, he was careful not to soil his white, silken gloves and with one sharp, deft stab he switched the lights on. At the sink he stopped, reached for a straight razor and began shaving, at once, so as not to waste any more time.

He shaved in long, bold strokes with supreme confidence, as though there was no room for error. He did not waver, even momentarily, to reconsider where to resume. Nor did the blade falter or claim a wound of any kind. It was as if it glided smoothly out of respect for the perfection of his countenance, and from a fear of blemishing it. Only when he was completely done shaving did he pause to examine himself. To do this adequately, and fully appreciate his work, he switched on an additional light situated next to the mirror. He leaned over, shamelessly close, so that his face loomed directly before the glass.

Cupping his chin in one gloved hand, as one might cradle a delicate vase, he proceeded to caress his cheeks lovingly with the other. He smiled to himself, quite pleased with the results. Then, he circled the outside of his face with both hands, coming in at the cheekbones and out at the jaw. He frowned. He was not particularly pleased with the shape of his jaw, tonight. He sighed and shut his eyes, dreamily massaging eyelids and eyebrows with both forefingers in a slow, circular motion.

Bringing the thumb and forefinger of his left hand together, he ran his fingers down his nose, over the bridge, pressing tightly at the base on either end of his nostrils. He scowled, again; this time it was even more pronounced. His nose was, unmistakably, bulbous this evening. In fact, he had harbored this suspicion for well over a week, but had not been certain.

There was also the weak chin to worry about. Something would have to be done, for tonight's crowd would be merciless.

He leaned even further into the mirror, so that his visage appeared to merge with it. Impatiently, he reached for the razor again, and began shaving with more vigor than before, remarkably closer. He brought the blade beneath his chin, shaving upward, adopting some caution, so as not to hurt himself. He buried the blade deep and with unnerving detachment, began to shave the outside of his face.

Working his way inward, the face came off in a meticulous coil that hung provocatively over the sink, not quite touching it. In one decisive stroke, he shaved off the last of his face and let it fall into the sink. He looked away as the running water cleared the skin, while the drainpipe consumed it, greedily. Before fleeing the house, uncharacteristically concerned with how late it was, he instinctively checked himself in the hallway mirror.

As he made his way into the ballroom, he came to adopt a much more leisurely gait. At the entrance, he cocked his head to one side and walked in, as if oblivious to the overwhelming commotion he was creating. He glided, directly, to his table and sat down. Upon his request, he had been seated alone. As soon as he took his seat, distinguished men and women from surrounding tables flocked around him to witness this phenomenon—gaping with unabashed awe and incredulous admiration.

One society lady was bold enough to actually touch his face. He did not pull back from this *faux pas*, but stiffened in place like a proud bird—looked on with chilly indignation as the poor woman fumbled through some intricate apology, praising his face, unreservedly, in the process. Apart from this hiccup, the evening proved to be yet another staggering success for him.

When the world was first introduced to the mystery of his face, decades ago, they were repulsed. Gradually this repulsion, spurred by fascination, metamorphosed into wonder and, eventually, gave way to admiration. His face had been his claim to fame, his ticket into high society. It bestowed upon him status, and the respect of the elite, distinguished members of the community.

In turn, it came to be that his whole world revolved around his face, and the next—so he, assiduously, took the finest care of each new face. The people had, albeit reluctantly, come to accept the fact that he was a man who, somehow or other, managed to transform his face from one day to the next. They had also come to expect the fact that, invariably, each new face was to be more physically attractive and artistically evocative than the last. Once they accepted and expected this, they did so with keen anticipation.

What's more, each successive face seemed to suggest a particular character or mood which people found themselves, helplessly, responding to.

At present, his face evinced an unmistakably leonine aspect. He felt invincible, at a personal peak, without peer—he could do no wrong. And, so, the-man-of-many-faces continued appearing at select events before an elect audience, parading his selves.

He grew exceedingly pompous, at times, refusing to change a face for months on end. The people complained but, despite themselves, still gathered in large numbers to catch a glimpse of him on his way to some rare outing at a reception or benefit dinner. They noted, too, that over time he paid noticeably less attention to his dress and would often fail to show up, altogether, some evenings. Finally, the elite in society grew impatient with his antics, and issued an ultimatum. If he did not appear, regularly, as before, dressed appropriately, as before, they wanted nothing at all to do with him.

As he was dressing the following night, post-ultimatum, he found himself paying especially careful attention to each garment. He also took additional time combing his hair, and setting it. Then, he decided to shave off his face, for he had outworn it during these last appearances. He no longer needed to shave before a mirror, having become adept at the art of shaving. Nevertheless, he thought he should consult the looking glass, afterwards, to see just how well he had done.

Surprisingly, he found it exceptionally painful to shave this time around; his face felt unusually exposed and stung, relentlessly. Before the mirror he staggered, mouthing a soundless cry. What stared back at him was a face like none of the others he'd masqueraded. It was not *remotely* attractive, arresting, or suggestive. This face was, quietly, devastating. Without features or color, it did not evoke any character or produce any emotion. He no longer had any other faces to hide behind. Frantically, the desperate man attempted to get beneath it, in vain. Instead, he cut himself shaving.

The Mosquito Landed

THE MOSQUITO LANDED. HE paced across the warm wooden door, care-lessly caressing its smooth, solid surface. The door stood its ground, did not flinch, while the mosquito moved up and down. When the mosquito reached the door's middle, to the left of the brass doorknob, he stopped. Languidly, he positioned his lower body in close proximity to a crack in the otherwise impregnable door, and penetrated it. The door seemed to offer little if any resistance as the stinger continued to its core. Then, when the mosquito had drained the door of its life, he withdrew his stinger, disgusted with himself and the door.

The mosquito landed. This time on a plush pink sofa (situated no more than a few feet from that drooping door). The sofa, the mosquito noted with faint fatigue, radiated color and life. So, wasting no time in his self-imposed task, the mosquito moved to the parting in the pink sofa. He started suck-ing, and sucking, and sucking. Each time he would consider stopping, he would detect some remaining color out the corner of his eyes. Either that, or he would actually feel the sofa pulsating with whatever little vitality his stinger had not yet deprived her of. Finally, unable to extract anymore, the mosquito wearily withdrew and flew past the panting sofa and out the worn door.

The mosquito landed, and landed, each time exhausting the life of some different object in the sparsely-furnished room. Not once did he allow himself the luxury of lingering—to savor the flavor of life—neither while he rendered the forceful four walls feeble, nor when he restlessly suckled the ceiling until it almost caved in. Only when the room looked as withered and lifeless as its occupant did the mosquito land onto the crumpled carpet, spent.

It was much later, and with great difficulty, that the mosquito managed to take to the air, weighed down by the overwhelming burden of life. He flew, full of hope, in the direction of the seemingly lifeless female curled up in the corner. Still, he flew cautiously close to the carpet for fear that his weakened wings might not continue to support his engorged body.

The mosquito landed, tenderly, on her left breast (the one cushioning her heart). Suddenly he felt apprehensive. Everything he had done up until this point had been comparatively common in comparison to what he was about to do, now. His assignment was one of resuscitation, and he was about to restore to the occupant the life that the room had taken from her.

More importantly, the mosquito was about to do something entirely out of his nature; he was about to give. Lovingly, he eased his stinger into her breast and began to return the life the room had rudely robbed her of. He did so begrudgingly at first, with the intention of disengaging at any moment and saving some of the life force he had retrieved for himself.

But, the sensation was startling, truly sensational. As he felt the life of the room slipping away from him and into her, he shivered with ecstasy and his wings beat wildly. Intoxicated by the rapture of giving, the mosquito surrendered all his gains, until he restored the woman to her usual lively self.

Nonetheless, the mosquito would not withdraw—he could not—for he still carried a little life within him: his own. The mosquito buried his stinger deeper into her bountiful breast and, selflessly, secreted his humble life. He felt satisfied as he sensed his life-blood ebbing away. The woman got up, her face flushed with intense vigor, and began fussing with her hair. Instinctively, she swatted the mosquito off her dress, grimacing at the blood stain that he left behind.

Reflections

Again, the young man lingers before the store window. Again, his eyes disinterestedly pass over the birds, the dogs, the cats, the fish, and rest upon a small, plain brown monkey. This time, the young man has brought with him a pocket-sized notebook in which to record his impressions. Intently, he studies the monkey, with furrowed brow and eyebrows knit in keen concentration. He writes:

Entry # 1

Monkey seems depressed: glance downcast, limbs limp.

Next day

Gaunt. Haunted, hunted. Grimace betrays pain. Abysmal melancholy. Prevailing air of despair.

One week later

Inscrutable expression; nondescript features. Inanimate, insentient, lifeless.

Some days later

Relapse. Paralyzed with grief, bereaved. Eyes tell of unceasing, relentless torment—signaling indescribable suffering. Of battles lost, and won, and lost again. Of harrowing hours spent in the proximity of death, in the breath of death, and narrow escapes. Still, there is a glimmer in the eyes, dim light playing on the surface of dark jewels. Hazy, lazy orbs travelling in vast space; stray stars from a far away universe. Glistening pieces of glass, slivers of silver sinking in a lake of crude oil. Smoldering eyes, glowing darkly, the last flickering flames of a great blaze. Still, a staunch resolution to persevere, to continue against the odds. Indomitable spirit.

The following day the monkey is no longer there. In its place sits a gray African parrot, red tale aflame. Hard, beady eyes stare back at the young man, hostile and suspicious. Suspecting the very worst, the young man anxiously hurries away. Later, when he returns in the evening, the young man is relieved to find the monkey. Much has changed, however. He notes:

Entry #5

A certain elasticity to the monkey's limbs. Arms outstretched, rest playfully atop its head. A discernible lightness, spiritedness even, marks the monkey's general mien. Wondrous eyes. Endlessly endearing artlessness. Is this willful forgetfulness or innocence revisited?

Next day

What a difference a day makes. Now, one arm drops by the monkey's side. The other, still raised, droops—a pitiable tribute to better days. Much else has fallen, and continues to fall. The mercurial monkey now slouches, slumps, sags as though beneath an imaginary weight, an unseen burden. Levity has been replaced by heaviness, vivaciousness displaced by numbness. Glazed, unseeing eyes echo a mute cry of world-weary remonstrance. Unenviable beast of burdens.

Following day

Today, the monkey sits bolt upright. Noble carriage, proud bearing, self-possessed. There is a faintly prophetic, soulful, look in the eyes. Premonitions of disaster, or a propitious fate? A newfound will, perhaps, a promise of eventual triumph? I wonder.

Few days later

Transfigured. Transported. Otherworldly. Venerable, serene demeanor, almost pious. A well of calm, an oasis of bliss. A sublime stillness surrounds him, emanates from him: the harvest of a lifetime passed in quiet pursuit of exalted, lofty ideals. The gaze is steady, tranquil, beatific—of one accustomed to looking down from dizzy heights. Of monkish abstemiousness. Of unfathomable depths. Unsullied, free of ill-will, guile, or self-interest. Arms and legs neatly folded, he sits: lost in thought, found in peace.

Two days later

Strange creature of infinite variety! Unwholesome comportment, lewd. Legs spread-eagle, shamelessly flaunt animality. Desperate sexuality. The obscene, brazen, drunken eyes of one who has lost to lust.

End of the week

Disquieting, sinister, ignoble.

A fortnight passes

Scarcely recognizable. Glancing askance, monkey hangs off a branch by one arm, grip slipping. Suspended above the Abyss, what does he see? Insufferably mocking expression. Half-hidden profile hints at caustic, bitter, sardonic mood. Lacerating eyes, bristling with insolence, uproariously lampooning Fate: his own and others'. Imperiously, contemptuously even, he sneers at the gaping Nothingness, below. Unimpressed and unafraid, he leers, violently defiant.

The very next day the young man returns. He does not linger before the store window. He enters. Once inside, the young man tremulously tells the shop owner he wishes to purchase the small monkey. The owner is gone for a few minutes, and returns with a wan smile. Sorry, he says, the monkey must have been sold earlier today. The young man recoils, visibly shaken. A look of profound dread passes over his face. Startled, yet concealing his uneasiness with some success, the shop owner reaches out for the young man's arm. He pats him on the shoulder, good-naturedly." Come, now," he says in a somewhat soothing, sing-song voice. "It's not the *only* stuffed animal in this store. . . "

Publication Credits

The Books We Were, *World Literature Today*
Every Subject Chooses Its Author, *Agni*
Rimbaud's Spiritual Battle, *World Literature Today*
That Particular Intense Gaze, *Rain Taxi*
Poetry and Journalism of the Spirit, *The Mantle*
Seeking the Light Through Literature, *World Literature Today*
Marianne Williamson & the New Spirituality, *The Mantle*
C.S. Lewis & the Spiritual Tipping Point, *Queen Mob's Teahouse*
Spiritual Tourism: A Confession, *Agni*
Radical Love: Mysticism in Islam, *World Literature Today*
Ballad of the Global Patriot, *Sundance Now*
What Makes for Good Conversation? *Queen Mob's Teahouse*
Short Meditations on Inspiration and Hope, *Fair Observer*
Reverence for the Visible and Invisible Worlds, *On Being*
Kneeling in Stages, *On Being*
Reborn in the USA: An Immigrant & Poet's Story, *Huffington Post*
The Failure of Misanthropy, *World Literature Today*
The Pornification of Popular Culture, *Truthout*
Virtual World: Life-Enhancing versus Soul-Destroying, *Best American Poetry*
Review of The Teeth of the Comb & Other Stories, *World Literature Today*
Review of By Fire: Writings on the Arab Spring, *World Literature Today*
Daring to Care: Notes on the Egyptian Revolution, *New Internationalist*
From Tahrir Square to New York Square, *New Internationalist*
Egypt: The Unraveling, *Salon*
Bassem Sabry, Voice of Egyptian Revolution, *2 Paragraphs*
July 4: New Independence Day for Egypt? *2 Paragraphs*
Egypt: Bread and Social Justice, *2 Paragraphs*
To Kill a Mocking Girl—An Artist in Kuwait, *2 Paragraphs*
Coming to America: The Remake, *Raconteur*
Questions & Aphorisms, *Idries Shah Foundation*
Unstuck with Brian Chappell, *The The Poetry*
Artistry Bordering on Meditation: Discussing The Artist As Mystic, *The The Poetry*

"If It Weren't For My Wound . . . " with Rob Vollmar, *Crosstimbers*
The City and the Writer: In Cairo, *Words without Borders*
An Artist's Story of the Arab Spring, *NPR*
Interview, *Poetry Nook*
Discussing Fever Dreams, *Tuck Magazine*
The Aphorist in Conversation, *Sufi journal*
The Contemporary Aphorist, *New Arab Review*
The Aphorism's Story: 4 Questions, *Arablit*
Aphorism: A Brief Art, *Fair Observer*
Trial by Ink: A Conversation with Tyler Malone, *PMc Magazine*
Poets Online Talking About Coffee, *Queen Mob's Teahouse*
The TNB Self-Interview, *The Nervous Breakdown*
Underground Revisited: with an Introduction by Brian Chappell, *The The Poetry*
Voices: Multiple Philosophies Speak Gently to Us, *Philosophy Now magazine*
Variations on Feet—Shoes or No Shoes, *Museum Exhibit (Belgium)*
Refugees, *Better Than Starbucks*
The Limits of Love, *The Punch magazine*
For Millennials, *The Punch magazine*

CPSIA information can be obtained
at www.ICGtesting.com
Printed in the USA
FSHW010938030720
71717FS

9 781725 264946